INTO THE
MOUNTAINS

STORIES OF NEW ENGLAND'S MOST CELEBRATED PEAKS

MAGGIE STIER AND RON McADOW

foreword by Neil Jorgensen

APPALACHIAN MOUNTAIN CLUB BOOKS
BOSTON, MASSACHUSETTS

Cover Photograph: Jerry Shereda
All photographs by author unless otherwise noted.
Cover Design: Ken Silvia Design Group
Book and Map Design: Carol Bast Tyler

Distributed by the Globe Pequot Press, Inc., Old Saybrook, CT.

Library of Congress Cataloging-in-Publication Data
Stier, Maggie.
Into the mountains: stories of New England's most celebrated
peaks / Maggie Stier and Ron McAdow.
p. cm.
Includes bibliographical references and index.
ISBN 1-878239-30-9 (alk. paper)
1. Mountains—New England—History. 2. New England—
History, Local. 3. New England—Description and travel. I. McAdow,
Ron. 1949–   . II. Title
F12.A16S75 1995
974—dc20   95-24578
                                                               CIP

The paper used in this publication meets the minimum requirements
of the American National Standard for Information Sciences—
Permanence of Paper for Printed Library Materials, ANSI
Z39.48–1984.∞

Printed on recycled paper using soy-based inks.

Printed in the United States of America.

10 9 8 7 6 5 4 3 2 1   95 96 97 98 99

For Hannah and Sophie
—M.S.

For Molly, Deep-Rooted Person Who Sees from Afar
—R.M.

Locations of New England's Most Celebrated Peaks

Contents ⩕⩕⩕

Acknowledgments

The idea for this book took shape for a year in my mind before I met Ron McAdow, who seemed to share my passion for understanding places. He had just finished two guidebooks for canoeists and was looking for a new project. Our collaboration began as one of researcher and writer: I the historian, hiker, and native New Englander; he the seasoned author and eager discoverer of mountain places. We spent a productive year in climbing, researching, and drafting the first few chapters, then reassessed the time involved in producing a complete book. The partnership changed. Building on a framework from Ron, and with the encouragement and patience of AMC Books Editor Gordon Hardy, I was able to complete the manuscript and see the project through to publication.

Many people contributed in significant ways to this book. At the AMC, we had early encouragement from the late C. Francis Belcher and were assisted ably by librarian Jessica Gill. Staff at other libraries generously provided access to resource materials and historical photographs; in particular I would like to thank the New Hampshire Historical Society; the Vermont Historical Society; the Maine State Library; Special Collections at Dartmouth College's Baker Library; the Society for the Protection of New England Antiquities; Shelburne Museum; Fruitlands Museums; and the public libraries in

Harvard, Princeton, Concord, and Holyoke, Massachusetts; Tamworth, New Hampshire; and Manchester, Vermont. The Massachusetts Department of Environmental Management generously granted permission to use its maps, as did the Green Mountain Club in Vermont and the New Hampshire Parks and Recreation Department.

I have been fortunate to work on a project that takes me to the mountains and introduces me to people who share a sympathy and love for these places. Some were gracious readers for specific chapters; others showed me their mountains or shared information that helped significantly to advance my own understanding. All deserve to be acknowledged and thanked for their interest and support.

Wachusett: David Crowley, Warren Sinclair

Holyoke and Tom: Dave Moore, C. John Burk of Smith College; Shelley Parker; Ginni Traub, Friends of the Holyoke Range

Greylock: Maureen Hickey, Deborah Burns, Dennis Reagan

Equinox: Mary Bort, Betty Manganiello, Equinox Hotel, Mrs. J. G. Davidson

Camel's Hump: Brian Lindner, William Gove, Hubert Vogelman

Mansfield: Kevin Graffagnino, University of Vermont; Charlie Lord

Ascutney: John Dryphout, Gregory Schwarz, St. Gaudens National Historic Site; Joan Bishop, archivist at Kimball Union Academy; Ruth Worden, Ascutney State Park; Morningstar Hang Gliding Center, Charlestown, New Hampshire

Monadnock: Michael Walsh, Ben Haubrich, New Hampshire State Parks; Barbara J. McAdam, Hood Museum of Art

Moosilauke: Robert Averill, J. Willcox Brown

Lafayette: Laura and Guy Waterman

Washington: Mike Courtemanche, Mount Washington Observatory; Douglas Philbrook, Laura and Guy Waterman

Cadillac: Lois Winter, National Park Service; Mary and Sohier Welch; Gladys O'Neil, Bar Harbor Historical Society

Katahdin: Irvin C. Caverly, Jr., Jean Howkwater, Baxter State Park; Pam Durrant

Neil Jorgensen has been a most supportive friend and critic in reviewing the entire manuscript and writing a foreword. Any errors that remain are completely my own; in a project of this scope they are inevitable.

Finally, my friends and family offered me the encouragement and support so crucial to any writing project. Evelyn Marcus provided thoughtful companionship and good humor over many miles of trail covered together. I drew frequently upon the collective mountain experiences of my brother, Frederick Moody, and sister, Carol Bush, as well as my parents, both New Hampshire natives. To William and Janet Moody I owe the greatest debt: to my father for instilling in me a love of mountains and to my mother for the courage to think I could put it all down in print someday.

Finally, I want to express my gratitude to my husband, Kurt Stier, who provided many of the fine photographs in this book. Both he and all the children, Sarah, David, Sophie, and Hannah, enthusiastically embraced any hiking excursion I proposed and patiently endured my absences and preoccupation during a long season of writing. I will always be grateful for their understanding.

Maggie Stier

Into the Mountains is, first and foremost, the work of Maggie Stier, who proposed the concept and who made the massive commitment of time and energy necessary to see the project through to completion. I am grateful to her for the opportunity to learn about the subject and for the implicit challenge to haul myself up some trails. Days spent on these mountains are days well invested; our shared hope in this book is to make your mountain time even richer through an added knowledge of mountain lore.

I would also like to acknowledge Bev and Don Essen for their suggestions at the outset, and Roger Baust for his interest in the project and for his reading of an early draft of the Mount Washington chapter.

Ron McAdow

Foreword

In human terms, the New England mountains have a venerable history. Native Americans dwelled in their shadows for thousands of years. By the mid-eighteenth century, European settlement had come at least to within sight of most of the higher mountains here. But until now this long association between the New England people and their mountains has received less attention than it should.

Scattered articles, old accounts, and even a small book or two on the lore and history of some of the more famous New England mountains do indeed exist but until now, no one had sifted through this information and gathered it together into a single volume. I am happy to report that *Into the Mountains*, Maggie Stier and Ron McAdow's graceful and fascinating account of fifteen New England mountains, admirably fills that void.

The book is much more than merely mountain history. The authors give us the character of these heights, and their geology and geography as well. But Maggie and Ron emphasize the historic, and herein lies the great value of *Into the Mountains*.

Although it is not difficult to perceive the role of human settlement on lowland New England, we tend to consider much of the mountain landscape as still pristine. A reading of *Into the Mountains* points out that the human hand has affected the mountain scenery–both in positive and negative ways–almost as much as it has those areas closer to civilization.

Often in the very shadow of high mountains we come across abandoned farmsteads, the pastures now grown to mature woods. The mountain landscape has been disturbed in other, much greater ways: the huge forest fire at Bar Harbor; the vast, turn-of-the-century logging operations in the New Hampshire mountains; and, later on, largely through the efforts of public-spirited citizens, public ownership of large mountain tracts and subsequent recovery of the forests.

Into the Mountains reminds us what a wonderful resource our mountains are. Just how much they contribute to the beauty and interest of the landscape here in New England became clear to me when, on a recent visit to Chicago, I looked out from the Sears Tower. Though dazzled by the magnificent Chicago cityscape around me on three sides, when I looked westward over the suburbs to the countryside beyond I was struck by the billiard-table flatness of the land. In vain I scanned many miles of horizon for even the slightest bump, anything to break the horizon. Our mountains, by contrast, offer us a pleasing relief, a constant variety of terrain.

Are the New England mountains high enough? Robert Frost didn't think so. True, when compared to the Rockies or Alps, the heights of New England's mountains are only modest. But they are high enough to present us with long views from their summits. People climb mountains for many different reasons. For me, the most compelling is what I will see from the top. From Mount Washington it is possible to see Portland Harbor; from Mount Monadnock, it is possible to see Massachusetts almost from one end to the other. Mountains high enough to provide hundred-mile views are perhaps high enough.

The great ice sheets that covered New England also enhanced the viewing aspect. Although they made much of the region inhospitable for agriculture and, by default, created the sometimes oppressive wooded landscape over 85 percent of the region, the glaciers also scraped off much of the soil from the mountaintops, leaving bare rock and open vistas. In the southern Appalachians, beyond the glacial reach, such extensive mountain vistas are rare.

All mountains demand respect; yet somehow I consider the New England mountains–with the possible exception of the Presidentials and Mount Katahdin–as less terrifying than the higher mountains elsewhere. Well-marked trails (thanks in large part to the Appalachian Mountain Club) and, of late, more reliable weather forecasting assure reasonably safe mountain travel for all but the most foolhardy or grossly inexperienced.

True, the massive and jagged peaks of the Rockies and Alps are splendid in small doses but–at the risk of sounding provincial–I think our softer mountain landscape wears better and feels more comfortable. I hate to disagree with a New England luminary such as Robert Frost but I find the height of New England's mountains to be just about right.

As is true with all good mountain books, the real value of *Into the Mountains* is that it inspires the reader to explore some of these famous peaks. Over the years I have climbed a number of the mountains chronicled here. Though my interest has been more in the natural history rather than the human history, I do recall how much a reading of the little book *Annals of the Grand Monadnock* enhanced my visit to that mountain. *Into the Mountains* now has provided the same degree of enrichment for the fourteen other peaks.

One additional advantage of the long history here is that many of New England's mountains now can be reached by means other than an arduous climb on foot. Roads, ski lifts, and even the cog railway on Mount Washington allow people unable to make the strenuous hike to experience the exhilaration of the high mountains. And for those who can still make it to the top by foot, there are many trails and many mountains waiting to be explored.

I was especially happy to see Mount Tom and Mount Holyoke included on the authors' list. It takes a stretch of the imagination to make these sharp little central Massachusetts hills into mountains. But even they can accord the visitor many of the same pleasures as do the high mountains farther away: wonderful views, interesting geology, and even a few unusual plant species. Mounts Tom and Holyoke remind us that it is not always necessary to venture into the remote areas in order to enjoy the mountain experience.

Now that they have finished this splendid book, perhaps Maggie and Ron will further reward us with a sequel volume on some of New England's other interesting mountains, both large and small. Of the latter, my own favorite is Streaked Mountain in the Oxford Hills of western Maine. At a height of only 1,700 feet above sea level, Streaked just barely qualifies as a mountain; yet even at this modest elevation, it provides almost everything anyone could want from a mountain. Great patches of bare bedrock account for its name, though in Maine parlance it is pronounced "streá ked," not "streaked." On a clear morning the view from these open ledges is magnificent: on one side, the shimmer of Casco Bay; on the other, the blue purple of Mount Washington.

Like other New England mountains, Streaked has evidence of habitation. Old stone walls and abandoned roads high on the mountainsides are evidence of farming during the nineteenth century. Viewing them, I wonder what stories could be told—what human tales are etched into Streaked's landscape.

Since it is a near-to-civilization mountain, Streaked's summit sports the usual assortment of small buildings, radio towers and other electronic junk. Just a few hundred feet away, though, lie hidden wonderful secrets of nature: open ledges, sphagnum bogs, wild blueberries, and dark spruce forest. It's a setting that seems far from all things human—and yet one can enjoy it for just a half-hour on the trail.

There are a hundred other mountains left for the authors to write about. Although some, like Streaked, do not receive recognition in the major mountain books, others are almost as well known as the peaks written about here. Each has a story.

Into the Mountains is a fine contribution to New England's mountain literature. The richness of Maggie and Ron's account cannot be digested in a single reading—it is a book to linger over and cherish. And I do hope another volume—perhaps including Streaked Mountain—will follow.

Neil Jorgensen

Introduction

What shapes a mountain's character? What gives individual peaks a sense of identity? Can we understand our mountains by taking a long view, not just from their summits, but into their pasts and ahead to their futures?

Trail guides provide the essentials—basic statistics and directions, perhaps even a taste of historical facts. But like the proverbial blind man and the elephant, can the whole be represented by these parts? Did Oscar Marshall, for example, by driving around the base of Mount Ascutney seven times and taking photographs of the mountain, come to understand the character of the place? Power hikers and Sunday drivers each form their own relationships to a mountain, but rarely through a single activity can the fullest appreciation be gained. Instead, through a combination of many different perspectives a focused picture emerges, and that, in turn, becomes unique as we each add our own experiences and sensibilities to what has gone before.

This book suggests that the story of our mountains is a story of ourselves, and by knowing what these mountains have seen—the bloodshed, the hardships, the commerce, the celebrations, the protection—we gain new insight into our own culture. It also suggests that current political battles over conservation and wilderness preservation need to be put into a deeper context, one that incorporates all that New England's mountains have represented and all we have wanted them to be over the course of their history. Once, summit hotels were ubiquitous; mountain roads and railways were not uncommon. Today, mixed use prevails almost everywhere, and attempts to balance commercial interests and recreational enthusiasts with wilderness protection have sometimes resulted in an uneasy peace. We are all a little self-conscious about the relatively small size of our peaks now that the Rockies, the Sierra, and even the Himalayas are so accessible, but many insist that wilderness, wherever it may be found, deserves serious preservation efforts.

Several years ago, my husband and I were preparing to take our two young daughters for their first overnight hiking trip. We had decided on Chocorua. I went to the bookshelf and pulled down a well-worn copy of Eva Speare's *Indian Legends of New Hampshire* that had belonged to my grandfather, feeling compelled to share the Chocorua legend with my family, just as my mother had done with me and her mother and father had probably done with her. The doomed Indian who jumped to his death from the rocky peak, the curse on the white man's cattle, the famous Thomas Cole painting of the scene—they should know about these as part of the experience of the place itself. Having the rocky cone of Chocorua pointed out to them as we drove up Route 16 was no longer enough. The place we were going to had to be understood, not just visited, and the only way to do that was to weave the rich tapestry of facts, legends, poetry and prose, heroic deed and ordinary days—all of which would add up to an idea of what had happened on Chocorua in the past and what its significance is in our culture today.

Once we were there, we talked about how it had changed in my lifetime, how one could no longer camp on its slopes, how I remembered on my first climb mixing lemonade concentrate in the water collected in a summit rock for something to drink. I'd read that the rangers never climbed the mountain now during the day because inevitably they had to go up at night to rescue some inexperienced straggler. We talked to other climbers and tasted mountain blueberries by the handful. And the children contemplated the view—a perspective so changed from their small-town life that the youngest blurted out, "Mommy, can we live here?"

So the stories of the famous mountains of New England, fifteen places so obvious there was almost immediate unanimity between coauthors and editor, are told in this book. The initial proposal to the AMC was more historical in nature, but they encouraged us to bring the story of the mountains up to the present by including conservation issues, current events, and contemporary development projects. The story of these places is more than just history; as cultural geography it encompasses the great swings of change in our collective consciousness and progresses from the past, through the present, and into the future. As a culture, we cannot make informed decisions, nor live as fully and richly as possible, until we have an understanding of what has gone before us.

New England's mountains are a unique and limited resource. Inevitably there are disputes about their use. Hikers generally object to roads, hotels, broadcasting antennas, memorial towers, and ski resorts because they erode the value of a mountain as a retreat where earth and its natural beauty can be appreciated. Conservationists wish to protect the mountains' natural resources that even the recreationists are gradually eroding. Private owners as well as state and local governments gain increased revenues by making the mountains more usable or productive, invariably attracting more people and often creating justification for more development.

The resulting political struggles can be hot. Mount Greylock, for instance, has faced almost every issue that conflicting values can generate. For nearly a half-century, conservative interests have faced off against developers offering economic improvement and wider access to mountain recreation. Tensions have run high, investors have gone bankrupt, and political maneuvering and profiteering continue to fan the flames of discontent. The search continues for an appropriate blend of uses for the mountain.

The fifteen stories told in this book share similar themes, beginning with the powerful spiritual connection between Native Americans and mountains. The European impulse, carried to these shores only 350 years ago, was to claim and subdue the landscape. Climbing mountains for physical challenge or rustic pleasure emerged as a distinctly nineteenth-century phenomenon. Mountains then provided a setting for social activity or a place to withdraw from the progress of a generally welcome industrial age. The contributions of early American artists in making the mountains into tourist destinations cannot be overstated. The images they created were the expression of the developing American consciousness itself and continue to influence the way we perceive our mountains today.

The era in which the Georgia-to-Maine Appalachian Trail took shape—in the 1920s and 1930s—represented a practical attempt to update the romantic, pastoral ideal of mountains. A growing urban population turned to nature for refuge and renewal. In a backlash against all that was wrong with the industrial age—the dehumanizing forces of the city and factory, the quickened pace of life in general—Americans took to the woods and mountains with determination and zeal. Today, we are struggling to deal with the legacy of that enthusiasm for the outdoors, mountaintop, backwoods experience. Overuse looms as perhaps the largest single issue in the mountains of New England today, and we struggle to provide protection even as we recognize how powerful, even essential, is the tonic that wilderness provides.

We have brought our high-tech knowledge to equipment, mapping, and gadget design, making it easier to survive and even be comfortable in the mountains. Yet as more and more people take advantage of opportunities for outdoor recreation in the mountains, the balance between man and nature grows ever more fragile. To the extent that we "use" New England's mountains, we jeopardize their very survival as wilderness; this is their paradox. The stories in this book are meant to provoke reflection on the changing dynamics of that uneasy balance over the last 500 years. If we can appreciate the present more and make wiser decisions for the future, this look into the past will have served us well.

Wachusett ⋀⋀⋀

Mount Wachusett, the highest point in Massachusetts east of the Berkshires, has rich historical associations. Stronghold of King Philip during the colonial Indian war that bears his name, and later idealized by the Concord poets, Wachusett's strategic location and natural beauty have been the star players in its colorful history. The popular 2,100-acre, state-run reservation includes an auto road and ski lifts that serve upwards of 300,000 people each season. Its hiking trails connect with Massachusetts Audubon's thousand-acre Wachusett Meadows Sanctuary and with trails in Minns Wildlife Sanctuary, delineating an important area of protected wildlife habitat and resource management.

Geology and Geography

Rising 2,006 feet in elevation, Wachusett is more than three times as high as the Great Blue Hill south of Boston (635 feet above the sea), and nearly twice as high as Mount Tom on the Connecticut River (1,202 feet). It divides the watersheds of the Connecticut River to the west and the Merrimack River to the east and lies approximately 50 miles west of Boston. The summit and most of the mountain are within the town of Princeton; the boundary line for Westminster sets off the mountain's northwestern slope.

1

Wachusett's historical importance stems largely from its geographical position. Wachusett is not part of a range of mountains—it is a monadnock, or isolated peak, the remnant of a great bulge of granite that weathered more slowly than the rock around it and therefore stands alone. The geological term comes from Mount Monadnock in southern New Hampshire, the most famous of these isolated mountains.

Wachusett has two shoulders on nearly opposite sides of the mountain, a long one to the south and a shorter one to the northwest, which give this mountain a distinctive profile when viewed from east or west. Two smaller monadnocks, Little Wachusett and Brown Hill, lie just to the south.

Like Mount Monadnock, Mount Wachusett is the result of an intrusion of erosion-resistant rock injected into the less resistant rock surrounding it (known as the "country rock"). This intrusion took place millions of years ago, perhaps then as much as five miles beneath the surface. Over the intervening ages, the infinitely slow force of erosion gradually wore down the land to its present topography, leaving the more resistant rock, called Fitchburg granite, that forms Mount Wachusett.

As recently as 12,000 to 15,000 years ago, a mile-thick sheet of glacial ice covered Wachusett's summit. The last dramatic event in the formation of the mountain as we know it, the retreat of the ice left behind rocks, boulders, and glacial debris in haphazard fashion. Two large rocks balanced one on top of the other at the foot of Wachusett stand as mute testimony to the power of that ice.

Early History

Wachusett is an Indian name, roughly translated from the Algonquin language as "the great hill." It is one of only three mountains in this book (Cadillac and Katahdin in Maine are the others) whose written history of the peak documents Native American and European interaction. Beginning with the 1630 settlement of the Massachusetts Bay Colony at Boston, early maps consistently refer to Wachusett as a landmark of the interior. English settlers, lured by the rich fields of hay along the river meadows, moved westward toward Wachusett as

Balance rock on Mount Wachusett reveals the erratic results of the last great Ice Age. Kurt Stier.

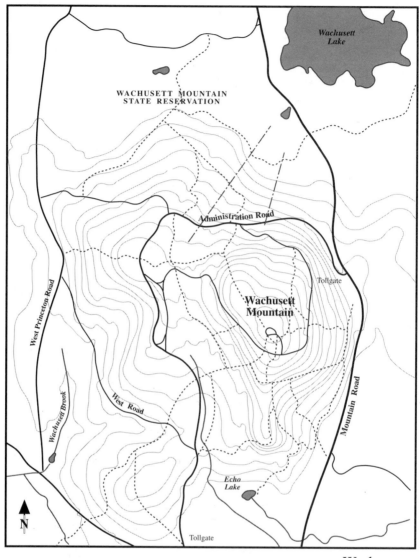

Wachusett

they bought and occupied Indian lands at Concord on the Sudbury River in 1640, and at Lancaster on the Nashua River in 1643.

Land purchases from natives were awkward, unsatisfactory transactions, however, for indigenous peoples held very different concepts of land ownership and currency values. The natives' frustration at the English desire for more and more land led to violence in 1675, when allied Indian forces made a final attempt to drive the English back to the coast. The bloody conflict that followed became known as King Philip's War, after the English name of its great native leader Metacom, sachem of the Wampanoags. From Wachusett, a vantage point that allowed him relative safety and physical advantage, Metacom directed raids on the towns of Lancaster, Sudbury, and Medfield.

The attack on Lancaster, launched from the foot of Wachusett, is perhaps the best-known event of the war, due largely to the account of one of those captured and taken prisoner by the Indians. *A Narrative of the Captivity and Suffering of Mary Rowlandson* details the ten weeks that the town minister's wife spent as servant and captive with King Philip's followers after the sacking of the garrison at Lancaster in 1676. It is the only historic source documenting the Indians' perspective of the war; for Mrs. Rowlandson, despite her Puritan rhetoric, had great sympathy

King Philip's war club was encased at the Fruitlands Museums overlooking the Nashua Valley and Mount Wachusett. Stolen from its case in 1970, it was recovered at a Worcester, Massachusetts yard sale in October 1994. Photo courtesy of Fruitlands Museums, Harvard, MA.

and respect for her captors. Her adventures, or "removes," as her ill-provisioned captors tried to evade the English by traveling from one campsite to another, make chilling reading.

During the early months of King Philip's War, the English suffered serious losses against the more successful guerrilla tactics of the native fighters. The colonists retaliated by confining on a Boston Harbor island all of the natives who had not joined Metacom, having received a tip that these "praying" or Christianized Indians could not be trusted to remain loyal. The result of their inhumane action, however, was to so anger the Indian tribes that the Wampanoags, Narragansetts, and Nipmucs formed an alliance for the sole purpose of eradicating the English from their territories.

At the height of his power, Metacom dispatched four hundred warriors from Mount Wachusett for the attack on Lancaster in mid-February 1676. Joseph Rowlandson, Lancaster's minister and leading citizen, was in Boston at the time, pleading for help in fortifying his town. When the raid began, Joseph's wife, Mary White Rowlandson, and thirty-seven others had taken refuge in an unfinished fortified house. "Quickly it was the dolefullest day that ever mine eyes saw," Rowlandson wrote of the fire and bloodshed with which she and her three children were soon surrounded. As they fled the burning garrison, Rowlandson and her youngest child, which she carried, were wounded by the same bullet. Twelve colonists were killed in trying to defend the house, twenty-four were captured, and only one escaped.

Thus began Mary Rowlandson's captivity. Now with a wounded baby, she and two more of her children were assigned Indian masters and taken to the Indian town called Menameset, near present-day New Braintree. There she met another captive who told her to apply oak leaves to her bullet wound, treatment she credited with her eventual recovery. Sadly, her youngest child did not survive. Rowlandson's son and a ten-year-old daughter, each assigned other masters, were separated from their mother. Rowlandson's band, who were mostly women, evaded the pursuit of colonial soldiers by building rafts to float across what the Indians called the Baquaug, now Millers River. In her account of her captivity, Rowlandson roundly criticized the ineptness of the English for failing to cross the same natural barrier.

For the first week Rowlandson was too distressed to eat. During the second week she was revolted by the unaccustomed fare of ground nuts (acorns) and scavenged meat, but by the third week she relished a broth of boiled horse's leg and a rotten scrap of bear meat given to her by a sympathetic Indian. Gaining her strength, she gamely crossed the Connecticut River in a canoe and on the far bank was presented to Metacom himself. Much to her surprise, she found him gracious, even charming, as he offered her his tobacco pipe. Metacom hired her to make a shirt and cap for his young son. The Indian leader paid cash for the shirt and rewarded the ill-nourished Mrs. Rowlandson for the cap with an invitation to dinner. "I went, and he gave me a pancake about as big as two fingers; it was made of parched wheat, beaten and fried in bear's grease, but I thought I never tasted pleasanter meat in my life."

Mary Rowlandson was finally ransomed in May 1676, at the time of the "great powwow," a gathering of Indians at the southern end of Lake Wachusett. For twenty pounds, a coat, and some seed corn, she was bought out of captivity and restored to her husband. Redemption Rock, at the eastern base of Mount Wachusett on a

The redemption of the famous Lancaster captive, Mary Rowlandson, took place at this rock at the base of Mount Wachusett. Kurt Stier.

preserve owned by the Trustees of Reservations, commemorates the spot where Mary Rowlandson was released.

The powwow was the pinnacle of Indian success. New England's natives, decimated by European diseases, eventually fell to the superior numbers of English. By the end of that summer Metacom was dead, his soldiers and their families captured or scattered, and almost all of the remaining southern New England Algonquins permanently estranged from the English colonists.

After King Philip's War, English colonists slowly moved into central Massachusetts. Lands around Wachusett were settled gradually during the hundred years before the American Revolution. The mountain itself was granted to Reverend Timothy Fuller, Princeton's first minister, and the first house in the town of Princeton was built in 1742.

From those early days, a legend arose of a lost little girl who is still said to haunt the mountain. Three-quarters of a century after King Philip's War, Princeton had only a few settled families on large farms far distant from each other. On the east side of Mount Wachusett lived Robert Keyes, his wife, and ten children. Young Lucy Keyes was only four years old in April of 1755 when she followed her sisters through the woods to Wachusett Pond. Straggling behind them, she disappeared from the trail and was never seen again. The woods were searched for weeks and the pond was dragged, but no trace of her was ever found. Lucy's father, believing she might have been taken captive by Indians, searched for her in New Hampshire and even in Canada. The poor child's mother, driven mad by grief, stood outside each night at twilight, calling for her child. Some say the plaintive echo of her voice, "Lu-u-u-cy!" can still be heard on dark nights on the slopes of the mountain.

The patriotic fervor of the young republic briefly drew Wachusett into notoriety once again in 1825. On the day of the inauguration of John Quincy Adams, sixth president and Massachusetts native, the people of Princeton held a great celebration. Bells rang at sunrise, cannons were fired from the mountain's summit, and a nighttime bonfire was lit, said to be visible even in Boston. The mountain was rechristened Mount Adams.

Four years later, after an unpopular presidency and Adams's failed bid at reelection, the *Massachusetts Spy* ran the following letter:

Mr. Editor:

It will be recollected that on the inauguration of John Quincy Adams to the presidency, four years ago this day, the good people of Princeton (hastily no doubt), at the suggestion of an old friend of mine, saw fit to honor me with a new name, that of Mount Adams. I had at that time very serious doubts as to the propriety of the course taken by my friends in Princeton, although I did not then remonstrate. During the four years last past, I have been in rather a disagreeable dilemma. Some of my friends and visitors have greeted me by my new name, while others have been determined to know me by no other than by my ancient and well established title, Wachusett. Now, my age, rank and elevation will, I trust, justify me in speaking for myself and settling this matter. I am satisfied with the administration of Mr. Adams....As Mr. Adams retires from office at this time, with due deference to him, I beg leave, through the medium of your paper, to inform the public that I have resumed my former name, by which, alone, I wish hereafter to be known and distinguished.

Respectfully, I remain your substantial friend,

Wachusett Mountain

Transcendentalism

Though Adams's connection to the mountain has been largely forgotten, other native sons and daughters have had a more lasting and lyrical influence on the mountain's story. The Concord Transcendentalists composed essays and poems about this mountain that are still read by students today. Henry David Thoreau had a particular affection for this place, often noting in his journals the round-shouldered summit crowning the western horizon from his hometown of Concord. He visited Wachusett twice, comparing himself to the mountain in a poem published as part of a longer essay called "A Walk to Wachusett." The last verse begins with a memorable phrase:

But special I remember thee,
Wachusett, who like me
Standest alone without society.
Thy far blue eye,
A remnant of the sky,
Seen through the clearing or the gorge
Or from the windows of the forge,
Doth leaven all it passes by.
Nothing is true,
But stands 'tween me and you,
Thou western pioneer,
Who know'st not shame nor fear
By venturous spirit driven,
Under the eaves of heaven.
And canst expand thee there,
And breathe enough of air?
Upholding heaven, holding down earth,
Thy pastime from thy birth,
Not steadied by the one, not leaning on the other;
May I approve myself thy worthy brother!

"A Walk to Wachusett" was first published as a newspaper essay, and remains in several modern anthologies of Thoreau's work. It begins on July 19, 1842, and chronicles a four-day saunter Thoreau took with his friend Richard Fuller, whose sister Margaret Fuller was at that time editor of the newly launched Transcendentalist magazine, *The Dial*. Written as Thoreau was recovering from the death of his older brother John, the essay is really a musing on the process of traveling and how, for all the differences one might encounter, people are essentially no different from one place to the next.

Subtle variations in speech fascinated Thoreau, and he noted "a truer and wilder pronunciation" of mountain names from their local inhabitants. "Not Way-tatic, Way-chusett, but Wor-tatic, Wor-chusett," making "us ashamed of our tame and civil pronuncia-tion....Their tongues had a more generous accent than ours, as if breath was cheaper where they wagged."

On Wachusett's summit, Thoreau and Fuller climbed "the foundation of a wooden observatory, which was formerly erected on the highest point," and from its stone walls, watched the sun set over a hazy landscape:

> We saw the shades of night creep gradually over the valleys of the east; and the inhabitants went into their houses, and shut their doors, while the moon silently rose up, and took possession of that part. And then the same scene was repeated on the west side, as far as the Connecticut and the Green Mountains, and the sun's rays fell on us two alone, of all New England men.

> It was the night but one before the full of the moon, so bright that we could see to read distinctly by moonlight, and in the evening strolled over the summit without danger. There was, by chance, a fire blazing on Monadnock that night, which lighted up the whole western horizon, and, by making us aware of a community of mountains, made our position seem less solitary.

After a light supper of milk and mountain blueberries they retired to their tent to read Wordsworth and Virgil. The following morning as they watched "the sun rise up out of the sea," Thoreau again analyzed the view. "There was little of the sublimity and grandeur which belong to mountain scenery, but an immense landscape to ponder on a summer's day. We could see how ample and roomy nature is."

The memory of Indians was faint but not forgotten here; though Thoreau makes reference to the captivity of Mary Rowlandson, he finds that "dark age of New England" to have a veil of shadow over it, as if the whole range of events of the Indian Wars had taken place in "a dim twilight or night."

In addition to Thoreau, Wachusett's illustrious visitors included Louisa May Alcott, also from Concord and author of *Little Women*, *Little Men*, and other children's classics. Another of the best-known writers of the nineteenth century, John Greenleaf Whittier, stayed at the old Roper Farm that nestled on the north slope of Mount Wachusett "like a bird's nest hung." Today only the cellar hole remains, located at the top of the current ski area's Indian Summer chair lift. But it was here that Whittier, at the height of his prominence as a poet and abolitionist, penned a sentimental ode to two celebrated mountains.

Monadnock from Wachusett

I would I were a painter, for the sake
 Of a sweet picture, and of her who led,
A fitting guide, with reverential tread,
Into that mountain mystery. First a lake
  Tinted with sunset; next the wavy lines
   Of far receding hills; and yet more far,
  Monadnock lifting from his night of pines
   His rosy forehead to the evening star.
Beside us, purple-zoned, Wachusett laid
His head against the West, whose warm light made
  His aureole; and o'er him, sharp and clear,
Like a shaft of lightning in mid-launching stayed,
  A single level cloud-line, shone upon
  By the fierce glances of the sunken sun,
   Menaced the darkness with its golden spear!

So twilight deepened round us. Still and black
The great woods climbed the mountain at our back;
And on their skirts, where yet the lingering day
On the shorn greenness of the clearing lay,
  The brown old farm-house like a bird's-nest hung.
With home-life sounds the desert air was stirred:
The bleat of sheep along the hill we heard,
The bucket splashing in the cool, sweet well,
The pasture-bars that clattered as they fell;
Dogs barked, fowls fluttered, cattle lowed; the gate
Of the barn-yard creaked beneath the merry weight
  Of sun-brown children, listening, while they swung,
   The welcome sound of supper-call to hear;
   And down the shadowy lane, in tinklings clear,
  The pastoral curfew of the cow-bell rung.

While poets romanticized the pastoral simplicity of rural farm life, the area was being transformed into a fashionable summer resort with the mountain as its centerpiece. To harried city dwellers, and especially those unfortunates suffering from tuberculosis, the clean mountain air offered welcome relief. But their demands for accommodations and services brought great changes to the area. By the 1870s, the uplands of the town of Princeton were attracting hundreds of well-to-do summer visitors to a dozen Victorian guest houses and hotels. Exploration of the mountain, perhaps for berry picking, perhaps to admire the view, was a popular day's outing for these visitors.

Buildings rose on Wachusett's summit. The summit had already shown some evidence of a tourist trade: Thoreau's old stone foundation from 1842 was probably the remains of a viewing platform erected sometime in the 1830s. After the Civil War ended in 1865, a small booth was constructed on the summit for selling candy and cigars, and it was later expanded to a small house. Then, in 1874, the privately owned Wachusett Mountain Company built a carriage road to the top of the mountain and erected a hotel called the Summit House.

Phineas Beaman bought the mountain in 1882 and built an even larger summit hotel, forty feet square. From its wide porches, guests could see east all the way to Boston, north to Mount Monadnock, and west to Greylock. Beaman built an ice pond and ice house to provide his patrons with chilled drinks after their ascent, stabled their horses in a nearby barn, and even provided a summit bowling alley for further diversion.

Conservation and Recreation

Then in 1899 came a major shift in the destiny of the mountain. Recognizing the diminishing resource of open lands, the Massachusetts Senate voted funds to create a publicly owned Wachusett Mountain Reservation. The following year, Beaman's heirs sold 533 acres and the Summit Hotel to the state for $20,060. Worcester County was supposed to provide funds for maintenance, but their local appropriations were rarely sufficient. Reservation commissioners barely had enough for routine maintenance of the four existing trails, the carriage road, and the sprawling hotel. Still, they were committed to preserving the natural aspects of the reservation, even as they were tempted by the promise of more revenue to help support the property.

The Summit House   Mt. Wachusett

Open from May
to October

E. W. NEEDHAM
Manager

On the top of Wachusett Mountain (2,015 feet above sea level,) Princeton, Mass.

Three different summit hotels stood on Wachusett; the final one succumbed to fire in 1970. Photo courtesy Anita Woodward, Princeton, MA.

Inspired by the success of the Mount Tom Railway, which opened in 1893, a group of private investors proposed building an inclined railway to Wachusett's summit from the terminus of the Gardner, Westminster & Fitchburg Street Railway. The proprietors of the Mount Wachusett Railway Company projected immediate financial success for the 1.3-mile-long attraction. Yet the state could not be convinced to implement the plan. Later, in 1902, they again took a firm stand against technology in the park, making two arrests for the same offense: entering the reservation with an automobile.

The state did continue to develop amenities on the mountain, building a new summit house in 1907–08 and adding electricity in 1925. But patterns of life were changing, and Wachusett's popularity was declining. Cases of tuberculosis dropped, and, with the advent of automobiles, the higher peaks of the White Mountains lured many travelers to a new mecca for post-World War I recreation. There were so few overnight guests on Wachusett that the reservation management saw little hope for the future of their hotel. They leased it to a private group, but its demise was inevitable. In its final years, the only public access to the once-grand hotel was a souvenir stand on the first floor. The Summit House was burned by arsonists in December 1971, having been scheduled for demolition the following year.

From the early years of the state reservation, forest management was a high priority. Not only did the commissioners vote to plant thousands of trees in an effort to restore the mixed forest that had been largely destroyed by logging and agriculture, but they began to reintroduce white-tailed deer to the park, a species long vanished because of lack of suitable habitat and food supply. The fenced enclosure also contained, for a time, elk and angora goats. Reports of the commissioners detail the concerted efforts to maintain wildlife and protect their habitats.

Much of this careful work was undone by New England's worst hurricane in September 1938. High winds wiped out thousands of the largest hemlocks and pines, leaving the reservation in ruins. Fortunately, help arrived from the Works Progress Administration (WPA), a depression-era public-works project, and much of the brush and deadwood were cleared and burned. This group also renovated the Summit House.

Forestry management could not replace lost tourist revenues, however. A new opportunity, downhill skiing, offered the promise of a popular, if not immediately lucrative, recreational enterprise on Wachusett. Charles Proctor, an Olympic skier from Pittsfield, cut the Balance Rock Ski Trail in 1933. It was 1.5 miles long, with a width of fifteen feet on the straightaways and twenty-five feet on the curves. A few years later, the Civilian Conservation Corps (CCC) came to Wachusett, improved the first ski trail, made another more difficult trail on the east face, and built Bullock Lodge as a warming hut for skiers. For twenty years these facilities, without any lift, served a small but dedicated group of skiers: Wachusett hosted the Massachusetts Downhill Championships frequently during the 1940s and 1950s.

Then in 1959, the superintendent of the reservation, Earle R. Vickery, successfully lobbied the Massachusetts legislature to develop a full-fledged alpine ski area on the mountain. Unfortunately, the state had little experience in running ski areas, and after adding trails, lifts, and snow-making equipment, found itself posting significant losses each year. Privatization was the answer. The state was relieved of its management problems in 1968 when it signed a lease for full operation of the ski area with Wachusett Mountain Associates, headed by Ralph Crowley of Worcester. There followed a decade of hard work and slim profit margins to build the ski area into a successful recreational enterprise.

Ten years later, the state reassessed the management of Mount Wachusett with a long-range planning process designed to extend into the twenty-first century. Their final report, issued in 1980, identified "priority zones" on the mountain, different classifications that would allow for multiple use at the same time that key areas of scenic, historic, or environmental significance would be preserved. One of the main outcomes of that report was clarification of how much further development the holders of the ski-area lease might be permitted.

Building on that report, the ski area created a master plan for their 450 acres. They hired Sno-engineering, designers of more than 250 ski areas worldwide, which proposed adding lifts and trails that would significantly expand the area's capacity and still conform to the regulations adopted by the state. Major expansion was undertaken in 1982–84, adding new lifts, trails, and snow-making equipment. Now operating with a new long-term lease, Wachusett Mountain Associates has invested its own funds in acreage adjoining the state-owned property at the base of the mountain. Expansion of the ski area continues.

An important component of the revitalized Mount Wachusett Ski Area is the award-winning base lodge designed by Lindsay Shives & Associates of Still River, Massachusetts and completed in 1981. Its rambling form recalls New England vernacular architecture. Its large decks overlook a small pond, welcoming visitors to the mountain at any time of year. The pond is really a multipurpose, man-made creation that was designed to fuel the snow-making system. Realizing the tremendous amount of heat generated by snow-making machinery, the architect located the primary machinery below the building itself. By means of an innovative heat-recovery system, excess energy from the snow-making process helps to heat the base lodge.

The state of Massachusetts leases part of its Mount Wachusett Reservation to a private company for a ski area. Photo courtesy Wachusett Mountain Ski Area.

From a couple of T-bars and a handful of trails serving 50,000 skiers a year, Wachusett has grown to five lifts, eighteen trails, and 375,000 skiers in its 1993–1994 season. Proof of its resounding success is the 1994–1995 addition of the only high-speed detachable quad chairlift in the state.

The Mount Wachusett State Reservation today works in partnership with the ski area to preserve and protect environmental resources. The state's basic management philosophy is to use the reservation for as many different forms of outdoor recreation as it will support "without allowing the pursuit of one form to encroach unduly on the enjoyment of other forms and without serious jeopardy to the resource itself."

The 1980 management plan for the reservation carried a renewed commitment to six goals—protecting environmental resources; providing high-quality, year-round recreational opportunities; maintaining scenic qualities; preserving habitat for flora and fauna; managing a sustainable program of timber harvesting; and continuing to respect the mountain's historical significance. A citizens' advisory group, the Mount Wachusett Advisory Council, wields significant clout as it reports directly to the state on matters regarding the operation of the reservation or the ski area.

Year-round use of the reservation goes beyond the north slope where the ski area is located. Much of it is concentrated along the auto road, where cars, boom boxes, and barbecue grills bespeak an urban way of life transported to the mountain. But in the reservation's woods, like an oasis of calm, one can still find delight for the senses and refreshment for the soul. Deer, partridge, and other wildlife are plentiful. In late spring, the woods are filled with the spicy scent of the pink-flowering azalea. Low-growing chokeberry carpets the summit rocks, and clintonia, Canada mayflower, and bunchberry bloom profusely along the mountain trails.

Mountains like Wachusett—accessible, friendly, laden with associations from the past—often inspire both poetry and prose. Clara Endicott Sears, facing the setting sun over Mount Wachusett from an elegant summer home to the east wrote both. She retold the story of King Philip's War for an early-twentieth-century audience because she felt it invested the landscape with resonance and meaning. Her poetry expressed similar sentiments. "The Valley of the Nashaway Indians" contained her plea to not forget:

> There stands lofty fair Wachusett
> Like a guardian at the gate,
> Silent watcher o'er the valley
> Through its varied turns of Fate.
> Once a stronghold of the Indians,
> Now it lets Time slip away,
> Dreaming of the by-gone warriors
> Of the vale of Nashaway.

Suggestions for Visitors

Mount Wachusett is a favorite location for watching spring and fall hawk migrations, especially on sunny days following cold fronts. The heaviest raptor traffic is usually in mid-April and in early October. In the spring, the Ledges, a little over halfway up the auto road, is a preferred lookout because it affords a good view to the south.

In June carpets of wildflowers, clintonia, and bunchberries border the Old Indian Trail on Wachusett. Kurt Stier

Four well-worn trails were already named and mapped when Wachusett Mountain State Reservation was established. On the north was the Old Indian Trail; Pine Hill Trail was on the east, the Mountain House Trail on the southeast, and the Harrington Trail on the southwest. All of these are still available for the hiker today, as well as many volunteer-built trails added later. The most notable of the more recent trails is the Jack Frost Trail, which was conceived, marked, cleared, and eventually named for a retired physician named Harold P.

Frost. It runs through a grove of hemlock on the south shoulder of Wachusett which, prior to his efforts, had not been reached by any trail. After his death, the Worcester Chapter of the AMC arranged to have the 1.5-mile trail named in "Jack" Frost's memory.

A combination drive and hike, especially good for families with small children, covers the lower half of the mountain by car. Parking is available at a turnout adjacent to a stone wall, and the trailhead is just beyond and to the left. Follow the Old Indian Trail up its last short but fairly steep pitch to the summit. Wildflowers and pink-flowering azalea bloom in abundance along this route.

The summit has been graded to accommodate a hundred-car gravel parking lot. Around the margins are a steel fire-observation tower, communications antennas for various state agencies, and a boarded-up WPA building called Parker Lodge. On peak weekends, cars fill even the overflow lots below the summit. While there is nothing to mark the spot of the summit hotel, the old ice pond and retaining wall are still visible, as are two viewing platforms constructed during the heyday of the hotel era. Off to the north are the 1954 cement remains of the hotel's sanitary facilities. Careful perusal of the rocks around the edges of the parking lot will reveal chiseled initials and names of mountaintop visitors of long ago.

Just a short walk down from the summit toward the top of the chairlift stands a memorial plaque to the Tenth Mountain Division. This elite corps of World War II ski troops helped fund the construction of the ski trail named in their honor, and every year, uniformed members reconvene at Wachusett for a day of skiing and remembrance.

One of the state's long-distance footpaths crosses the summit of Wachusett. The Midstate Trail, which runs through the middle of Massachusetts, goes over Wachusett on its way north from Rhode Island. A 3.9-mile segment of the trail lies within the reservation. From Redemption Rock, the trail winds over Wachusett, through Ashburnham, then over the state line into New Hampshire, connecting there with another long-distance hiking route, the Wapack Trail.

Altogether the reservation contains twenty miles of marked and named trails, maintained in part through the volunteer efforts of members of the AMC's Worcester chapter. The paved summit road is open from May through the end of October, 10:00 am to 8:00 pm.

Modern structures and the nineteenth-century ice pond stand just below the summit of Wachusett. Kurt Stier.

Hikers, snow-shoers and bird watchers can park at the Hitchcock Visitor's Center on Mountain Road, just beyond the entrance to the ski area. There trail maps, bathrooms, and information on the social and natural history of the mountain are available. No camping or snowmobiles are permitted in the reservation; hunting is allowed only in specially designated areas. Dogs must be leashed. For more information, contact the Visitor's Center at 508-464-2987.

Information on skiing and year-round special events at Wachusett Mountain Ski Area may be obtained toll-free by calling 800-SKI-1234.

Holyoke and Tom

High above the oaks and sycamores of the Connecticut valley loom the dark cathedrals of Mount Holyoke and Mount Tom, celebrated outlooks over the rich farmlands bordering the wide river. Native Americans worked in riverside fields here, then were succeeded by colonists whose industry and agriculture transformed the landscape. The scene of rural prosperity to be seen from the high ridge of mountains above the towns of Holyoke, Hadley, and Easthampton brought these peaks early attention; the first mountaintop structure in the United States was built on Mount Holyoke in 1821. Later, ingenious uphill conveyances carried thousands of city dwellers up Mount Holyoke and Mount Tom, there to be entertained in spacious summit houses and rewarded with wide vistas of the winding river and picturesque towns below.

The Tom and Holyoke ranges, born of intense geological change, home of rare and endangered species, gateway to New England's larger mountains, have seen extensive use in their long history. Thanks to preservation efforts in the present century, the distinctive geography of these places continues to offer diverse recreational activities and scenic rewards.

Geology and Geography

Mount Tom, at 1,202 feet, crowns a ridge of basalt that projects sharply upward from the floor of the Connecticut River Valley in western Massachusetts. This ridge runs north to south along the western edge of the river in the towns of Holyoke and Easthampton until it reaches Mount Tom, then turns eastward. The Connecticut River cuts through at the pivot point; to the east of the river the mountains are called the Holyoke Range, to the west the Tom Range. The subordinate peaks of Mount Nonotuck, Goat Peak, Whiting Peak, and Dead Top on the western side of the river share the ridge with Mount Tom.

On the east side, straddling the towns of South Hadley and Hadley, are the summits of Holyoke and Hitchcock. Mount Norwottuck, farther to the east, is the highest point in the range at 1,106 feet. Extending along the ridge to the Amherst/Belchertown line are the lesser summits of Rattlesnake Peak and Long Mountain. Mount Holyoke, closest to the river and rising to an elevation of 878 feet,

As seen from Mount Tom, the upraised highlands of the Holyoke Range show the ridge of the Connecticut River Valley fault line. Kurt Stier.

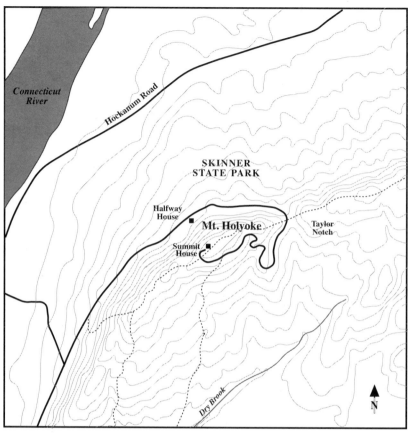

Holyoke

has given its name to the entire ridge. While these elevations may seem comparatively low, the mountains rise so sharply from the valley floor at only about 100 feet above sea level that their overall height seems more impressive.

The ridge and the valley were actually formed together, a rift made several hundred million years ago when tectonic forces tore North America away from Africa. Rivers deposited layer upon layer of sand and mud, which, over millions of years, gradually hardened into sandstone and shale, respectively. Lava spilling out of deep fissures in the earth poured across these sediments, cooling and hardening into thick layers of a dense, chocolate-colored stone called basalt or traprock.

As the rifting continued, the whole east side of what is now the valley gradually subsided, tilting the once-flat beds of basalt and sedimentary rocks on an angle. After that, the infinitely slow process of erosion gradually etched away the rock, attacking the softer shales and sandstones more effectively and leaving the more resistant basalt as the series of craggy ridges we see today.

In comparatively recent times, successive invasions of huge ice sheets have further modified the scenery. Rocks and sand frozen in the ice left still-visible scratches and gouges in the basalt on the summits of these hills. As the ice melted, about 12,000–15,000 years ago, it left its cargo of rocks and debris as a scattered layer on the ground. A great mass of this mixture dammed the valley below present-day Middletown, Connecticut, and meltwater from the ice sheet filled the upper 157 miles of the valley as far north as Lyme, New Hampshire. This huge body of water, known as Glacial Lake Hitchcock, lasted 4,000 years. Sediments deposited on the bottom of the lake, enriched by annual flooding of the river that succeeded the lake, created the most fertile agricultural land in New England.

History

The native peoples of this region farmed the rich bottom lands of the valley long before the coming of European settlers. They were all members of the Algonquin-speaking Nipmuc tribe, the band near Mount Tom called the Nonotuck and the group near Holyoke the Norwottuck. Norwottuck means "in the midst of the river," suggesting not only the physical location but also the central importance of the river in the lives of these early inhabitants.

In 1653, English settlers paid a hundred fathoms of wampum and ten coats, and plowed sixteen acres of land for use by the Native Americans, to obtain title to a hundred square miles of land lying north of Springfield. Mounts Holyoke and Tom are generally believed to have been renamed by these first white settlers. The story goes that two groups of explorers headed northward from Springfield on

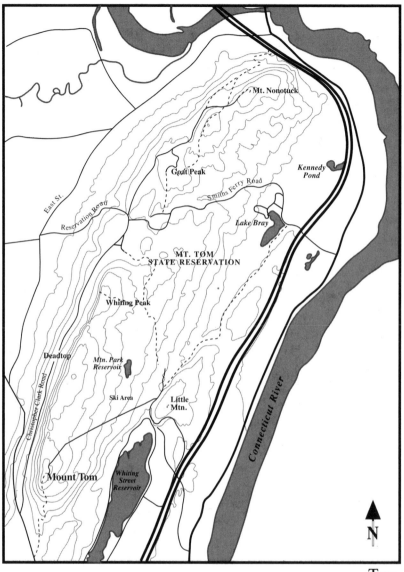

Tom

opposite banks of the Connecticut River. One group, led by Captain Thomas Rowland, marched up the west bank, and another party, led by Elizur Holyoke, proceeded up the east bank. What transpired as they reached the mountain range was immortalized in "Mountain Christening," a verse by Dr. J. G. Holland:

Holyoke, the gentle and daring, stood
 On the eastern bank, with his trusty four,
And Rowland Thomas, the gallant and good,
 Headed the band on the other shore.

The women were weeping to bid them good-bye,
 And sweet Mary Pynchon was there (I guess),
With a sigh in her throat, and a tear in her eye,
 As Holyoke marched into the wilderness.

The morning dawned on the double group,
 Facing each other on opposite shores,
Where years ago with a mighty swoop,
 The waters parted the mountain doors.

"Let us christen the mountain," said Holyoke, in glee.
 "Let us christen the mountain," said Thomas again,
"This mountain for you and that mountain for me."
 And their trusty fellows responded, "Amen."

Others dispute this bit of history, suggesting instead that Mount Tom's name may have been derived from an Indian word; or that, because town records contain no mention of a Thomas Rowland, perhaps a surveyor named Thomas Cooper, a member of Holyoke's militia, was the actual protagonist on the west bank.

Whatever the origin of its name, Mount Tom's peaks were not appreciated as a scenic outlook by seventeenth- and eighteenth-century farmers, who perceived such hilly terrain as utterly valueless. One Yankee's estimate of mountains in general, that "they might be good land if they were flatter," was typical and only slightly less positive on the subject than another's: "They look nice, I guess, but we often have them here."

That attitude was to change rather quickly along the Connecticut River. Reverend Timothy Dwight, a Northampton native who served as president of Yale College, was one of the first Americans to celebrate the virtues of landscape scenery. Every summer from 1795 to 1807 he toured the countryside, and in 1821-22 he published a five-volume narrative account, *Travels in New England and New York.*

Dwight's book almost instantly popularized specific places as destinations worthy of travelers' pilgrimages.

One of those places was the Mount Holyoke region of the Connecticut River Valley, the premier outlook from which to contemplate the progress of American civilization. Dwight, and those who followed in his footsteps, admired not only Holyoke's picturesque scenery, but its panorama of tidy homes, industrious villages, white churches, and well-tended fields. Dwight's enthusiasm for this European ideal of landscape is captured in his description of the view.

> From Mount Holyoke...is seen the richest prospect in New England, and not improbably in the United States....On the highest part of the summit, the inhabitants have cleared away the trees and shrubs so as to open the prospect in the most advantageous manner....The variety of farms, fields, and forests, of churches and villages, of hills and valleys, of mountains and plains comprised in this scene can neither be described nor imaged.

Dwight's word pictures conditioned Americans to the civic pride and panoramic beauty he thought they ought to be experiencing when they climbed mountains. Thanks to his advance publicity, hundreds of visitors made their way to these relatively accessible summits after 1820. Other guidebooks, published in succeeding decades, reiterated Dwight's assessment. One extolled the view from Mount Holyoke as "probably the richest in America, in point of cultivation and fertile beauty." The climb itself was considered only a means to an end, and within a few short years even that arduous element of the trip could be avoided.

The Hotel Era

Mount Holyoke not only had the most appreciated view in the United States, but it may have had the first mountaintop building in North America, certainly the first in New England. A one-room house was erected on the summit of Mount Holyoke in 1821, used mostly as a drinking spot by local hunters and outdoorsmen. By the 1830s, however, it was a bit more genteel. A guidebook from that era advised those who would climb Mount Holyoke: "The ascent at the side is easy; and it is a fashionable climb for tourists, whose patronage of ginger-beer and sunrises maintains a shanty and a hermit on the top, and keeps in repair a series of scrambling but convenient ladders at the difficult points of the enterprise."

An ambitious couple, John and Fanny French, bought the summit property in 1849, and within two years it offered grander accommodations in a two-story, eight-room structure they called Prospect House. By 1851 they had added a unique cable railway that conveyed people directly from the Connecticut River up to their establishment on the summit of Mount Holyoke. Variously labeled a funicular, chairlift, covered cable railway, or tramway, the lift operated in two distinct parts. On the lower half, passengers were carried from the steamboat dock on the river up a moderate grade to another new building, French's Halfway House. There the lift entered a wooden tunnel and continued for 400 feet up the nearly vertical face of the traprock, where the three-seat cars emerged directly into the lobby of Prospect House.

A typical outing to the mountains in the nineteenth century might require crossing the Connecticut River on the horse-powered Hockanum Ferry. Photo courtesy Historic Northampton, Inc.

Horses originally furnished the power for the lower section, working one-hour shifts to turn a giant windlass. But the rope on the windlass had a tendency to stretch, so this part of the system was scrapped and horse-drawn carriages were used to ascend a road instead. The wooden tunnel between the Halfway House and Prospect House continued in service, using steam power and ultimately electricity to power the cars.

This unorthodox system was subject to frequent redesign. In its last incarnation, the tracks were 600 feet long and rose 365 feet, a gradient much steeper than that of Mount Washington's cog railway. It carried an estimated two million passengers without a serious accident until it was shut down after the start of World War II. Henry Wadsworth Longfellow, John Quincy Adams, and Alexander Graham Bell all rode French's tramway up Mount Holyoke. The guest register of the summit hotel contains other famous names, too, such as Jenny Lind, the "Swedish Nightingale," and a record of dozens of outings from nearby colleges.

Prospect House was an elegant destination, and the proprietors expanded and remodeled to keep it in the height of fashion. Enlarged first in 1862, it was refined to Victorian tastes in 1890, when large balconies and porches were added. From the telescopes in the observation room, one could read the time on the Hartford, Connecticut, clock tower sixty miles away.

French sold the hotel to New York businessman John Dwight in 1871, but continued to operate it until his death twenty years later. Dwight then ran it for awhile, but the house's fortunes were in decline. Local businessmen rescued it in 1908, when they formed the Mount Holyoke Hotel Company and purchased the property from Dwight's heirs. One of the stockholders of this new venture was Joseph A. Skinner, a wealthy silk manufacturer from Holyoke. In 1916, Skinner assumed full ownership of the mountain property.

The hotel's continued survival in the twentieth century was threatened by damage from the epic hurricane of September 1938. The four-story, thirty-five-bedroom wing that had been built in 1894 was razed following the storm. That same year, Joseph Skinner deeded the summit house and 375 acres to the commonwealth of Massa-

The restored summit house on Mount Holyoke is the centerpiece of the Joseph Allen Skinner State Park. The Friends of Skinner State Park sponsor free or low-cost events and activities, including the Mountain Fest each June. Kurt Stier.

chusetts, to be used "for the enjoyment of the public." In 1940 the Holyoke Range State Park was dedicated, and the park continued to operate Prospect House and auto road to the summit.

The summit house became notorious locally as the place where Mount Holyoke College students went to slow-dance, but by the 1970s it was a ravaged wreck. There followed several years of controversy about the future of the old building. Finally, in the 1980s, the Massachusetts Department of Environmental Management made a commitment to restore the main structure. The project was completed and the building once again made available for public use in 1987.

French's cable car did not fare so well. The popularity of automobile travel made it less used and therefore unprofitable to operate, and the old wooden tunnel and tracks were expensive to maintain. The death knell was sounded when heavy snowfall accumulations in the spring of 1948 collapsed the tunnel, making the lift totally inoperable.

The glory days across the river at Mount Tom lagged well behind Mount Holyoke, although a house had been built on Mount Tom's South Peak (elev. 1,218 feet) sometime prior to 1827. In 1893, a new corporation called the Mount Tom Railway Company purchased land on the southeast slope of the mountain and built a trolley line from the Holyoke Street Railway to the base of the mountain. Despite criticism from skeptics, the railway company constructed an electric cable car leading straight up the mountain to a spacious and elegant summit house.

In 1894 the company opened a 400-acre amusement park located between the river's edge and the mountain's base. Mountain Park and the cable cars drew hundreds of mill workers and farmers to its rustic enclave on the outskirts of the city, where they could enjoy a dance pavilion, a roller coaster, and a carousel. Fossils of long-extinct dinosaur footprints were discovered in sandstone deposits within the park, adding another natural attraction to the man-made ones.

The Mount Tom Railway took visitors from the park to the mountaintop by means of an innovative two-car counterweighted system different from Mount Holyoke's lift. Two custom-made trolley cars, "models of taste and finish," were named for the legendary namesakes of the mountain range, Elizur Holyoke and Thomas Rowland. These were attached to an inch-and-a-quarter-thick steel cable that turned around an eight-foot sheave, or pulley, at the summit. One car climbed the mountain while the other descended and counterbalanced the first. Halfway up the grade, a turnout allowed the cars to pass each other.

Souvenir books of photographs and texts, published by the railway company, reassured passengers of the safety of the line. "The cars move up the rocky slope of the mountain by a grade so easy as not to suggest even the fear of giddiness to the most timid." Indeed, the maximum grade was only 21 percent.

At the top of the mountain stood an architectural wonder, a three-story summit house, seventy-six feet wide by ninety-two feet long, including fourteen-foot-wide piazzas surrounding the lower two stories. As at Holyoke's Prospect House, an observation room on the

Three large summit hotels stood on Mount Tom. The first, shown here, burned in 1900; the second even grander structure burned in 1929. A final concrete and steel edifice enjoyed much less architectural acclaim. Photo courtesy Holyoke Public Library, Holyoke, MA.

first floor was furnished with telescopes and detailed maps of the surrounding countryside. A second-floor concert hall contained an imported orchestrion, graphophones, and the very latest stereopticon and photographs, according to an 1897 newspaper article. Mount Tom had its share of famous visitors, too, including President and Mrs. McKinley, who were photographed at the Summit House in 1899.

The Summit House suffered an early demise: a huge fire destroyed the entire building in 1900. Unfortunately, that night the brakes were locked on the counterweighted cable car at the top, preventing potential assistance from below. Observers in the valley helplessly watched the conflagration as a sole night watchman on the summit valiantly tried to extinguish the flames. A rebuilt summit house, nearly identical to the first, opened the following year and operated until 1929, when fire claimed the mountaintop structure for the second time. By then, changes in economics and the increased popularity of weekend automobile travel were making local amusement parks and recreation areas such as Mount Tom's obsolete, so there was no attempt to rebuild on the former scale.

A much more modest summit house, made entirely of steel and concrete and lacking the architectural sophistication of the first two, was constructed in 1930. Without an auto road, however, Mount Tom's attractions were increasingly overlooked by travelers, and the third mountain house was ultimately razed at the same time the cable railway was sold for scrap. Mountain Park is now closed and the remaining buildings are boarded up, but the carved horses of the carousel have been preserved in downtown Holyoke's Heritage Park.

The attraction of the Mount Tom Railway's summit experience echoed the same ideals Timothy Dwight had found so compelling at the beginning of the century. The glory of the view, according to the railway company's publicity, was not just the vast panorama of the landscape, but in the particular attributes that showed the region's prosperity and status. Highlights worth noting included nearby Smith College and Mount Holyoke College, and at a further distance the two colleges of Amherst and the great gilded dome of the Hartford, Connecticut, statehouse. The mills that contributed to the region's strong economy were also itemized—Holyoke's paper making,

Chicopee's cotton cloth and bicycles, Westfield's whips and cigars, and Easthampton's button manufactory.

Conservation

In addition to taking pride in the well-ordered and prosperous civilization that could be seen from the mountaintop, the largely urbanized visitor population noticed something else about the mountain—its natural beauty and wildlife. At the beginning of the twentieth century, the state assumed an active role in protecting these qualities and in reaping a share of the profits from tourism.

In 1903, the commonwealth of Massachusetts purchased the entire northern section of Mount Tom adjacent to the amusement park and created the Mount Tom State Reservation. Reservations at Greylock and Wachusett had been established a few years earlier, but Mount Tom's was delayed because the state wanted the local counties to have responsibility for maintenance. Since Tom straddles two counties, there had to be consensus. Although Hampden County wanted the reservation established, the smaller Hampshire County was very reluctant to take on the financial commitment. The two counties finally agreed to manage the reservation cooperatively and did so until 1990 when the Massachusetts Department of Environmental Management assumed full control.

On the Mountain Park side of the mountain, the Civilian Conservation Corps cut ski trails beginning in 1933. Throughout the mountain areas of New England this public-works program, authorized by Congress during the Great Depression, put groups of unemployed young men to work developing natural resources for outdoor recreation. They cut hiking and ski trails, built roads, and constructed fire towers, camping facilities, and picnic areas.

After the CCC's efforts, the Mount Tom Reservation requested that the state purchase about 600 acres of the former Mountain Park to add to the existing state reservation. When the state declined, the property passed into private ownership.

The Mount Tom ski area now occupies the face of the mountain that once had cable cars running up and down. Fueled by the postwar boom in skiing and supported by the urban centers close by, it opened for business in 1960, utilizing the old CCC trails. That same year it became the first ski area in the country to install lighting on its slopes and offer night skiing. Mount Tom's natural snowfall is unpredictable, and, even with artificial snow making, the management had to look for other sources of income after the late-1980s downturn in the New England economy. In 1991, Mount Tom revived the amusement-park concept with a 4,000-foot alpine slide descending the face of the mountain, a mechanized wave pool, and an outdoor cafe. Visitors who show the same enthusiasm for these recreational "sports," like those of an earlier era on the roller coaster, seem oblivious to the more natural charms of the mountain.

Mount Holyoke, on the other side of the river, has enjoyed greater protection under state ownership. The 375 acres given to the commonwealth in 1938 by Joseph Skinner became the nucleus of what is now Skinner State Park. Recognizing the need to protect the entire range, a group of dedicated citizens proposed an expanded Holyoke Range State Park that will eventually encompass the entire ridge. Already, about two-thirds of the proposed lands have been purchased.

Within the park, the privately occupied Halfway House has been restored, and refurbishment of the historic Prospect House at the summit is nearly complete. No overnight accommodations are offered, but when it is open on weekends, the house conveys a powerful sense of its former glory. Down in the notch where the north-south Route 116 passes through the Holyoke Range, a new visitor's center has also opened.

Natural Attractions

The geology of these mountains makes for interesting exploration. Edward Hitchcock, president of Amherst College, first documented the peculiar geology and botany of the region in the 1830s, and both a peak in this range and the glacial lake that flooded this valley following the Ice Age are named after him. Rocks here look unlike those of the mountains farther to the north; the basalt breaks into shoebox-shaped solids or odd tubular eminences where molten rock once thrust upward. North of the ski area on Mount Tom is an old quarry where stone was removed for paving the streets of Holyoke, and where gravel is still being taken out in small quantities and sold for road use today.

The dramatic geologic fault that created these mountains has yielded a distinctive ecology here. Copperheads and even timber rattlesnakes make their homes on the traprock ledges, and rare marbled salamanders and box turtles may be found in moister habitats beneath the ledges. Surrounding development and highways have fragmented these ranges into biological islands, where animals and plants have survived in small, isolated ecosystems long after their elimination in the nearby countryside. These include an endangered orchid called the lily-leafed twayblade and an unusual forest mix of hop hornbeam (a relatively low-growing understory tree also called ironwood for its tough, heavy wood) and hickory.

Perhaps the best-known element of Tom and Holyoke's natural environment is the hawks that are drawn to these uplands. During the spring and fall, Tom and Holyoke are premier locations for watching migrating hawks along the Connecticut River corridor. In the fall, the Holyoke Range has the effect of funneling the southbound birds toward Mount Tom.

Hawks migrate on nearby updrafts. These winds arise because the mountains deflect surface winds upward and also act as solar collectors that generate columns of warm air. Two towers have been constructed on Mount Tom to elevate hawk watchers above the trees. In the fall, especially during the middle of September, the Goat Peak Tower is the best vantage point for viewing the thousands of raptors that pass by. Species include broad-winged, sharp-shinned, red-tailed, and red-shouldered hawks; harriers; ospreys; eagles; and falcons. Spring migration is best observed from Bray Tower; the spring flights are not usually as concentrated as those in the autumn, but take place over a longer period from mid-March through early May. Mount Holyoke's summit affords an equally rewarding site for hawk watching, where birds are often observed flying well below the summit elevation.

The peregrine falcon nested until the middle of this century on the jagged and precipitous traprock ledges on the western side of Mount Tom. A living thunderbolt whose unsurpassed powers of vision and flight gave it command of the broad fertile valley, it preyed

The falcon aerie on Mount Tom, located in 1864, was the first confirmed peregrine nesting site in Massachusetts. Photo courtesy Massachusetts Division of Wildlife and Fisheries.

on domestic fowl so heavily that it was hunted and trapped almost to extinction. Able to fly at speeds up to 150 miles per hour, the peregrine can kill on the wing and frequently knocks birds larger than itself, including other birds of prey, right out of the air. Mount Tom, first confirmed in 1864 as one of about a dozen documented nesting sites in Massachusetts, has received much attention for its peregrines over the years.

Another early threat to these majestic birds was egg collecting, a hobby that has thankfully all but disappeared. The Fish and Game Department began a program in the 1920s to locate nests and label each egg with a painted number inscribed on a white spot that had been sandpapered on the egg. This effectively discouraged collectors, and if any stolen eggs did turn up, they could easily be traced to a certain nesting site. Other threats—hunters and later the pesticide DDT—eliminated the peregrine falcons entirely from their Mount Tom location, a loss keenly felt by bird lovers and conservationists.

In the 1970s, Cornell University attempted to reintroduce these birds to the cliffs of Mount Tom. In 1976, three chicks were successfully raised, but an equal number the following year yielded only one survivor. Six birds were placed in the historic aerie in 1978, and this time the success rate was excellent—only one of the fledglings failed to survive. But a major disappointment in 1979 finally stopped the Mount Tom project: Four young birds introduced to the site disappeared under "very suspicious circumstances," according to the coordinator.

Successful fledging of peregrines ultimately was achieved on the twenty-first-story window ledge of an office building in nearby Springfield. The activities of one of only two nesting pairs in Massachusetts have been broadcast around the clock on a local cable-television channel for several years.

Art and Artists

Typical of any tourist mecca, these mountains have attracted prominent literary and artistic people, including many foreigners, who delighted in the great beauty of the view from either summit. In 1834, the visiting Harriet Martineau wrote admiringly of the town of Northampton: "It lies in the rich meadows which border the Connecticut, beneath the protection of high wooded knolls and terraces on which the village stands....The celebrated Mount Holyoke and Mount Tom are just at hand...while the brimming Connecticut winds about and about in the meadows, as if unwilling, like the traveler, to leave such a spot." Nathaniel Hawthorne visited here, as did Massachusetts Senator Charles Sumner, who declared, "I have been all over England, have traveled through the highlands of Scotland; I have passed up and down the Rhine. I have ascended Mount Blanc and stood on campagna in Rome; but I have never seen anything so surprisingly lovely as this."

Ironically, the most famous painting of this view portrayed it in just the opposite way, not as a celebration of a cultivated land of peace and plenty, but more like the chaos of creation. Thomas Cole (1801–1840) painted *View from Mount Holyoke, Northampton, Massachusetts, after a Thunderstorm* in 1836. Now in the collection of the Metropolitan Museum of Art in New York, it is the quintessential expression of his philosophy of landscape painting—that wilderness

Thomas Cole's celebrated 1836 painting View from Mount Holyoke, After a Thunderstorm, *paired contrasts of wilderness and civilization in a potent metaphor for the American experience.* Photo courtesy Metropolitan Museum of Art, New York, NY.

and untamed nature were meant to evoke a feeling of helplessness in the face of God's power.

Cole, often considered the father of American landscape painting and acknowledged as the founder of the famous Hudson River school, contrived the view from Mount Holyoke to fit a formula he and his followers began to develop in the 1820s. They traveled during the summer and early fall along the Hudson and into the Catskills, through the White Mountains and east to Katahdin and Mount Desert Island, all the while filling sketchbooks with dramatic and awe-inspiring landscape scenery. Then, back in their New York or Boston studios for the winter, they translated these sketches into oil paintings, often of monumental proportions.

Cole's widely known Mount Holyoke image is one of dozens painted or drawn of the famous oxbow bend in the river. Other artists often depicted the scene more realistically by including the rustic hermit's shanty or well-dressed visitors. But just a few years after Cole's visit, the view was changed forever. In 1840, an ice jam formed within the oxbow and the backing waters found their way across the neck of land, cut a more direct channel, and converted the oxbow into a crescent-shaped lake.

Suggestions for Visitors

Auto roads give easy access to the top of Mount Holyoke and Mount Tom's Nonotuck peak, but the gut-level experience of these and other mountains is reserved for those who walk up their grades. Skinner State Park (413-586-0350) and Mount Tom Reservation (413-527-4805) charge a small entrance fee and offer extensive trail networks, good maps, and picnic and restroom facilities.

Mount Tom Reservation's entrance is off Route 5 at Smith's Ferry, a few miles south of Northampton. Visitors can park near Lake Bray and follow the Teabag Trail up to Goat Peak's lookout tower and on to Mount Nonotuck. There, the trail runs past the fortresslike stone ruins of Eyrie House. Built by an eccentric man named Street who wanted to operate his own cable car to the summit, Eyrie House was aptly named. Though the woods around it are now overgrown, it perches on a very steep outcropping high above the valley floor.

Hiking trails and roadways radiate from the Robert Cole Museum of Natural History within the Mount Tom State Reservation. Kurt Stier.

A pleasant drive follows the winding paved park road through the woods to the Robert Cole Museum of Natural History, open seasonally. Just beyond the museum is a picnic area with playing fields and swing sets.

The Mount Tom Ski Area (413-536-0416) is not in the reservation; its turnoff is just off Route 5 a few miles south of the entrance to the Mount Tom Reservation and near Interstate 91. The boarded-up Mountain Park is visible to the left along the mountain access road. Commercial interests are very much in evidence on the true summit of Mount Tom: ski lifts and several broadcast towers.

Mount Holyoke, at the eastern end of Skinner State Park, can be climbed via the Metacomet-Monadnock Trail, which leaves the west side of Route 47 a short distance south of the main entrance to the state park. The trail begins at the Connecticut-Massachusetts border and follows a north-south axis through the central part of the state into New Hampshire, ending on the summit of Grand Monadnock. It follows the traprock ridge along the west edge of the Connecticut valley over Mount Tom, veers east and travels the length of the Holyoke Range, then turns north again at the eastern end of the ridge at Metacomet Lake.

A paved road affords another means of ascent to the summit and the historic Prospect House. Once there, picnic tables, outdoor fireplaces, and interpretive signs are maintained by the park. Just a short walk from the summit stands a granite memorial to the twenty-five victims of a 1944 plane crash there—a World War II training mission from nearby Westover Air Force Base. The explosion of the plane's fuel tanks caused a fire that burned about an acre of woodland here.

An all-volunteer organization, the Friends of the Holyoke Range, offers no- and low-cost hikes, talks, and other activities for the public. Every June they sponsor an annual "Mountainfest" at Prospect House which includes music, dances, and a presentation about native birds of prey. Throughout the year they work to encourage interest in and support for conservation and recreation here. Membership, program, and newsletter information may be obtained by writing to the Friends of the Holyoke Range, P.O. Box 728, South Hadley, MA 01775.

Greylock

Mount Greylock, the highest point in Massachusetts, lies in the northwestern corner of the state within an enclosure of mountains that sets the Berkshire region apart from the rest of the commonwealth. One hundred and fifty years ago industry sought the power of falling water in the Berkshire hills, spawning dozens of mills and factories that brought the promise of economic independence to scattered agricultural settlements. At the same time, a burgeoning upper class found the beauties of the natural landscape the perfect setting for summer cottages, and their presence complemented a host of artists and writers. Greylock, perhaps because of its sheer size or the presence of other, more approachable mountains close at hand, did not earn full celebrity status from these visitors. Nor did it yield its riches freely to entrepreneurs, though through difficult times in the region's economy Greylock has often been called upon as a commercial asset.

Greylock's fame has accumulated gradually, and events in the twentieth century have confirmed the paradoxes of this mountain as a place for both commerce and sanctuary. As the state's first natural reservation, Greylock has been characterized as having a limited capability to attract tourists, yet great potential for wilderness

Mount Greylock's eastern side as seen from Adams in this early photograph.
Photo courtesy Berkshire County Historical Society.

preservation. The ironic reality is that those who wish to preserve the mountain have often been those who invited more development.

Geography and Geology

Mount Greylock is 3,491 feet above and 130 miles away from the Atlantic Ocean. The summit is in the town of Adams, but the entire mountain encompasses parts of North Adams, Adams, Williamstown, Cheshire, New Ashford, and Lanesborough. The massif, a ridge eight miles long and about half as wide running parallel to the New York State border a short distance to the west, contains ten named peaks. The summit is called Mount Greylock. Its subordinates include Cole Mountain, Ragged Mountain, Mount Fitch, Mount Prospect, Rounds Rock, and Jones Nose. At various times in its history, the mountain has been known by other names, including Saddle, Saddle Ball, and Saddleback. From the south, the summit and the next northerly peak, Mount Fitch, do indeed bear a strong resemblance to the out-line of a saddle.

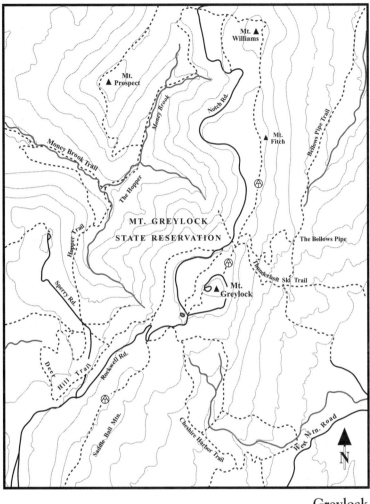

Greylock

Many of the rippled sides and valleys along the ridge are known by colorful names that chronicle the early history of the mountain. Rounds Rock and Jones Nose were named for the farmers who first cleared these outlooks. The Hopper, a prominent ravine on the mountain's west side believed to have been created by glaciers, is so named for its resemblance to the inside of a coal hopper. Bellows Pipe, at the upper end of the Notch on the east side of Greylock, takes its name from the thundering wind current that forms inside the narrow, steep walls of this valley. And, according to Greylock lore, Money Brook got its name because a den of counterfeiters lurked in its valley about two hundred years ago. Their cave, which has eluded modern investigators, is said to be guarded by ghosts, and the ringing concussions that echo from the hills are the sounds of deceased counterfeiters hammering unauthorized coins.

The valleys around Greylock are made of accumulated sea-floor sediments, rich in limestone created from the coral beds underlying what was once an ocean. There is also sandstone and shale, which is produced by mud; all are sedimentary rocks formed under tremendous pressure. The collision of North America with Europe and Africa created a great force that thrust upward the Berkshires, forerunners of the Appalachians. Extraordinary heat and pressure metamorphosed some of these sedimentary rocks: limestone became marble, sandstone became quartzite, and shale became schist and slate. Both sedimentary and metamorphic rocks are found on the mountain today.

Although generally regarded as part of the Berkshires, Mount Greylock is geologically a spur of the Taconic Range, of which Mount Equinox farther north is also a part. The Green Mountains and the Berkshire Hills are east of the Taconics, across the valley of the Hoosic River. A curious geological inconsistency exists here: the rocks of the Taconics appear to be upside-down in age—that is, the older ones lie atop the younger. Some geologists believe that what is now the Berkshires was at one time covered by the Taconics, and as the Green Mountains and Berkshires buckled upward, the Taconics broke off the top, flipping over and sliding to the west.

Mount Greylock's thick woods are filled with a rich variety of trees. At high elevations the principal tree is the red spruce, but on the mountainside the forest is of mixed hardwoods dominated by sugar maple, beech, and yellow and black birch. White birch, black cherry, basswood, white ash, and poplar are also present, and hemlocks crowd into ravines creating winter shelter for white-tailed deer. The understory is primarily striped maple and hobblebush. As elsewhere in New England, the virgin timber on these slopes is long gone, except for one notable stand of hemlock, perhaps 250–300 years old, in the Hopper. The steep sides of the ravine there prevented loggers from taking out the trees. Elsewhere, the slopes of Greylock were nearly denuded in the mid-nineteenth century by farmers clearing trees for fields, lumber, and for charcoal to fire iron-smelting operations and power railroad locomotives. This deforestation reached a peak after the Civil War; by the 1870s trees were reclaiming many of the hillside pastures, and farmers were abandoning unproductive fields for the relative promise of factory work in the cities.

Early History

Mount Greylock lay within the domain of the Hoosac Indians, a subgroup of the Mahicans, and until 1838 bore a version of the name they probably gave it, Grand Hoosuc Mountain. Written records from colonial days reveal little about their relationship to this, the highest mountain in their territory. The Mahicans were among the westernmost of the New England tribes speaking an Algonquin dialect. To their west were the Mohawks, part of the Iroquois federation and the Mahicans' bitter enemies. The mountain was thus a logical boundary for the two groups.

Early exploration of Greylock did not immediately precede settlement, as proved to be the case with many of New England's other peaks. In 1739 Massachusetts sent Ephraim Williams, Sr., to survey townships in the northwest corner of the commonwealth in order to claim this territory as part of its province. (Members of the survey team are believed to have been the first English-speaking people to have climbed the summit of Mount Greylock.) Although the surveyors drew township boundaries on paper, it was not considered safe for colonists to settle here until 1763, when the Treaty of Paris effectively ended the French and Indian Wars and gave control of Canada to Great Britain. Without pressure from their French allies, local Indian tribes willingly negotiated a peace, bringing security for English-speaking settlers to begin to populate New England's frontiers.

An energetic immigrant from Rhode Island named Jeremiah Wilbur was the first to claim ownership of Mount Greylock, building a bridle trail to the summit of Grand Hoosuc Mountain. Wilbur lived in the area known as the Notch, on the east side of Mount Greylock. Although his 1760s farmhouse is now gone, it was probably located near the beginning of the present Bellows Pipe Trail. Wilbur's farm eventually totaled 1,600 acres; the stone walls that bordered his extensive sheep pastures are still in place as high up as the 2,200-foot contour.

On the western side of the mountain, streams suitable for mills attracted industrious settlers into small village centers. The first mill in the Greylock area was built in 1767 at the place where Hopper Brook enters the Green River in present-day Williamstown, just downstream from one of the earliest houses built in the scenic valley called the Hopper. That house at the end of Hopper Road, erected by a Quaker couple named Elkahan and Grace Parris, stood for nearly two hundred years, from 1761 until it was destroyed by fire in 1950.

Higher on the mountain's west slope, Reverend Aaron Wright built a house in the valley of Money Brook, a tributary of Hopper Brook that drains the steep gulf between Mounts Prospect, Williams, and Fitch. While the foundation of an old sawmill still stands at Money Brook, Wright's house met an early demise, being carried off in a 1784 landslide. The Wright sawmill cut the lumber used to build one of the first towers on Greylock's peak.

While farmers Wilbur and Parris grazed their livestock on Mount Greylock's high pastures, a less tangible claim to the mountain was emerging in the valley. The son of the original surveyor was laying the base for an educational institution whose students would adopt Greylock as an unofficial outdoor classroom. Ephraim Williams, Jr., killed in the French and Indian Wars, had made provision in his will for a college. Williams College was founded in Williamstown in 1793.

Teachers and students almost immediately began to climb the mountain for recreation and to study natural history. A succession of enthusiastic Williams professors forged a strong bond between the mountain and the college that persists to this day. Professors Chester Dewey and Amos Eaton led botanical excursions, and Ebenezer Emmons, a geologist, made a list of Greylock's birds. One day in May 1830, the college president, Edward Door Griffin, dismissed all classes and formed a student task force to cut a trail up the west side of the mountain. The day's exertions resulted in the Hopper Trail, as well as an "observatory," the first building on the summit. (As on Wachusett, this was probably little more than a raised platform from which to "observe" the view.)

As interest in the mountain increased, so did dissatisfaction with its lack of one consistent appellation. The many variants of the name Hoosac in the area, and the further confusion over the mountain's other names, led to open controversy in 1838. Williams College professors took the lead in favoring the name Greylock, though its origin was vague. One Berkshire historian asserted that "it takes the appellation of 'Greylock' from its hoary aspect in the winter," while others argued it was named for an Indian chief named Gray Lock. In the final decision Greylock prevailed, a lesser peak to the south was officially given the name Saddle Ball Mountain, and the much-used Hoosac was reserved for the river and eliminated from the mountain range altogether.

As Williams College helped rename the mountain, so it took the lead in utilizing the mountain for physical education and recreation. The most notable of the early mountain-tramping Williams professors was Albert Hopkins. In 1841, with a college tutor named James H. Coffin, he spearheaded an effort to construct a three-story summit tower on Greylock. Replacing the old observation platform built by students, this was to be a real "meteorological observatory," and money was raised from the towns of Williamstown and North Adams. Wright's sawmill cut the lumber; students hauled it up the Hopper Trail. Though Hopkins' observatory suffered from occasional vandalism, it survived until fire completely destroyed it in 1878.

Hopkins is better known, however, for forming the first of New England's hiking clubs, the Alpine Club, in 1863. An astonishing nine of the twelve founding members were women, an indication of the early enthusiasm local women had for hiking. The club's activities centered on Greylock, but over its two-year span, members of the Alpine Club ranged farther afield to climb many other New England mountains as well.

Meanwhile, the wilderness aspect of Greylock was disappearing, and those who would speak out in favor of preservation had not yet found a voice. Human migration to the Ohio valley and the construction of the Erie Canal reduced the competitive position of New England agriculture. Lumbering for pulp, charcoal, and railroad fuel almost completely deforested Berkshire County before

Williams College students built this observation tower on Greylock. Henry David Thoreau climbed it in 1844.
Photo courtesy Berkshire Athenaeum, Pittsfield, MA.

the abandonment of farms and the use of coal for fuel reversed the trend. Industrialization seemed to offer the only hope of economic salvation for the depressed rural economy. As early as the 1850s, towns around Mount Greylock had paper mills, textile mills, iron and copper mining, sawmills, and tanneries, all powered by the streams rushing off the mountain's sides. Quarries for marble and slate opened huge gashes on the hillsides.

A further boost to economic development came in 1875, when the longest railroad tunnel in America, the 4 3/4-mile Hoosac Tunnel, was built through the Berkshires to North Adams. The last of the timber resources on Greylock would soon fall prey to the cities to the east, and demand for goods and raw materials from the Berkshire area spurred even greater economic development.

Tourism and the Arts

Up to this point, if Greylock enjoyed celebrated status, it was mostly among the Williams College crowd and those who had a particular interest in it because it was economically profitable. Artists and writers who brought fame to other mountains and contributed to their development as tourist meccas for the most part bypassed Greylock in favor of other attractions. Southern Berkshire County locales such as Mount Everett and Monument Mountain, Bash Bish Falls and Pontoosuc Lake, satisfied the aesthetic cravings of this elite group and their patrons who vacationed in tasteful summer homes in the area.

Williams-educated William Cullen Bryant and the writer Catherine Sedgwick formed the nucleus of the social life centered in Stockbridge and set a highbrow tone for the Berkshire experience. Bryant first opened a law practice in Great Barrington, then gradually turned to poetry, ultimately moving to New York where he became editor of the *Evening Post* and one of the most influential writers in America.

One of Bryant's best-known volumes, *Picturesque America,* described for aspiring travelers the highlights of American scenery. His characterization of the Berkshires bespoke a strong personal affection: "In village nooks, in glens and by-ways, upon near crests and remote hilltops, the lover of the beautiful will find innumerable views to gaze upon, to sketch, or happily to daguerreotype only on his memory." Bryant did not recommend the logged and mined slopes of Greylock to his readership.

Furthermore, Stockbridge, Lenox, and Lee were serviced by a railroad line and offered grand scenery of their own. Mount Everett and Monument Mountain received a great deal of attention from seasonal vacationers in these fashionable resort towns. It was here, therefore, that the great writers and artists of the day congregated, and although many made reference to Greylock, many more took the less strenuous path and rambled about Mount Washington (as Everett was then called) or Monument Mountain. In contrast, the northern corner of Berkshire County was difficult to reach, Greylock was a more difficult climb, and one was never guaranteed of appropriately genteel company.

Landscape artists of the nineteenth century, like the writers, accorded Greylock only moderate recognition. Most of the major figures of the Hudson River school painted in Berkshire County at some point in their careers, but they favored the southern Berkshires, where, according to Herman Melville, "no boy climbs hill or crosses vale without coming upon easels planted in every nook, and sunburnt painters painting there."

Only Thomas Cole produced a significant view of Greylock during this period—a typical composition of placid lake, grazing cows, and the dark, cloud-ringed heights of the mountain. Significantly, it was drawn from a southern vantage point, sketched during an 1833 trip and later painted in the studio. Called *View of Hoosac Mountain and Pontoosuc Lake Near Pittsfield, Massachusetts*, the artist found a buyer for the painting and it faded into private obscurity. Then a few years ago, curators at the Berkshire Museum noted something vaguely familiar in a picture known as *View of Mount Merino* in the collection of the Newark Museum. Compared to the present-day view from Pontoosuc Lake in Pittsfield, there was convincing evidence that the Cole painting of Greylock, long lost to the art world, had finally been "found." It was featured in an exhibition and catalog on the artistic ideals of the region's landscape, *A Return to Arcadia*, presented by the Berkshire Museum in 1990.

Greylock has a more impressive roster of literary associations. Three years after his walk to Wachusett, Henry David Thoreau went alone to Greylock and climbed it in the summer of 1844. There, he passed an interesting night on the summit: "As it was cold, I collected quite a pile of wood and lay down on a board against the side of the building, not having any blanket to cover me, with my head to the fire, that I might look after it, which is not the Indian rule. But as

Thomas Cole's View of Hoosac Mountain and Pontoosuc Lake Near Pittsfield, Massachusetts, *is one of the few nineteenth-century American landscape paintings to celebrate Greylock, though many artists were aware of the mountain.* Photo courtesy Newark Museum, Newark, NJ.

it grew colder towards midnight, I at length encased myself complete-ly in boards, managing even to put a board on top of me, with a large stone on it, to keep it down, and so slept comfortably."

Compensation for the discomforts of the night came with the dawn, when he climbed the tower built by Williams College to observe "an ocean of mist, which by chance reached up exactly to the base of the tower, and shut out every vestige of the earth, while I was left floating on this fragment of the wreck of a world, on my carved plank in cloudland."

Herman Melville, who spent thirteen summers in nearby Pittsfield at a farm he called Arrowhead, wrote much of *Moby Dick* within sight of Greylock. The dark outline of the mountain, he said, reminded him of the vast bulk of the great white whale. To mark the completion of his great saga of the sea, Melville and friends held a night-long party on the summit of Greylock. Another novel, *Pierre*, carried a dedication to "the majestic mountain Greylock—my own more immediate sovereign lord and king."

Nathaniel Hawthorne ventured beyond the comfortable hospitality of the mountain's southern side to find inspiration in Greylock's dark valleys. After a summer spent in North Adams observing local townsfolk, he composed a typically dark, brooding morality tale called "Ethan Brand." The plot involves the return of a lime-kiln owner who for eighteen years has been on a spiritual quest for the Unpardonable Sin. His search finally ends with a discovery from within. Hawthorne sets the stage for the ultimate revelation of eternal damnation by describing the woodland scene with eerie precision:

> There are many such lime kilns in that tract of country, for the purpose of burning the white marble which composes a large part of the substance of the hills. Some of them, built years ago, and long deserted, with weeds growing in the vacant round of the interior, which is open to the sky, and grass and wild flowers rooting themselves into the chinks of the stones, look already like relics of antiquity, and may yet be overspread with lichens of centuries to come. Others, where the lime-burner still feeds his daily and night-long fire, afford points of interest to the wanderer among the hills, who seats himself on a log of wood or a fragment of marble, to hold chat with the solitary man. It is a lonesome, and, when the character is inclined to thought, may be an intensely thoughtful occupation; as it proved in the case of Ethan Brand, who had mused to such strange purpose, in days gone by, while the fire in this very kiln was burning.

Some unusual activities have taken place on the summit of Mount Greylock. Around the turn of the century, ballooning was something of a rage. Edith Wharton claimed in her will that her chauffeur was the first to drive a car to the summit, in 1897. The only other legitimate claim to that record was made in 1902, when two steam-powered cars were reported to have made it to the top. Around 1917, the first winter ascent by car was reputedly made; most likely a light-snowfall year.

But by far the most bizarre of the many incidents associated with the mountain's history is the physical phenomenon known as the Specter of the Brocken. This rare meteorological occurrence is named for the highest of Germany's Harz Mountains, where it was first observed and recorded. It has also been noted at Mount Mansfield and Mount Washington. At Greylock, early in the twentieth century, it was experienced by the reservation superintendent and his guests as they stood on the summit at sunset. Looking down, they saw their own larger-than-life-size images reflected on a fog bank that was rising from the valley. In other reports, the Specter of the Brocken appears as a shadow projected onto clouds with a corona of rainbow colors. Whether shadow or reflection, the so-called specter can be explained as the product of sunlight striking objects horizontally with a cloud bank for projection.

Conservation and Exploitation

The built environment added a rich antiquity to the character of the place, but the lure of the mountain, for others, was its abundance of natural history. William Brewster, ornithologist and writer, ascended Greylock on horseback in June 1883, to catalog its bird population. His enthusiastic account, published in *The Auk* for the following year, lists sixty-six species, four never before recorded as nesting in the state. Brewster reported seeing a golden eagle, a bird that once nested in Massachusetts on this peak and now is only rarely sighted in the state.

In the great naturalist tradition of Brewster, many others have found rich sources for the study of natural history on Greylock. Williams College has played a key role in such efforts, as have local and state environmental groups including the Massachusetts Audubon Society. The mountain's varied habitats and limy soil today provide refuge to an estimated forty species of rare plants including the northern mountain ash, a tree that grows nowhere else in Massachusetts.

Mount Greylock had not, up until the 1880s, developed a wide reputation as a tourist destination, but conflicts inevitably surfaced between those who enjoyed Greylock for outings on foot or on horseback and those whose primary aim was to exploit the mountain for profit. Ironically, the peak of the artistic interest in Greylock coincided with the period during which the environmental degradation was the worst. Heavy logging, for instance, caused disastrous landslides and forest fires, especially on the mountain's east side.

A group of local businessmen formed the Greylock Park Association in 1885 in hopes of somehow preserving the mountain. Developing its potential for recreation seemed a perfect solution, one that would boost the economic fortunes of the region and at the same time reclaim the mountain's natural state. The association bought 400 acres of land at the summit, hired a superintendent, built a small house for him to live in, opened a toll road from Adams for horse-drawn vehicles, replaced with a metal tower the old wooden observation tower (it had burned a few years earlier), and even built a tennis court on the top of the mountain. In 1896, they completed a second road, called the New Ashford Road, that originated on Greylock's southern side and ran to a spring just below the summit.

Despite its frankly commercial approach, the mountain enterprise still could not establish any significant increase in tourism nor make a profit. The Greylock Park Association gave up and turned over ownership of its land to the state in 1898, expressing the hope that the state would "protect forever Greylock and its adjacent peaks" from exploitation and development. Massachusetts' first wilderness park, the Mount Greylock State Reservation, opened that same year.

One of the first proposals under the new state management was to run a trolley-car line up Mount Greylock from the town of Adams. Citing the successful examples of Mount Holyoke and Mount Tom, the commissioners thought such a plan surely would attract more visitors than were willing to take the uncomfortable four-hour horse-drawn carriage ride to the summit. Despite initial enthusiastic support, the plan eventually foundered in 1913, and the commissioners turned to other ways to develop the mountain for wider use.

Automobile access to the summit seemed to be the logical next step. Neither one of the two existing carriage roads ran right to the top of the mountain, so in 1906 the Rockwell Road was added, providing a half-mile connection between the summit and the junction with the New Ashford Road. The newly completed route quickly proved the most popular way to ascend the mountain. The wood-frame superintendent's cottage on the summit provided limited overnight accommodations, and just below the summit, a productive spring was dammed to create an ice pond and reservoir. Hiking and camping were also encouraged.

The Greylock commissioners aggressively acquired additional mountain acreage as it became available. State appropriations made possible the purchase of more than 3,324 acres before 1920. Today, the reservation includes nearly 12,000 acres, acquired through both purchase and donation and extending over parts of six towns.

Almost since the park's inception, the commissioners perceived a need for adequate summit facilities to provide meals and lodging to those who hiked or drove to the top of Mount Greylock. Many of New England's principal mountains already had accommodations at or near their summits, argued John Bascom, an influential Greylock commissioner. Beginning in 1901, he led the drive to create such a facility on Greylock. Bascom did not live long enough to see construction begin on the building that was named for him, but one wing of Bascom Lodge was completed in 1935. The 107th Company of the Civilian Conservation Corps (CCC), for a total cost of $11,000, finished the sprawling structure in 1937.

Unlike the other Victorian summit hotels, Bascom Lodge followed an unobtrusive, simple design. The building is made up of two single-story wings projecting in a Y-shape from a two-story center, not crowning the summit but set off to the side and slightly below it. It is made of stone and wood—a harmonious blend of siting and native building materials that compares favorably with the original stone Tip Top House on Mount Washington. The CCC built the walls of the building with rocks they had cleared from the mountain's trails and ski runs, and fashioned a huge stone fireplace for one of the common rooms. Timbers cut on the mountain were sawn nearby and hauled into place. Upstairs, simple dormitory rooms provided overnight accommodations for thirty-four people.

Meanwhile, a second structure had been built on Greylock's summit, dramatically transforming the open clearing there. As the highest point in the state, Greylock was chosen as the site for a

Bascom Lodge, at the edge of the summit clearing on Mount Greylock, was built by the Civilian Conservation Corps. Photo courtesy Appalachian Mountain Club.

monument to honor Massachusetts soldiers who had fought and died in World War I. A $200,000 state appropriation funded the War Memorial Tower, a ninety-two-foot granite lighthouse originally intended to stand by Boston Harbor.

In 1933, the curious new memorial was dedicated on Greylock "to the hope of everlasting peace." It replaced an 1885 ironwork fire tower that the Greylock Park Association had built. Within its tapered circular walls, a small chapel on the ground floor welcomes all visitors, and a winding stairway leads to a high observation room above which powerful searchlights shine in honor of the war dead and as aviation beacons. During World War II, however, the lights were shut down to avoid attracting attention from enemy aircraft. Today, in deference to the rhythms of nature, they are inactive during the major spring and fall bird migrations.

The War Memorial Tower crowning Mount Greylock's summit was designed originally as a lighthouse for Boston Harbor. Kurt Stier.

The War Memorial Tower recently received a complete face lift. Severe mountaintop weather had eroded the mortar and other structural problems ensued. In 1973, the entire structure was taken apart and then painstakingly reconstructed, block by block.

Development on the summit matched development on the mountain itself in the 1930s. Greylock played a leading role in the advancement of the sport of downhill skiing in Massachusetts. The Mount Greylock Ski Club, formed in 1932, chose the steep eastern face of Greylock above the town of Adams for a ski trail they called the Thunderbolt. Constructed in 1934 by a thirty-man CCC crew, it drew the best skiers of the time to "the most thrilling wooded run yet built," even surpassing "anything in the Rockies," according to its promoters.

The first state downhill championship was held on the Thunderbolt in 1935 and was won by Dick Durrance of Dartmouth College. Races were run for more than a decade thereafter, but the frequent lack of sufficient snow cover on the steep, 1.6-mile trail often caused scheduled races to be moved farther north. By 1956, the

Skiing on Mount Greylock began in 1934 when the Thunderbolt Ski Trail was constructed. Photo courtesy Berkshire Athanaeum, Pittsfield, MA.

Thunderbolt was largely abandoned. Today the trail is still hikable but unmaintained, and is an experts-only climb. It lies completely within the boundaries of the park.

Greylock's attraction for hikers took a quantum leap forward in the 1920s, when the Appalachian Trail (AT) was conceived and laid out over its summit. Massachusetts was the first state to take the proposed AT seriously, back in 1922, and planned a specific route that included a traverse of Greylock. In 1928 a newly formed local trails committee set to work on the southern portion of the trail. The Appalachian Trail over Greylock was in use by 1931.

The entire 2,000-mile footpath running from Georgia to Maine was completed in 1937, linking most of the East's preeminent peaks into a single trail network. The AT's route through western Massachusetts runs along the ridge of the Taconics, where Greylock marks the gateway to the big peaks of New England. It is the first mountain over 3,000 feet in height encountered by northbound end-to-enders since leaving northern Virginia, although the feat of hiking the trail's entire length was not envisioned by the trail's founders and would not be accomplished until ten years after its inauguration.

For a time, the Mount Greylock Ski Club devoted summer weekends to trail work, but most of the responsibility for maintenance lay with the state reservation. Today, a well-organized group of volunteers from the AMC works with the state to maintain this historic route.

Modern Development

Greylock, in the twentieth century, has seen its share of hard-nosed practicality as well as visionary and aesthetic appreciation. Battles between preservation and capitalism are often hardest fought in areas with few other resources from which to make a living. Such has been the case in northwestern Massachusetts, where one of New England's most drawn-out and bitter contests over a development project has been played out on the lower slopes of Mount Greylock.

Since the 1950s, Greylock has been the focus of attempts to offset the failing economy of the northern Berkshire region with tourism and large-scale recreation and convention facilities. One of the ironies of these many-faceted plans is that throughout the nineteenth century, Greylock's remote location and its difficult access by roads and railroads prevented its becoming overcommercialized. Yet under the aegis of a state protection agency, commercial interests have seemed to prevail over aesthetic or environmental issues.

Business leaders in Adams and North Adams, faced with serious unemployment problems left by departing mills and closed manufacturing plants, sought assistance from the state as early as 1953, when the government of Massachusetts, acceding to the wishes of Berkshire politicians, created the Mount Greylock Tramway Authority. The self-financing, independent entity proposed building a cable car up Greylock's steep eastern face, the base of which would be located in the most economically disadvantaged town of Adams.

In 1960 the state's Greylock commissioners awarded the authority a long-term lease on half of the 8,800-acre state reservation. Fireworks began in 1964 when the tramway authority revealed it planned not just a cable car, but an enormous multifaceted resort development that included four chairlifts and many ski trails, plus shopping, lodging, and dining facilities. The tramway would take passengers to a huge terminal on the mountain's peak.

A previously silent constituency angrily protested the scope of the proposal, leading a groundswell of opposition. Those who wanted to preserve wildness on the mountain revived the Greylock Protective Association, which had once prevented the commissioners from allowing commercial logging in the reservation. The protective association engaged the Greylock commission in head-to-head legal combat, arguing successfully in court that the commission had violated its trust to protect reservation lands. That victory was followed up in the legislature, which dealt the commission the *coup de grace* in 1966. It abolished the tramway authority and placed the Mount Greylock Reservation under the Department of Environmental Management (DEM).

A compromise measure, requested by the representative whose district included Adams, authorized the alternate lease of Saddleball Mountain at the southern end of the Greylock massif. This opened the door to a group of developers who acquired private lands adjacent to Greylock and in the 1970s put forward a plan known as Greylock Glen. After constructing the rudiments of a ski area, the developers lost their financing. Hoping to draw new backing, they made a bid to legalize casino gambling, which failed after opposition from Governor Michael Dukakis.

But the Berkshires continued to lose manufacturing jobs and the state sought a route to development that was less of a threat to Greylock's natural character. State officials, in consultation with citizen groups and developers, brought forward a new plan for east-slope development called Heritage Greylock. This plan began as a modest recreational area but grew until it also threatened to harm the public's long-term conservation interest in Greylock. In 1991 Governor

William Weld's administration announced that it would not support this proposal and withdrew all funding support that had been promised.

Work has continued to find a formula for development that is acceptable to all concerned, and in the fall of 1993, the state secretary of environmental affairs announced approval of a new development plan for Greylock Glen. The 1,000-acre, privately owned tract of woodland will have a modestly sized conference center and an environmental-education center, along with such recreational amenities as cross-country skiing, tennis, golf, and trails. No lifts or downhill ski trails will be built on Greylock. According to a press statement, "the advisory committee feels the conference and environmental-education center could become the star attraction of the Berkshires, drawing people from the Boston area, New England, and the entire Northeast." The state DEM continues to work toward soliciting appropriate proposals from qualified developers, with about $6.5 million in state funds available to help support the project.

Today, Greylock poses a distinctive challenge. Its potential for economic profit cannot be overlooked by the depressed area towns, yet advocates of wilderness preservation see it as a public trust that must be preserved intact. Plans for a tramway and ski area on its east side have been the source of conflict for more than forty years. Amid all the conflicting pressures of government, business, special-interest groups, and conservationists, compromises finally are being forged to maximize Greylock's use by the public yet limit the encroachment of man-made distractions on this high ridge.

Suggestions for Visitors

Today, the Mount Greylock Reservation contains 11,611 acres of preserved land. An attractive stone-and-glass visitor's center, constructed in 1972 near the beginning of the auto road on the southern end of the mountain in Lanesboro, off Route 7, offers maps, orientation, and education programs. There are free, informative exhibits on the mountain's geology and history, and a fascinating large scale model of the mountain showing its various topographical features and trails.

In an unusual partnership, the state leased operation of Bascom Lodge to the Appalachian Mountain Club in 1983, an organization already well experienced in mountaintop hospitality with its chain of high huts in the White Mountains. In return for operating the lodge, the AMC was to provide two naturalists to the reservation to help with interpretive programming, and organize trail-maintenance crews in the summers. Then in 1993, the AMC agreed to fully staff and manage the visitor's center. Reservations for lodging at Bascom or for nature programs can be made directly through the AMC at Greylock (413-443-0011).

Near Bascom Lodge on the summit, but partially screened by trees, is another small building that houses communications equipment and a tall antenna used by local television stations. The Rockwell Road, which arrives at the summit at this point, receives heavy use on weekends through the summer and fall. The Williams College cross-country ski team skis up the road on roller-skis as part of their fall training regimen.

The Hopper Trail, originating at the Haley Farm in Williamstown, is a popular and historic route for hikers. Just off the trail, about halfway up, is a spur leading to the Sperry Campground, which can also be reached by car. This facility provides a more remote base for campers, who are not allowed to pitch a tent elsewhere within the reservation. For those who wish to hike only the upper part of the mountain, there is a parking lot at the campground, and the Hopper Trail leads from there to connect with the AT near the summit.

Equinox ∧∧∧

Mount Equinox, the highest peak in the Taconic Range, is something of an eccentric among New England's mountains. It has remained completely in private ownership, an aloof, towering presence above the small town of Manchester, Vermont. The celebrated status of Equinox owes much to the hotel of the same name at the foot of the mountain, which, since the mid-nineteenth century, has been responsible for attracting the public to this mountain. In stark contrast to the elite resort character of the town, a small brotherhood of Carthusian monks live and pray high on the mountain, 7,000 acres of which they own. The Carthusian Foundation owns the public auto road and summit hotel on Equinox, and operates wind turbines to help decrease reliance on expensive and nonrenewable energy sources. This beautiful mountain thus seems an assemblage of opposites, the opulent residing alongside the ascetic, ancient custom commingling with high-tech energy projects.

Geography

Equinox lies on the far western border of New England, along the narrow Taconic range, which stretches from Massachusetts into central Vermont. The Taconics are studded with three high peaks—Greylock in Massachusetts, at 3,491 feet; Dorset Peak to the north at

3,804 feet; and Equinox, the largest of them all at 3,816 feet. It is the highest peak in Vermont that is not crossed by the state's north-south footpath, the Long Trail.

On the east lies the Valley of Vermont, an area of soft sea sediments eroded away by rivers ancestral to the present-day Housatonic and Hoosic rivers. Beyond the valley stretching to the north lie the more resistant rocks of the Green Mountains. New York State is immediately to the west.

Early History

Mount Equinox has borne several names during its history. Early references indicate the mountain was frequently called West Mountain, and outsiders sometimes referred to it as Manchester Mountain. The exact origin of the present name is somewhat obscure. One theory involves an Indian origin for the name, citing peoples in the area by the name of Ekwanoks or Awaknocks. One misguided editor went so far as to call it Esquimaux Mountain, in George's *Pocket Gazetteer of the State of Vermont*.

A more logical explanation derives from one of the earliest explorations of the mountain. A young West Point graduate named Alden Partridge in 1823 led an expedition of cadets from Norwich Military Academy (in Norwich, Vermont) to climb the mountain and determine its height. They ascended on September 19, accompanied by their host, Vermont Governor Richard Skinner, and twenty other Manchester residents. It has been speculated that because Partridge's visit was close to the time of the autumnal equinox, and because he served as surveyor general of Vermont that year, he might have christened the mountain Equinox. Zadock Thompson's 1824 edition of the *Gazetteer of the State of Vermont* still refers to it as Manchester Mountain, but by the time of Thompson's 1842 *History of Vermont*, the name Equinox was used in print.

New Hampshire's provincial governor, Benning Wentworth, granted the charter for the town of Manchester in 1761. As was often the case, the original proprietors were investors with no intentions of settling there. Instead they found others to validate the grant by clearing land and erecting dwellings, usually just simple log cabins. The main north-south road through the valley ran through the new

Sheldon's and Slason's Marble Quarry, from the 1861 Report on the Geology of Vermont, *shows some of the techniques for cutting and lifting stone.*
Photo courtesy Wilbur Collection, Bailey Library, University of Vermont.

town and connected with a major road to the east. At this important crossroads, at the base of Mount Equinox, a two-story wooden tavern opened its doors in 1769.

The Marsh Tavern became a well-known gathering place for the Green Mountain Boys, those independent-minded Vermonters who fought against the British in the American Revolution. At a 1772 meeting of the Vermont Council of Safety, the tavern's owner, William Marsh, steadfastly proclaimed his loyalty to the British, provoking Ira Allen to confiscate his property. The tavern, in fact, was the first Tory-owned property seized by the revolutionaries to help support the war. After the war, Thaddeus Munson bought the property from the state and expanded by adding another inn next door in 1801. His original establishment is now part of the Equinox Hotel.

The principal industry in early Manchester was farming. Abundant water power coming from the high mountain meant industry

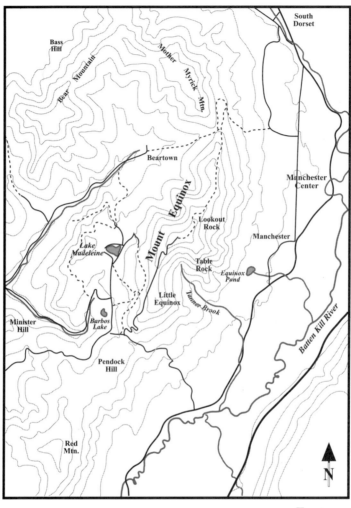

Equinox

could develop, too, and the local marble deposits were the perfect product. The prized stone was so abundant that it was used liberally for building foundations, hearthstones, steps, and gravestones. Manchester Village has more than four miles of marble sidewalks. The best-quality marble came from the nearby town of Dorset, but quarries on Mount Equinox yielded a lesser-grade marble that was burned for lime to be used in the tanning process or for mortar. The huge blocks of marble sawn in Manchester were hauled by wagon or sled to

Burr & Burton Seminary, the oldest coeducational secondary school in Vermont, is built of marble quarried on Mount Equinox. Kurt Stier.

Philadelphia, New York, and Boston. The village of Factory Point, after the arrival of the railroad, developed into a central location for stone dressing and shipping operations.

Local limestone was quarried for building as well. An impressive structure made of huge blocks of this stone still stands at the base of Mount Equinox in Manchester. Founded as Burr Seminary to educate young men for the ministry, it was built in 1833 of light-gray marble from the Taconic Quarry on the side of Mount Equinox. A few years later, a local citizen bequeathed money to the all-male academy on the provision that girls be admitted. In 1849, the school was renamed Burr & Burton Seminary and became the first coeducational secondary school in Vermont. Now the town high school, Burr & Burton is the starting point for the only hiking route to the summit of Equinox from the town of Manchester.

Alden Partridge

The first recorded climb of Mount Equinox was the previously mentioned "march" of Captain Alden Partridge in 1823, though local residents may have made the ascent much earlier. Partridge was the original "power hiker," one of the earliest Americans to climb mountains purely for pleasure and the physical and mental challenges they presented. His determination and stamina were unusual in his own time, but his feats seem truly impressive today.

Partridge was born in 1785 in Norwich, Vermont, just across the Connecticut River from Dartmouth College. He studied at Dartmouth, then transferred to West Point, where he graduated in 1806. He stayed on to teach mathematics, then, at the young age of thirty, was appointed superintendent at West Point in 1815. When this popular and brilliant leader found that his position would not be renewed, he moved back to Vermont and founded the American Literary, Scientific, and Military Academy in his hometown in 1819. At the same time, Partridge began leading his young students on climbs of New England's mountains, coming up with the term "physical education" to describe his unorthodox, nonclassroom methods.

On their climb of Equinox in 1823, Partridge and twenty-seven cadets covered the 150-mile distance from Norwich to Manchester in four days. Each person carried a heavy pack containing bedroll, food, and supplies. After crossing the Green Mountain Ridge, Partridge boasted that on the final day, "a youth of 16 years of age walked by my side 45 miles." In fact, the captain would regularly travel similar distances for several days in a row, often setting off several hours before sunrise. Partridge covered 152 miles in three days to climb Mount Monadnock and 220 miles in four days to climb Greylock. He also climbed Mount Washington, Lafayette, Moosilauke, Ascutney, Camel's Hump, Killington, Mansfield, remote peaks in Maine, and dozens of other mountains. Through newspaper accounts of his explorations, Partridge inspired a new generation of Americans to conquer distances and heights for pleasure.

Tourism and the Hotel Era

Meanwhile, the house that was once called the Marsh Tavern had been replaced by a large inn called Munson's Tavern, expanding to meet the needs of the area's growing population in the years from 1800 to 1850. An addition by a new owner in 1854 marked a name change to the Taconic Tavern. At the same time, a local man named

Franklin Orvis combined his family home and store into a competing hotel next door which he called Equinox House. Here was the nucleus of a summer resort that would soon be without parallel in Vermont. Aggressive in his plans, Orvis bought another building, Straight's Tavern, which contained a courtroom and jail, rebuilt it, bought another house as an annex, added a music hall in 1868, and in 1880 or 1883 purchased the Taconic Tavern and joined it to the Equinox by a second-story bridge.

Orvis's investments were not just speculation. His hostelry (ultimately comprised of seventeen different structures) was located at the junction of several major stagecoach routes, and after 1853 railroad service connected it to Troy, New York. Orvis astutely foresaw that not only would he receive increasing business travelers, but that the fresh mountain air and inspiring scenery would provide a great incentive for vacationers as well.

Equinox House started taking summer guests in 1853, and within a few years, Manchester grew to be one of the premier summer resorts for America's elite. Doubling the rates within a few years of taking over

The Equinox Hotel anchors the resort town of Manchester Center at the foot of Mount Equinox. Kurt Stier.

the hotel, Orvis still found himself with no shortage of well-heeled guests from New York who stayed for the entire summer. Servants and children were generously offered half-price arrangements.

The reputation of Manchester's Equinox House was assured with the two-week visit, beginning August 25, 1863, of Mrs. Abraham Lincoln and her son Robert. The vacation was such a success that Mrs. Lincoln made plans to return with her husband, and the hotel constructed a special presidential suite in anticipation of the honor. But in April of 1865, her husband was assassinated, and Mrs. Lincoln returned to Manchester a widow.

Robert Todd Lincoln became an attorney, was secretary of war under Presidents Garfield and Arthur, and served as president of the Pullman Train Car Company. He chose Manchester for his summer home, building a twenty-four room Georgian Revival mansion called Hildene on 300 acres of land facing Mount Equinox in the west. Hildene remained in the Lincoln family's possession until 1975, when it was purchased by a private foundation that now operates it as a seasonal museum and National Register Historic Site. Lincoln's presence helped to attract other illustrious individuals to the area, including

Robert Todd Lincoln chose Manchester as the location for this summer home, a twenty-four-room Georgian Revival mansion called Hildene. Kurt Stier.

four sitting or former presidents—Ulysses Grant, Benjamin Harrison, Theodore Roosevelt, and William Taft. President Taft came to Manchester and stayed at Hildene while in office in 1912.

To treat Equinox House guests to summer outings up Mount Equinox, Orvis built a wagon road sometime between 1860 and 1870. It ran over the northern flank of the mountain to Lookout Rock directly above the town of Manchester. In the 1870s, Manchester's most popular stage driver, John Stockwell, made the trip up Equinox several times a week, driving his coach and four. Another driver, Manchester shoemaker O. G. Felt, devised a special method for adding extra braking power on the way down—he tied a big log to the rear axle.

One of the elegant touches at the Equinox Hotel was the European-inspired tradition of serving fresh mountain-spring water. Equinox Spring Water, offered still or sparkling, and later Equinox Ginger Champagne (a forerunner of ginger ale) made from the same clear water, became so famous that the hotel bottled the water for retail sale. Even as late as 1920, a tiered fountain in the center of the dining room served the still-popular beverage to hotel guests.

The hotel's prized spring was located about halfway up Mount Equinox, 1,500 feet above Manchester. Advertising brochures claimed the water was 38° F at all seasons, and the prodigious output of the spring, at one and a half to two barrels per minute, was unaffected by rain or drought. The Equinox Company bought 1,000 acres around the spring and piped water down to a large bottling plant they built directly behind the hotel. From there it was shipped to all the best hotels in Boston and New York.

While the Equinox Spring's owners made no claims about the health benefits of their water, in those days water cures were all the rage. Medical fashion proved a boon to spring-water sales. In 1894, Equinox Spring Water's marketing efforts relied heavily on physicians' testimonials: "Gentlemen: I have studied the effects of EQUINOX SPRING WATER for the past three years and I am greatly pleased with its beneficial action. It has proved to be of great value in diseases of the kidneys and bladder, and in cases of gouty rheumatism, its free use has relieved pain very markedly. No one can make a mistake by using it freely."

Franklin H. Orvis added other pleasures for his guests. Sometime before 1880, he constructed a specially designed, ten-acre trout pond partway up the eastern slope of Mount Equinox. Fed by three streams, Equinox Pond became the centerpiece of the hotel's holdings on Mount Equinox itself. In 1994, wishing to assure preservation of the pond and the surrounding woods, the hotel established the Equinox Preservation Trust and donated the entire 900-acre parcel to a partnership of the Vermont Land Trust and the Nature Conservancy. Programs about nature and environmental issues are an important feature there today.

Sharing his brother Franklin's interests, Charles F. Orvis developed a distinctive fishing rod which he began to sell by mail order. The Battenkill River, running through Manchester, was, then as today, famed for its trout fishing, and the combination was unbeatable. A huge retail and mail order business has sprung from those simple beginnings, and today both the Orvis Company and the American Museum of Fly Fishing are favorite attractions in the town of Manchester.

Around the turn of the century, recognition of Manchester's languishing tourist business prompted a group of local businessmen to organize the Manchester Development Association. In 1901 this group undertook a formal program of advertising and promotion of the town as a summer resort. Encouraged by these plans, Franklin Orvis's wife, Louise, who had taken over operation of the hotel after her husband's death, commissioned a championship golf course in 1925, then added an airport and skeet field. Tourism was just reviving when the crash of 1929 hit—the beginning of the end for the Orvis family holdings. The heyday of Manchester's success as an exclusive summer resort seemed about over. Summer guests decreased dramatically, and Louise Orvis finally sold out of the hotel business in 1937.

Trying again to revive the tourist economy, a new campaign to promote winter sports began in 1935. The Manchester Outing Club, with WPA help, opened two ski trails near Deer Knoll on Equinox, and held ski races there in 1936. They had a ten-year lease on the use of the mountain but were unable to compete with another WPA-supported ski area on a much larger mountain nearby, Bromley Mountain, where the first ski trail was cut in 1936–37. The following year, skier and businessman Fred Pabst built a tow on Bromley, effectively shifting enthusiasm for skiing away from the short, steep runs on Equinox to a larger mountain, a better location, and better snow conditions.

Undaunted, local boosters found yet another scheme to use the mountain as the centerpiece for attracting tourists. In August 1938, forty local businesspeople met to discuss the possibility of building an auto road to Equinox's summit. Before their plans got off the ground, a single investor purchased nearly the entire mountain. Two years after his purchase, in 1941, Dr. J. G. Davidson began the first stretch of a road to the top. The project was completed in 1946.

Opened to the public in 1949, the toll road called Sky Line Drive did help to increase tourism in Manchester. It begins in the town of Sunderland, south of Manchester on Route 7A, and climbs 5.2 miles over the summit of Little Equinox Mountain to the spectacular summit of Equinox. Sky Line Inn, a two-story motel on the mountaintop, provides a place for meals and overnight accommodations. Throughout the 1950s, it was known for its superb views and especially for its sunsets. The Adirondacks, Berkshires, White Mountains, Green Mountains, and even Canada's Mont Royal in the city of Montreal can all be seen from Equinox's summit. During foliage season, it is a particularly popular spot. The "Hill Climb," an auto race of pre-1960 sports cars, has become an exciting annual event on the Sky Line Drive, which has some pretty tight turns on the switchbacks.

Davidson's plans for his holdings did not end with the Sky Line Drive and inn. To provide power for his mountaintop facilities, he impounded a stream just below the summit. The Lake Madeleine Dam, named after his wife, was dedicated on October 1, 1957. The thirty-acre lake created by the dam holds a total of 216,000,000 gallons of water at an elevation of 2,179 feet.

The Carthusians

During the late 1950s, Dr. and Mrs. Davidson became acquainted with a small group of Carthusian monks who recently had been sent to establish the first Carthusian order in America. Saint Bruno founded the Carthusians in 1084 when, with a few companions, he withdrew to a deep valley in the French Alps near Chartreuse. There they built the mother house of the order, the first Carthusian

From the Sky Line Inn, the spectacular view from the summit of Equinox looks out over the valley of Vermont toward the Green Mountains. On very clear days, Mont Royal in Canada is visible. Kurt Stier.

monastery, and developed a religious practice founded on the principles of silence, seclusion, and prayer.

When the Davidsons met them, the Carthusians were living at a donated site near Whitingham, Vermont. Intrigued by the devotion and piety of the group, the Davidsons learned more through visits to some of the two dozen surviving Carthusian monasteries in Europe. Affirming their own faith and the good works being done by monastic orders, the Davidsons decided to offer their property on Mount Equinox for the first permanent Carthusian sanctuary in America.

In 1960 construction of the monastery, or charterhouse, began. Following tradition, it was to be built to last for centuries, and so specially cut nine-and-a-half-foot blocks of granite from the Rock of Ages quarry in Barre, Vermont, were set on end to form the building's outer walls. Completed in 1970, the Charterhouse of the Transfiguration is home to a family of about twenty brothers and cloister monks.

The Carthusian philosophy is summarized in a booklet describing their life. "By virtue of his call to a solitary life, the Carthusian is separated from the world and to a large extent from his brothers within the Monastery. Still, he does not live for himself alone. On the contrary, he embraces this life for love of God and for His glory and in accordance with His will, but also, more than for himself, for the world which he has left and yet whose well-being he desires intensely."

Interrupting normal sleeping hours at midnight for several hours of chants and worship, working at cutting wood or gardening, taking occasional communal walks in the surrounding woods, the life of these monks is lived in strict separation from the tourists daily passing their abode. The monastery, gardens, and surrounding grounds are never open to visitors but are clearly visible from the Sky Line Drive in the saddle between Equinox and Little Equinox.

Because of Davidson's gift of his entire mountain property to them, the Carthusians have inherited Lake Madeleine and its hydropower plant, which they use to good advantage. They generate enough surplus power at their hydro plant to sell the extra kilowatt hours to the Central Vermont Public Service Company (CVPSC). Besides generating electricity through water power, the Carthusians,

Built in 1960 of Vermont granite, the Carthusian Monastery on Mount Equinox is the only one of its kind outside Europe. Kurt Stier.

who have a strong commitment to the use and development of renewable energy sources, have recently become a principal investment partner in a wind-powered generating station located on their land on Little Equinox Mountain.

In 1981, the first wind turbine on the mountain was christened with Carthusian-made chartreuse liqueur, but it was too big and blew over. Two smaller turbines, 120 feet high, replaced the original one and now generate enough power for seventy homes, which is also sold through CVPSC. At a cost of about $500,000 to install turbines, transmission lines, and control house, the pay-back was projected to take about a decade.

A third tower, located on the main summit of the mountain, is operated by the Federal Aviation Administration as a peripheral communications station. It receives and transmits communications between nearby aircraft and Boston's Logan Airport. There is also a University of Vermont transmitting station near the Lookout Rock Trail.

The winds on the summit of Little Equinox, privately owned by the Carthusian Foundation, have powered wind turbines since 1981. Kurt Stier.

Recreation and Preservation

In the hiking boom of the 1960s and 1970s, the steep slopes of Equinox were all but forgotten as Vermont's Long Trail, the Appalachian Trail, and the White Mountains lured the majority of enthusiasts. Coupled with the decline of Manchester as a summer resort, the few who did ascend Equinox were mostly tourists passing through, or local residents. The once-grand hotel fell into decline and in 1972 was abruptly condemned and ordered to close its doors permanently. Feverish attempts to preserve the historic structure were rewarded with its nomination to the National Register of Historic Places later that year. Various proposals to revive the hotel operation hinged on the development of other profit centers, most notably a ski area on Equinox. Local residents were almost unanimous in their outspoken opposition to that alternative, with the result that new zoning laws were passed to make the Equinox Pond area part of a district in which commercial development was forever prohibited.

Then, in 1974, investors called the Galesi Group purchased the shuttered, vacant building that had been the Equinox Hotel. With some $20 million in restorations, the once-grand edifice reopened in 1985, this time for year-round operation. During the renovation process, a spectacular fire seriously jeopardized the resurrection of the historic structure. A propane truck making a delivery to the construction site sprang a leak in its tank, creating a fireball that ignited one whole side and the roof of the hotel.

Since 1991, a new group of owner/investors has worked to bring back the former glory of the elegant columned hotel, striving to make it "the premier resort destination in the Northeast." Now managed by Equinox Resorts Associates, which is partially owned by Guinness spirits and beers, the completely refurbished hotel combines modern hotel and spa facilities with a respectful pride in the building's historic heritage. Old photographs of guests in the horse-and-buggy age and fly-fishing memorabilia decorate the halls and common rooms, and most of the guest rooms offer a close-up view of the mountains.

Equinox Spring Water's notoriety extended into the 1990s, too, and was indirectly responsible for a 120-unit condominium development, Equinox on the Battenkill, at the base of the mountain. Sewer permits would not have been obtainable had not Great Waters of France, parent company of Perrier Water and investor in resurrecting the spring-water business on Equinox, relinquished its 220,000-gallon-per-day permit. With that, any hope of a Perrier-related spring-water product named Equinox seems to have completely vanished.

The "air of rich and cultured living" surrounding the mountain spawned a colony of artists who make Manchester their summer residence. While few of the great landscape painters of the nineteenth century found their way to the Taconics, in the twentieth century the area has welcomed many artists, including Reginald Marsh, best known for his robust depictions of city life in New York. The wooded estate of Gertrude Devine Webster, on the northern slope of Equinox, became the Southern Vermont Art Center in 1950, due largely to the efforts of Dean Fausett, perhaps the best known of Manchester's modern landscape artists. Here one may find exhibits of the work of local artists, sculptors, and craftsmen, as well as music performances year-round.

Equinox welcomes a varied constituency today. Mostly it is tourists who come to drive its scenic roadway and perhaps wander on the circuit of footpaths around the summit. Some, especially the locals, seek out that solitary path behind Burr & Burton Seminary that climbs steeply up the face of the mountain. From below in the village of Manchester, the mountain rises as a beautiful backdrop, and from the mountains to the east perfectly frames the valley of Vermont. Its rich history, from the revolutionary meetings at Marsh Tavern to the visits of presidents, has been affirmed by many who have worked hard to maintain the beauty and integrity of the landscape. Unique and progressive, the Carthusian presence on the mountain affirms for us all the value of solitary contemplation in such wild places.

Suggestions for Visitors

The town of Manchester comes in two parts, the historic center where the imposing Equinox Hotel faces a granite revolutionary battle monument on the common; and the downtown, now rife with upscale shopping outlets. The historic district surrounding the hotel retains its nineteenth-century flavor and the integrity of its old buildings, several of which contain shops or fine restaurants. The white-marble sidewalks add a touch of luxury, and profuse gardens and plantings in summer create an aura of romantic nostalgia.

For many, the presence of Equinox's toll road makes climbing almost unnecessary, and with the Carthusian sanctuary being off-limits, and the wind turbines and communications towers whirring away on Little Equinox, the views are the only compelling reason to leave the comfort of the Equinox Hotel's front porch. Equinox's Sky Line Drive is open from May 1 to November 1, 8:00 A.M. to 10:00 P.M. The toll house at the road's beginning is on Route 7A just south of the town of Manchester (802-362-1114). The Sky Line Inn, after a few closed seasons, reopened in the summer of 1993 (802-362-1113).

Driving up the road and then hiking around the summit is perhaps the best way to approach this mountain. Not only is Equinox relatively steep to hike from the bottom, but the Burr & Burton Trail is not always reliably marked or maintained. A nice walk around the summit makes a loop on the Red Trail and the Yellow Trail to the Lookout Rock and back, a distance of a little over a mile. Along the way, you will pass an unusual monument, placed there by Dr. J. G.

J.G. Davidson, who owned the mountain, built the road, and deeded 7,000 acres of this property to the Carthusian Foundation in America, chose a quiet spot near the summit for a memorial to his favorite dog, Mr. Barbo. Kurt Stier.

Davidson in memory of one of his favorite dogs, Mr. Barbo. When these trails were cut, the old carriage road from Lookout Rock down through Beartown Gap to Manchester was still passable, but now the route is completely overgrown and neglected in favor of the 1940s' toll road.

For those undaunted climbers, the Burr & Burton Trail can be picked up from behind the limestone seminary building at the far end of the athletic fields. It passes near the famed Equinox Spring on its way up, and through stands of white birch and dense evergreen balsams.

Other sights to see in the area include the Imperial Quarry, operated by the Vermont Marble Company, which is the largest underground marble quarry in the world and covers more than twenty acres of open space deep within Dorset Mountain. Hildene, once the home of Robert Todd Lincoln, is open seasonally just south of Manchester, and the grounds are open in winter for cross-country skiing (802-362-1788).

The Southern Vermont Art Center (802-362-1405), located north of the town of Manchester, occupies a restored mansion with a sculpture garden on its grounds. Trails radiate up the slopes of Mount Equinox from here, too, but it is best known for its varied programs of art-and-craft exhibits, music performances, and summer art classes.

Camel's Hump

Camel's Hump, in the Green Mountains of Vermont, has such a distinctive shape that an outline of the mountain forms part of the background design on the official state seal. There is no tourist development or commercial activity on Camel's Hump's slopes or around its base, and most people are unaware that such things once existed there. It is perhaps Vermont's best-loved mountain, owing not just to the friendly animal imagery of its name, but because it is the state's highest undeveloped peak. Camel's Hump is a mecca for serious hikers. It may be the state's most-studied mountain, also; under the aegis of the University of Vermont's Biology Department, data collected here has furnished some of the earliest and best-documented evidence of the forest-destroying effects of acid rain.

The tallest part of the double-humped summit rises above treeline to 4,083 feet; the forested southern hump is several hundred feet lower. Camel's Hump ranks as the third-highest mountain in the state, after Mansfield and Killington, and is tied with Mount Ellen to its south. Motorists along Interstate 89 in Vermont cannot fail to be impressed by the sheer bulk of this mountain, for it lies close to the road, and if its summit is not sheathed in fog, the curves of its distinctive outline present a memorable sight.

The distinctive double-humped profile of Camel's Hump was first named Le Lion Chouchant by French explorers on Lake Champlain about 1609. Kurt Stier.

The Name

Samuel de Champlain and his party, on a summer expedition from Montreal in 1609, are believed to have been the first Europeans to see the towering peaks of the Green Mountains as they explored the large lake that would later bear Champlain's name. "Very high mountains capped with snow," Champlain wrote, a somewhat mysterious observation since snow on these peaks in July is highly unlikely. The explorers perceived a resemblance to a sleeping lion in this double-summit mountain, and called it Le Lion Couchant, a term from French heraldry. The Anglicized version of this name—the Couching Lion (sometimes mistakenly called the crouching lion)—is definitely not the same attitude of repose that Champlain had in mind. Its usage prompted some rather acrimonious debate in the 1920s. Since then, the term has diminished in popularity, but the Couching Lion is still a well-known nickname for Camel's Hump.

Ira Allen appears to have been the first to see a camel, not a lion, in the mountain's image, and his 1798 map referred to it as The Camel's Rump. Zadock Thompson's 1824 *Gazetteer of the State of Vermont* used that name, too, indicating that it had probably become common usage. But by 1830, propriety introduced a more genteel part of the camel's anatomy to the nomenclature, and the name was changed to Camel's Hump. There are still advocates of the older name, touting it as not only more authentic and original, but more colorful in its associations.

Though mountain lions were native to Vermont, camels have always been exotics in the landscape of the Western mind, and several fanciful stories have evolved to explain the name of this peak. In 1890, a humorous poem played up the incongruity of camels in the Green Mountains to explain the origin of two of the highest peaks.

The Talk of the Mountains
The "Camel's Hump" is there on high; his head, as you might think,
Is by the river's bed where once he ran to kneel and drink,
But, stumbling in his thirsty haste, he threw his rider high,
And there lies "Mansfield" as he fell, a-staring at the sky:
This dashing youth, a giant in his pride, (say naught of birth,)
Had laid a bet on time to ride the "Camel" round the earth,

But—weary, being over-driven—here ended all his pacing;
And th' Fates condemned them there to lie, as a warning
against racing.

—Rev. Perrin B. Fisk

Well before the time of Champlain, however, the mountain carried another name, given to it by the native peoples of the region, the Abenaki. Their name, Tah-wak-be-dee-ee-so Wadso, meant "the resting place mountain," or "place-to-sit-down mountain." Another source translated Tawabodi-e-wadso as "a mountain to sit upon" or "the saddle mountain."

Geology and Natural History

The formation of the Green Mountains occurred about 440 million years ago, making them the oldest mountains in New England. Sedimentary and volcanic debris deposited during the early Cambrian age (about 550 million years ago) was forced together by heat and pressure, then raised and folded upward to form the high range that runs the entire length of the state of Vermont. The Taconian and Arcadian uprisings, or mountain-building events, created a group of metamorphic rocks collectively known as Green Mountain schists, or green schists. Many of the rocks on Camel's Hump actually have a greenish color, created by the presence of minerals such as chlorite. Over eons of weathering, the harder rocks of the mountains resisted erosion as the surrounding valleys wore away.

One of only two arctic-alpine zones in the state of Vermont (the other is on Mount Mansfield) covers about ten acres on the summit of Camel's Hump. Occurring on the high peaks of New Hampshire and Maine as well, these rare botanic communities are relics of the Ice Age and contain plants that normally occur in climates much farther north. As the ice melted and receded, plants that were once common in that frigid climate retreated to the highest mountaintops, and have persisted there for thousands of years. Today, their presence is threatened by careless hikers and foot traffic that can undo hundreds of years of sturdy growth in one season.

The arctic-alpine plant community consists of low-growing grasses, sedges, mosses, and lichens that have made unique climatic

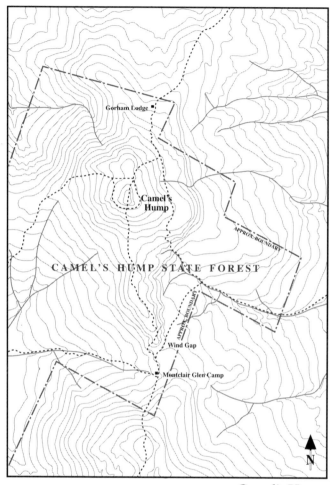

Camel's Hump

adaptations. Able to grow in very thin soils, these plants have each evolved their own unique mechanism to resist potentially damaging wind and cold. Common plants on Camel's Hump include the narrow-leafed Bigelow's sedge, mountain sandwort, Labrador tea, alpine bilberry, and mountain cranberry.

Early Exploration and Hiking

Few explorers came through these mountains before about 1800. The high terrain of the Green Mountains was so inaccessible that towns in the area around Camel's Hump, though they were mostly granted shortly after the Revolution, were slow to be settled. Even today, only small villages exist in the dark mountain valleys of the towns of Duxbury, Huntington, and Fayston surrounding Camel's Hump. Most early residents eked out a living by farming and timber harvesting, keeping to the valleys and lower mountain slopes where the terrain allowed the easiest travel.

The arrival of Alden Partridge into these parts must have seemed just short of incomprehensible to the local inhabitants, who thought that mountains were to be circumvented, not climbed over. In 1818, Partridge walked the seventy-six miles from his home in Norwich, Vermont, to climb Camel's Hump and Mount Mansfield. It rained nearly the entire week he was on the road. Bushwhacking up the northern ridge of Camel's Hump during a furious rainstorm on September 16, Partridge wrote in his journal afterward, "Not a dry thread in my clothes, and somewhat fatigued, having ate nothing nor drunk anything but water during the day." Bright and early the next morning, however, he was on the road to Stowe, where he met a friend and climbed Mansfield. Bushwhacking again, they completed their trip at 5:00 P.M., and Partridge started toward home, arriving at Waterbury, where he spent the night, at 10:00 P.M. after thirty-four miles and at least fifteen hours of walking.

Partridge carried scientific equipment to measure the altitude of all the peaks he climbed, using a simple barometer that measured the air pressure, which decreases in relation to increasing altitude. By comparison with a chart of air-pressure readings from other known heights, he could estimate relatively accurately his elevation above sea level. On Camel's Hump, he was only five feet over today's standard, with an elevation reading of 4,088 feet.

Alden Partridge may have been a fanatic about climbing mountains, but his ideas caught on among his students and those who read his widely disseminated newspaper columns. This little-known figure, with his unorthodox prescription for good health, should rightly be credited with pioneering the mountain-climbing craze that today has reached full-blown proportions. He also contributed in no small way to the development of the New England mountains as tourist destinations in the nineteenth century, influencing artists who ventured into the mountains in search of awe-inspiring scenery, and through them, thousands of appreciative Americans.

Though Partridge's advice sounds a bit unrealistic today, it is also not hard to believe that it did indeed, contribute significantly to better health and longevity. "Walk about 10 miles per day at the rate of 4 MPH; about 3 or 4 times each year shoulder your knapsack and with your barometer, etc, ascend to the summits of our principal mountains and determine the altitudes, walking from 30 to 80 miles per day, according as you can bear the fatigue."

The Tourist Era

Those who followed Partridge's recommendations and climbed Camel's Hump before 1850 probably did so without benefit of any trail. Then the railroad arrived, and with it a station at North Duxbury. A friendly hotel proprietor named Samuel Ridley, Jr., entertained mountain-bound tourists and worked to develop Camel's Hump as a popular destination spot. Soon, the summit of Camel's Hump had a carriage road winding partway up its north side. Guests at Ridley's Hotel could ascend the mountain to a point just below the steep upper slope in relative ease; from there the guests rode on horseback over the last stretch of trail to the hotel. Once on the summit, they were rewarded with spectacular views of Lake Champlain, the Adirondacks, and the whole Green Mountain range.

In the late 1850s, a modest, clapboarded "hotel" went up at the terminus of the carriage road. The Summit House, really more like a camp, could accommodate thirty people overnight, though with little privacy for anyone. Water was brought in to the building in buckets, and supplies were hauled the five miles from Ridley's by ox cart. It was not a successful enterprise, and after its failure in business the Summit House burned and was never rebuilt. Today, only the clearing where it once stood remains, just below the summit at the junction of the Forestry Trail and the Long Trail.

The popularity of Camel's Hump as a tourist destination was modest and short-lived. Mansfield, larger and more accessible, had better-financed promoters and very quickly surpassed Camel's Hump as the premier mountain resort in the state. Following the Civil War, which took a devastating toll on Vermont's population, Camel's Hump faded into a period of relative obscurity. It was neglected until the first decade of the twentieth century, when climbing the mountain again became a primary source of interest.

Art and Literature

Part of the lure of this particular mountain stemmed from its romantic associations, and while the mountains of New Hampshire far surpassed all others in the number of literary works published about them, there were a few authors who found Camel's Hump an interesting source for artistic inspiration. Some visitors were amused by Camel's Hump's colorful name and wrote verse, as was cited earlier. Daniel Pierce Thompson composed a story about buried treasure on Camel's Hump's thickly wooded slopes. "May Martin: or the Money Diggers" was serialized in the *New England Galaxy* in 1835 and for a brief time spurred interest in the mountain. But by the 1840s, two-thirds of Vermont's land had been cleared for farming or sheep raising, and the mystery and intrigue of the story's locale could not be sustained.

Only a few artists of the mid-century Hudson River school found Camel's Hump a picturesque subject for landscape painting. Ranging through northern New England and favoring the Adirondacks and the White Mountains, adherents of this painting style found surprisingly little inspiration in the Green Mountains. Yet Camel's Hump still proved compelling, with the view of it from Lake Champlain being particularly favored. John Frederick Kensett painted at least two versions of it in 1850–51. His *Camel's Hump from the Western Shore of Lake Champlain* faithfully reproduces the scenery of the place, even as he struggled to express the more powerful and awe-inspiring aspects of pure nature.

In 1861 Charles Heyde, a Burlington artist, was commissioned by the Vermont Historical Society to create a coat of arms for the state. He sketched the outlines of Camel's Hump and Mansfield from the lake, just as they might have looked to Samuel de Champlain in 1609. A state seal was adapted from Heyde's design, further simplifying the coat of arms but inexorably linking the mountain with the state's identity. Heyde, and others of his generation who painted in

John Frederick Kensett's Camel's Hump from the Western Shore of Lake Champlain *(1852) shows the distinctive outline of the Vermont peak amid a civilized, pastoral landscape.* Photo courtesy High Museum of Art, Atlanta, GA.

the 1860s and later, accepted the more civilized aspect of the Vermont landscape. It is this image, of rolling hills and open fields, that visitors then as now have sought most often in Vermont.

William Dean Howells, editor of the *Atlantic Monthly*, and one of America's most popular novelists at the end of the nineteenth century, was fascinated by rural life in Vermont and set one of his novels at Camel's Hump. In *The Landlord at Lion's Head* (1897), Howells uses the landscape, and the mountain in particular, as a metaphor for human character. His hero, Thomas Jefferson Durgin, is likened to the "primitively solitary and savage" mountain that keeps constant watch over the Durgin farmhouse. The heroine, Cynthia Whitwell, is identified with different, more feminine moods of the mountain. In their story of facing difficult times and finally being forced to turn to summer visitors to survive, Camel's Hump is at center stage throughout.

If you looked at the mountain from the west, the line of the summit was wandering and uncertain, like that of most mountain-tops; but seen from the east, the mass of granite [Howells was mistaken here—the mountain is not granite] showing above the dense forests of the lower slopes has the form of a sleeping lion. The flanks and haunches were vaguely distinguished from the mass; but the mighty head, resting with its tossed mane upon the vast paws stretched before it, was boldly sculptured against the sky. The likeness could not have been more perfect, when you had it in profile, if it had been a definite intention of art; and you could travel far north and far south before the illusion vanished. In winter the head was blotted by the snows; and sometimes the vagrant clouds caught upon it and deformed it, or hid it, at other seasons; but commonly, after the last snow went in the spring until the first snow came in the fall, the Lion's head was a part of the landscape, as imperative and importunate as the Great Stone Face itself.

As in Hawthorne's story, *The Great Stone Face*, about the Old Man of the Mountains in Franconia Notch, Howells's characters grow to assume the rugged and beautiful qualities of the landscape that surrounds them.

Recreation

Economic stagnation in Vermont around the end of the last century directed attention, here as elsewhere, to the mountains as a potential source of new income. A group of local businessmen formed the Camel's Hump Club in nearby Waterbury in 1908, their objective being "the exploitation of the mountain that it may be better known and its beauties more fully enjoyed." The club's first main project, begun that same year, was to open a road from the highway to the summit. Ridley's old road was completely overgrown, so the club chose instead to follow part of a Vermont Department of Forestry route on the southeast side of the mountain, cut earlier for reforestation projects in an area hard-hit by forest fires in 1903.

Then, just below the Hump, in a grassy clearing where the earlier Summit Hotel had stood, the Camel's Hump Club set up a

14 x 16-foot tent for mountain hospitality, complete with a small heating stove and two others for cooking. These initial efforts expanded to include four tents with beds made of boughs; one slept twenty, and the others accommodated twelve each. In the 1910 season there were 700 visitors. The following year, business was even better, and 1,100 people took advantage of the tents to spend the night on the mountain. Permanent facilities were needed by 1912, so a 14 x 20-foot hut replaced the tents. Eventually, three tin huts served the hiking public, and these were used until the early 1950s.

While the accommodations, by all accounts, fell far short of the elegance found on mountaintops elsewhere, the view remained outstanding. A brochure from the Vermont Bureau of Publicity tempted potential visitors: "The view of Lake Champlain from the Hump is the finest that can be obtained from the Green Mountains. All the hills seem to dip toward the lake and at sundown, when Champlain reflects the colors of parting day, each is touched with delicate hues, leaving the valleys sunk in deep black. The changing glories of a sunset over Lake Champlain never can be adequately pictured with pen or brush; they must be seen from the summit of this mountain to be fully appreciated."

The Long Trail

The burgeoning interest in hiking and camping after the turn of the century supported a radical new idea—a hiking trail running the entire length of the state of Vermont. James P. Taylor launched the concept of the Long Trail in 1910, and it immediately caught on. Influenced by the regimen of Alden Partridge, Taylor had led hikes for his students while serving as headmaster of the Vermont Academy for Boys at Saxtons River. But adequate hiking trails were hard to find. He had the visionary idea to build a series of trails and connectors that would form one trail spanning the entire distance of his home state. The trail system would be built and maintained by an organized group of hiking enthusiasts, to be called the Green Mountain Club (GMC).

The gregarious and well-spoken Taylor, who had experience not only as a school administrator but also as a teacher and Chamber

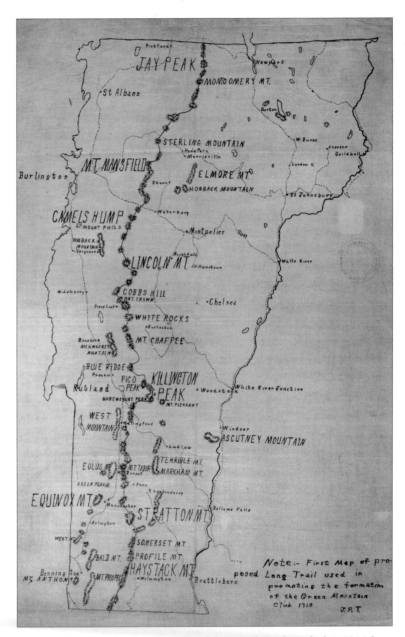

James P. Taylor's idea for a state-long hiking trail was launched in 1910 by the newly-formed Green Mountain Club. The first section of the Long Trail to be constructed was the segment from Camel's Hump to Mansfield. Photo courtesy Vermont Historical Society.

of Commerce executive, went to work full-time to spread the word about his new plan. He held a series of meetings all over the state, and on March 4, 1910, sent a call to about two dozen prominent citizens to form the Green Mountain Club. The next week, the group met in Burlington and officially organized, with their purpose "to make the Vermont mountains play a larger part in the life of the people, to encourage mountain climbing, to make trails, build shelters, and aid in preparation of maps and guide books." They started constructing the Long Trail right away.

The first stretch of the Long Trail connected Camel's Hump and Mansfield, fifteen miles apart as the crow flies but almost thirty miles by trail. Bowing to pressure from the Forestry Department, the trail turned out to be a low-lying fire-fighting access road, and most hikers disliked it. A fortuitous intervention by Will S. Monroe changed the course of the trail in 1915. Trained as a psychologist and a member of the summer-school faculty at the University of Vermont, Monroe thought the 1913 trail was an embarrassment to the Green Mountain Club. He volunteered to fix it, scouting, marking, and clearing a new trail on Camel's Hump.

Monroe named one of two GMC camps on the Camel's Hump section of the trail Montclair Glen in honor of his former home in New Jersey. He built the trail over Ethan and Ira Allen mountains and Burnt Rock Mountain, altogether creating a fifty-mile stretch of the Long Trail from Middlebury Gap north to Mount Mansfield. According to Laura and Guy Waterman's *Forest and Crag: A History of Hiking, Trail-blazing and Adventure in the Northeast Mountains*, "hikers on that 1916-vintage skyline from Montclair Glen south over the Allens and Burnt Rock are rewarded with the first sample of Monroe's artistry as a trailsman. He painstakingly combed the ridges for spots of exceptional interest or beauty, then linked them together for his trail, so that the miles roll by in a dazzling succession of rock outcrops, mossy glades, secluded hollows, airy ledges, arching hogbacks, boulder heaps and caves with mysterious openings leading to unfathomed recesses, or exposed rock slabs commanding sweeping views of rugged mountainsides....His work elevated the Long Trail from one that was merely long to one that was a classic for beauty and interest as well."

Montclair Glen Lodge is one of two shelters maintained by the Green Mountain Club on Camel's Hump. Historic photo courtesy Green Mountain Club/Kurt Stier.

Monroe bought property high on the east side of Camel's Hump in 1925, naming it Couching Lion Farm. He lived there until 1939, with one sister and his many dogs. This eccentric visionary chose to be buried there, too. Near his grave is another cemetery unique in New England mountain history—the final resting place for Monroe's beloved collies, Saint Bernards, Newfoundlands, and Great Pyrenees, each with its own granite marker.

The Long Trail would take several years to complete, although by 1920 it extended from the Massachusetts border north to Johnson, Vermont. Many felt a trail along the main ridge of the Green Mountains would be sufficient, but hard-core supporters pushed for the trail to encompass the entire length of the state, right to the Canadian border. In 1927, the stretch to Jay Peak was finished, and the final ten miles to Canada were completed in 1930. But the heart of the Long Trail, the section for which Will Monroe was responsible and which is the most heavily used today, is now known as the Monroe Skyline. From Camel's Hump south through Lincoln Gap to Middlebury Gap, this twenty-seven-mile stretch offers some of the most interesting and scenic hiking to be found anywhere in Vermont.

Will S. Monroe was famous for trail building and also for his devotion to his many dogs. At his Couching Lion Farm at the base of Camel's Hump, he even created a special cemetery for his pets, giving half a dozen animals their own grave markers. Photo courtesy Green Mountain Club/Kurt Stier.

Parkway Controversy

The construction and popularity of the Long Trail threatened to be dwarfed by the scope of a public-works project proposed by the federal government in 1935. As part of the New Deal to help America recover from the Great Depression, Vermont was offered $18 million for the construction of a scenic highway for automobiles running along the Green Mountain ridge. The Skyline Drive, as it was to be called, would extend 260 miles, and all that Vermont had to do was contribute the land—a right-of-way along the ridgeline that would be turned over to the federal government to become a national park.

Such a spectacular scheme could not help but provoke fierce debate, and for a year there were intense arguments all over the state about whether such an idea would bring economic salvation or total ruin. Vermonters stubbornly and angrily defended their views, some, such as James P. Taylor, championing the proposal, and others vowing never to sell out their mountains.

The Vermont legislature put the final decision to the public in March 1936. In a vote monitored by all the major newspapers in the country, only four of fourteen counties in the state accepted the government's proposal for an economic bail-out, and the Green Mountain Parkway was rejected. Camel's Hump, along with all the other high peaks of Vermont, had been spared.

An editorial in the *New York Sun* summed up the controversy: "Uppermost in the minds of most Vermonters, perhaps, was a strong desire to preserve the ancient beauty of their hills. If a large part of the territory through which the broad parkway was to run is now a wooded wilderness, so much the better....Apparently the old-fashioned idea still survives in Vermont that a man who prefers to fare forth afoot to see the world is entitled to some protection."

Plane Crash

Another incident in the history of the mountain did not have such a happy ending. On the night of October 16, 1944, on a routine training flight from Westover Air Force Base in Massachusetts, a B-24 bomber crashed into the mountain. There were nine fatalities, but miraculously, one man survived. The determined investigations in the 1970s of a local Vermont man, Brian Lindner, have yielded a complete record of the causes and consequences of this bizarre and fascinating story.

The flight pattern directed the pilots on a routine, four-leg training mission before going overseas. Starting from their home base at Chicopee, Massachusetts, they headed to Albany, New York, and from there were to go to Burlington, Vermont; Manchester, New Hampshire; and back to Chicopee. The night was clear and there was no moon. The first snowfall of the season had dusted the high peaks of the Green Mountains. To gain experience in instrument navigation, the copilot had pulled a retractable canvas shield down over the windshield so he could not see out, while another crew member visually checked their position at all times.

Perhaps the early snowfall on that moonless night distorted their perception. Perhaps because of the night's cold temperatures, they tried to keep warm by flying at a lower altitude. Traveling 215 MPH at only 4,000 feet instead of the standard 8,000 feet, the plane slammed into the top of Camel's Hump just west of the summit. Upon impact, the aircraft cartwheeled to the south, ripping off its tail section against a tree, hitting the left wing and belly, then smashing the

During World War II, the crash of a U.S. Air Force bomber on a routine training flight catapulted Camel's Hump into the headlines. Brian Lindner.

nose. The forward part of the plane completely disintegrated, and nine members of the crew were killed instantly. Only James Wilson survived, spending two frigid nights on the mountain before rescue crews were able to reach him. He lost both hands and feet after his forty-one-hour ordeal, but with artificial limbs went on to become a lawyer in Colorado and an inspiration to other amputees.

Rescuers at the crash site carried off the bodies of the air-force men who were killed, and a special delegation from Westover made a hurried trip to Vermont to recover what some speculate may have been a top-secret Norden bomb sight. The 36,000 pounds of wreckage has gradually disappeared to souvenir hunters and scrap-metal salvagers, some of the aluminum being used in the Korean War. For many years after, a hand-painted sign directed hikers to the wreckage and the crash site, but for the last twenty years or so there has been virtually no trace of the World War II disaster left on the mountain.

Conservation

The preservation of Camel's Hump is one of the success stories of the mountain. Developed as a tourist area along with Mansfield, then targeted by the federal government and opportunistic businessmen in the twentieth century, the fate of the mountain might have been quite different. A major turning point was the generous and far-sighted gift to the state of 1,000 acres on Camel's Hump's summit by Colonel Joseph Battell of Middlebury in 1911. Battell, who made money in the publishing business, specified in his gift that the whole forest was "to be preserved in a primeval state." A brochure published by the Camel's Hump Forest Reserve Commission poetically affirmed their commitment to the preservation of Camel's Hump: "A Promise was made to the mountain that the only changes it would undergo are Spring, Summer, Fall and Winter." Vermont continued to acquire Camel's Hump lands, and by 1951 the state forestry agency had 7,478 acres.

Today, it owns and administers almost 19,500 acres. Because so many of the state's other big mountains have ski areas and communications towers, the state of Vermont strictly limits the building of structures and other development there, and has turned down several development proposals for Camel's Hump. Designation as a natural area in 1965 gave the mountain further protection, and in 1968 it was registered as a National Natural Landmark. Camel's Hump State Park was established in 1969 specifically to preserve this last of the high Green Mountains in a natural state.

Camel's Hump State Park is part of the Camel's Hump Forest Reserve, which lies within the towns of Duxbury, Fayston, Huntington, and Waitsfield. Restrictions on hikers and campers limit their impact on the area. No fires are permitted and the only overnight camping is in the Green Mountain Club lodges, which during the busy season must be reserved in advance. The Ecological Area, set aside as a special-use district, extends from the 2,500-foot elevation to the summit. From mid-May to mid-October, the state and the GMC cosponsor ranger-naturalists to patrol this area and assure that hikers understand the fragile alpine tundra ecosystem and help to preserve the rare plants growing there.

High-level politicians, including (from left) EPA head Lee Thomas, Senator Patrick Leahy, and Vermont Governor Madeleine Kunin, inspect a red spruce tree core for potential environmental damage on Camel's Hump. Photo courtesy Conservation and Research Foundation.

The University of Vermont (UVM), located in nearby Burlington, has forged a strong partnership with the state on Camel's Hump. Students from UVM have been gathering data on this mountain for many years. A graduate student's baseline survey of the forest community between 1964 and 1966 provided data against which another survey in 1979 could be compared. The number of red spruce and other seedlings taking hold to replace mature trees as they died proved to be surprisingly reduced—by a dramatic 50 percent. As scientists have tried to assess the causes for this decline, they have analyzed not only atmospheric factors but soil properties as well.

Camel's Hump is shrouded in fog for nearly 2,000 hours a year, or about 22 percent of the time, and fog carries more intense levels of acid than rainwater. Coal-burning power plants in the Midwest, with their extra-tall stacks to reduce local air pollution, pump tons of sulfuric acid and other harmful chemicals into the high atmosphere. These high concentrations of sulfur, lead, and cadmium condense over New England, affecting soils and ground water, causing a severely inhibited uptake of minerals and nutrients by trees, and poisoning fish and other aquatic life. Where once there was a dense forest canopy, whole areas on Camel's Hump are filled with dead and dying trees, and an entirely different forest-floor community is taking hold in the unexpected sunlight furnished by the lack of mature shade trees.

Dr. Hubert Vogelmann coordinated Vermont's Acid Rain Research Project, which studied the effects of acid rain on the environment. One prime suspect in explaining the forest die-back is aluminum, which appears to be released in the soil as part of a chemical reaction triggered by higher acid levels in the ground-water. While scientists have studied tree rings from red spruce and sugar maples and can document that annual growth began to shut down around 1950 (at the same time the concentration of aluminum began to climb), they can only advance theories about how acid rain, heavy metals, and mobile aluminum work to kill trees.

The inconclusive nature of lab experiments in proving these theories has stalled federal-level policy changes that would force reduction of the emissions that cause acid rain. For now, there may be some satisfaction in the fact that most Americans, according to a recent poll, not only believe that acid rain is a serious problem, but have expressed a willingness to pay up to $100 per year to help eliminate it.

The view from Camel's Hump is said by many to be the best in the state. Here the view to the north shows the ridge of the Long Trail as it winds toward Mount Mansfield. Kurt Stier.

Suggestions for Visitors

Camel's Hump is a strenuous climb yet offers unsurpassed views, and is among the most popular in the state. Current Green Mountain Club figures estimate that 10,000 to 12,000 people per year climb the Hump. The preferred route is the historic Forestry Trail, which begins at the former Couching Lion Farm site near North Duxbury. The Burrows Trail from Huntington is the shortest route to the summit, and the Long Trail, running north and south, offers a way to do a circuit hike on more than one trail.

The GMC maintains Montclair Glen Lodge, south of the summit and within two hundred yards of Professor Monroe's original Montclair Glen shelter. An overnight hike that begins on the east side of the mountain follows the Forest City Trail to this point, then picks up the Long Trail from there to the summit. Of note along this route is Wind Gap, where the tall cliffs of Camel's Hump's southern end funnel the wind into strong currents. The exposed layers of folded rock look like gnarled driftwood in some places, and the precipitous cliffs are truly breathtaking.

Information on hiking Camel's Hump may be obtained at the Green Mountain Club's headquarters just north of Interstate 89 on Route 100. The mailing address is RR 1, Box 650, Waterbury Center, VT 05677; 802-244-7037.

Mansfield

Mount Mansfield, the highest point in Vermont, lies fifteen miles north of Camel's Hump in the Green Mountain chain. The aspect of the two could not be more different; while one is protected from development, the other has seemed to attract and encourage it. Mount Mansfield's name, and that of its ski area, Stowe, has become synonymous with winter recreation in Vermont. Today, the fragile alpine plant community on the summit of the mountain sees between 30,000 and 50,000 visitors annually (not including skiers), who arrive via a toll road, ski lifts, or on the many hiking routes (including the Long Trail) that ascend the 4,393-foot-high peak.

Mansfield is actually a two-mile-long ridge, with an irregular outline that, viewed from east or west, appears to form the features of a human face in profile. The various peaks along this ridge are named accordingly—the Forehead, Nose, Upper Lip, Lower Lip, and Chin. The highest point on the mountain is the Chin, located at the northernmost end of the chain. Samuel de Champlain, the French explorer who is believed to have named Camel's Hump in 1609, likewise is credited with being the first European explorer to record seeing Mansfield.

The traditional Abenaki name for the mountain, Moze-o-de-be-wadso, is translated "mountain with a head like a moose." One

The high profile-like ridge of Mount Mansfield dominates northwestern Vermont; ski trails criss-cross its eastern slope. Kurt Stier

Indian legend, recorded in the 1800s, gives a different origin for the face on the mountain. It explains that the son of a chief, in order to inherit his father's position, had to prove himself by climbing to the summit of the mountain. Despite crippling disabilities, the young Indian succeeded in making it to the summit, only to be engulfed by a violent storm and swirling clouds. For several days the summit was thus shrouded, and when the storm finally abated and the mountain-top was again revealed, it had taken on the features of the determined but doomed young man.

Early History

The Green Mountains and Lake Champlain formed a natural boundary between the Algonquin peoples of New England and the Iroquois of New York. Indian settlement in Vermont was primarily in the valley of the lake. To the east, Mansfield and the Green Mountains effectively separated the indigenous inhabitants of the Champlain valley from the Connecticut River Valley. The separation and tension between these three groups foreshadowed similar conflicts between colonial Americans. The mountainous area containing

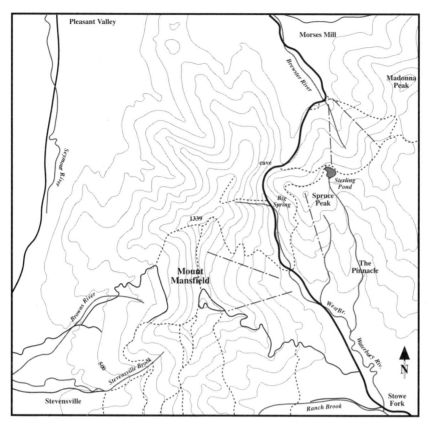

Mansfield

Mount Mansfield, between Lake Champlain and the Connecticut River, was the subject of a long political tug of war between New York and New Hampshire.

In 1763, New Hampshire Governor Benning Wentworth laid claim to the unpopulated territory by dividing it up into townships and distributing 138 grants of land. Wentworth issued the charter for the town of Mansfield on June 8, 1763, naming it for Lord Mansfield, English solicitor general, who was involved in the New Hampshire–New York dispute over Vermont's ownership. A large portion of the new town of Mansfield passed into the hands of Ira Allen, brother of Ethan Allen, who was to lead that renowned American Revolution band, the Green Mountain Boys.

In 1772, his fellow proprietors hired Allen to survey the town. Since the northern boundary of the town crosses Mount Mansfield at the Adam's Apple, Ira Allen probably became the first provincial to climb this high ridge. In his autobiography, Allen recorded that doing the survey gave him a good chance to size up the fertility of the town. "At this time, I was owner of very near one third of the town, and could not discover lands that would [make] one good farm." In good Yankee fashion, he concealed the true nature of Mansfield's topography until after he had sold his own holdings.

Not surprisingly, Mansfield attracted only the hardiest and most determined of early settlers. Zimri Luce arrived in 1799 with his wife and ten children, followed by Samuel Henderson, Isaac Knight, and Zimri's brothers Moses and Ivory. Many from these earliest families remained loyal to the area, but the town grew so slowly that it did not have enough residents to organize officially until 1815. In 1820, there were but sixty residents. Suddenly the population grew rapidly, so that by 1830 Mansfield had reached its nineteenth-century high of 279 citizens, still scattered on fragmented subsistence farms. It was said that Ivory Luce was elected to represent the town in the state legislature because he was the only man in town with a proper pair of shoes.

The promise of better agricultural lands in New York and the Midwest lured away much of the population of Vermont in the middle of the nineteenth century, and Mansfield was no exception. Mansfield's situation was complicated further by the huge ridge of mountain running down the middle of the town. The town officially dissolved in 1839. The western part of Mansfield was annexed to Underhill, and nine years later the remainder joined Stowe, completely obliterating the former town. Today, the southern portions of Mount Mansfield lie in Underhill and Stowe; the northern portion is in the town of Cambridge. Only the mountain, and numerous other local organizations, have kept the honorable memory of Lord Mansfield alive.

Geology and Geography

One of the Mansfield area's intriguing features is Smuggler's Notch, a passage at the head of the Lamoille River between Mount Mansfield and its neighbor to the east, Mount Sterling. Smuggler's Notch, unlike the famous passes in the White Mountains, was not glacially formed and lacks the characteristic U-shaped cross section that marks ice-gnawed valleys. Instead, it appears to be the work of water in its liquid state, and is thought to have been cut by glacial meltwater that poured from the Champlain valley into the Stowe valley, perhaps because other outlets were blocked by ice.

The name of Smuggler's Notch derives from events that led to the War of 1812. In an effort to reduce international tensions, President Thomas Jefferson imposed an embargo on United States trade in 1807, crippling the New England economy, which was dependent on shipping raw materials and receiving finished goods and commodities. As a result, a clandestine commerce with Canada developed, much of it by way of Lake Champlain. The high mountain pass just north of Mansfield provided a little-known overland route for goods and livestock from cities and towns in eastern New England. Contraband goods and cattle were said to have been hidden in caves on the side of Mount Mansfield. The steep road through Smuggler's Notch, bordered by dramatic high cliffs from which huge chunks of rock regularly fall, was improved for auto traffic in 1921. One last section remained gravel until 1963. The well-traveled scenic roadway is never open in the winter because it is too narrow and too steep to plow.

The highest point on the floor of the pass is 2,100 feet, with the mountains rising a thousand feet skyward on either side. The cliffs of Smuggler's Notch are made of 380-million-year-old metamorphic rock characteristic of the Mansfield massif. It is schist, specifically mica-albite-quartz schist (albite is a white, chalky member of the feldspar family). Because the proportions of the schist's constituent minerals vary, its appearance changes from place to place.

The raw materials of Mansfield's rock were sediments deposited on the floor of an ancient sea. When these layers were subjected to great heat and pressure, their mineral components migrated and recrystallized into larger grains. These crystals formed with their long dimensions perpendicular to the pressure, giving them an unusual layered, or foliated, appearance, which was contorted by subsequent folding. At places on the summit, these folds are so pronounced that the layers of rock look like giant drapery. In other places, bright impurities such as garnets—small red twelve-faced crystals—and lumps of milky white quartz appear in the schist.

Mansfield's surface was formed from an ancient sea floor, where heat and pressure folded the sediments into rocks resembling giant drapery. Kurt Stier.

Cracks or rifts, which geologists call joints, have shaped many of Mansfield's other natural features, such as the north-facing cliff known as the Nose. This abrupt cliff just above the top of the toll road was created as pressure on the rock layers diminished and they broke apart, rising at different rates. In other places, deep canyons have formed where a huge block, separated by joints from the neighboring ledge, has crept down the mountainside.

The Cave of the Winds is one such deep cleft in the rocks, just below the summit. Early explorers of this cave conveyed themselves in with ropes, and for a time there was a ladder leading down into it. Carrying the anthropomorphic analogy to a logical conclusion, one writer in the 1870s concluded: "Whether this opening be the path to the Old Man's stomach has not been determined. Thankful not to be swallowed by the giant, visitors are glad to leave this chilling cavern believing the Old Man's heart to be as cold as stone."

Joints also gave glacial ice finger-holds to pluck loose boulders for distribution through the neighboring countryside. Glacial striae (or grooves) caused by the grinding of ice-carried rocks against the bedrock, indicate that ice moved diagonally across the mountain. While the most recent continental glacier is thought to have flowed straight south through the Champlain valley about 12,000 years ago, some of it evidently spilled sideways from the main flow over Mansfield.

Glacial ice and geologic formations have created a fascinating array of natural features on Mount Mansfield, and each generation of hikers has made new entries into the catalog of sights. Cantilever Rock, apparently discovered by an off-trail hiker on the Underhill side in the 1960s, is a spectacular thirty-nine-foot-long shaft wedged at right angles to the mountain itself. Today, hundreds of people pass the rock on a new, well-marked trail. An elephant head is outlined in rock outcroppings in Smuggler's Notch, and a turtle-shaped rock keeps watch over the Chin.

Wampahoofus Rock, shaped like a fanciful beast, juts out from the southern end of Mansfield's summit. The story goes that this quadruped once ranged freely over the Green Mountains. Adapted for

Unusual geological formations, including anthropomorphic rocks, add some interesting highlights to a hike of Mansfield. Turtle Rock is located on the Chin; in the background are the trails of the ski area on the mountain's east side. Kurt Stier.

chasing prey on steep slopes, its downhill legs grew longer than its uphill ones. But all the males were born left-handed (and went clockwise around the mountain), while the females were right-handed and did the opposite. Mating became impossible, and the wampahoofus died out.

Mount Mansfield is also endowed with Vermont's highest-altitude lake. Lake of the Clouds, a several-acre pond just north of the summit, is fed by rains and mountain snows. To avoid confusion with the Lakes of the Clouds on Mount Washington, an attempt was made in the 1860s to change the name to Crescent Lake, but the new name never stuck.

The Advent of Tourism

The era of mountain tourism and recreational hiking began much later in Vermont than it had in Massachusetts or New Hampshire. Notwithstanding the ascent of Mansfield by Norwich's indefatigable Captain Alden Partridge in 1818, it would be almost three decades before there was a proper hiking trail on the mountain.

The first known route was cleared by citizens of Underhill Center in 1847. Still known as the Halfway House Trail, it led partway up the west side of the mountain to a small hotel called the Halfway House, built in 1850. From there, a bridle path extended to the Nose, where the summit's first shelter, a tent and platform, was raised in August 1856. Fire probably claimed the Halfway House about 1876, but a second one was built and continued to exist until the mid-1880s.

Although Underhill on the west side of Mount Mansfield first attracted tourists, Stowe was destined to become the primary focus of recreational activities on the mountain. Stillman Churchill launched the trend in 1850 when he opened the Mansfield House (now part of the Green Mountain Inn in downtown Stowe) and encouraged "rusticating" in a pleasant country village. Five years later, the beginning of development on the mountain's east side forever altered the character of the place.

Stowe attorney William Henry Harrison Bingham built his own Halfway House (not to be confused with the similarly named place on the opposite side of the mountain) at a large spring partway up the east side of the mountain. Then, in 1857, Bingham erected his first mountain hotel on a plateau called the Height of Land, just a half-mile from the summit. The next year, Bingham built an even larger hotel at this location, and then the following summer moved the building farther up the mountain to the Nose, where, known variously as the Summit House, Tip Top House, Mountain House, and Mount Mansfield House, it remained in continuous service for a hundred years. The eight-sided warming shelter called the Octagon stands today on the site of Bingham's first hotel.

Mount Manfield's Summit House was featured in many nineteenth-century stereograph cards. In July 1926 a windstorm broke every single window on the west side of the Summit House—220 panes in all. Photo courtesy Society for the Preservation of New England Antiquities, Boston, MA.

Bingham, capitalizing on Stillman Churchill's original investment, and holder of much of Mount Mansfield's acreage himself, went on to become the presiding genius of Mansfield's commercial development. Incorporating as the Mount Mansfield Hotel Company, Bingham and a group of investors opened another hotel in 1864, this one located on Stowe's main street and called the Mansfield House. After about 1870, carriages carried guests to the summit of the mountain via another Bingham enterprise, the Mount Mansfield Turnpike Company's toll road. The log roadbed and hairpin turns must have contributed to a memorable ride.

Promoters also pursued the idea of a cable car or track-based conveyance for getting up the mountain. D. C. Linsley, an engineer from Burlington (most likely the same person who built the 1857 Linsley Road on Ascutney), mapped out a route for a cable car in 1865. When this idea failed to take hold, Linsley countered the next year with a proposal for a toll road along roughly the same route, up the west side from Underhill to end at the top of the Chin. This scheme made it as far as the state legislature, where it died.

Railroad-building plans surfaced again around the end of the century. Lack of broad interest seems to have undermined all these proposals. Happily, the prediction that a landing field for aircraft ought to be laid out between the Nose and the Chin, made after the first flight over the summit in 1920, came to naught as well.

Though it never matched the popularity of the White Mountains, Mansfield was easily the busiest mountain destination resort in the state, attracting mostly middle-class families and traveling businessmen. The arrival of the railroad in 1850 had opened Vermont's mountains to a steady influx of vacationers, mostly from New York and northern New England. The wave of tourism all over the region crested in the 1880s and 1890s with resorts in the White Mountains, the Berkshires, and along the Maine seacoast offering stiff competition to Vermont's mountains. The railroads tried hardest, promoting "the power of a locale or building...to convey the spirit of the past through association." But it was precisely this lack of historical association that proved to be Mansfield's greatest weakness as a tourist attraction. Vermont's mountains were not immortalized in any great literary or artistic works; no great natural disasters or episodes of human heroism or tragedy took place there. As we shall see, such credentials helped create the White Mountains' fame and overwhelming popularity.

As if to substitute for this lack of story, there was a long debate to establish that Mansfield was truly the highest peak in the state, the designation of the highest being something of a prize that might help attract more tourists. Following Partridge's estimate of 4,279 feet, other well-known mountain figures came up with their own readings. Geologist Edward Hitchcock got 4,329; Arnold Guyot of Princeton measured it at 4,430, and promoters of the Summit House boasted in one brochure that Mansfield was "about 5,000 feet."

Each time a new pronouncement came out, there was a scramble to see how Mansfield stacked up against Camel's Hump and Killington, farther to the south. Raphael Pumpelly, working for the U.S. Geodetic Survey, at one point announced that Camel's Hump was highest, but another reading on Killington surpassed this, making Mansfield third on the 1901 list. Finally in 1924, the debate was settled with a U.S. Geological Survey. Their copper disc is firmly embedded in the Chin, officially Vermont's highest point at exactly 4,393.3 feet.

Ralph Waldo Emerson, one of the few Transcendentalists to climb Mansfield, produced no memorable prose about the mountain. Instead, his journal records a rather disappointing visit to the Summit House with his daughter Ellen on August 24, 1868: "We were not quite fortunate, as we found a party of amateur players on the top of Mansfield Mount filling the house, too, all night with violent fun. And as they were good young people...perhaps the contretemps was not better. If I could have spared the time, we should have outstayed the company, and made our religious visits to the crags later."

Time spent on Mansfield was certainly convivial, nineteenth-century accounts agree. A group of hikers in 1863 witnessed that unusual phenomenon known as the Specter of the Brocken, and later described their adventure in a newspaper account excerpted in Robert L. Hagerman's *Mansfield: The Story of Vermont's Loftiest Mountain*. "We had time to change our positions, throw our arms about, and toss up our hats, and watch the same performance by the dumb imitators in the cloud. We went wild with excitement at the glorious scene, and we were sorry that it did not 'hold on,' for it lasted but little more than a minute."

Artists of the era did not entirely overlook Mansfield as a subject but tended to exhibit much the same perspective as had Emerson—a pleasant place for people to enjoy natural scenery. Jerome Thompson's *The Belated Party on Mansfield Mountain* shows a relaxed group of picnickers on the Lower Lip looking toward the Chin. The painter must have been impressed with the unusual contours of the summit ridge, too, balancing his fashionably dressed group of figures with the looming elevation of the rocky Chin.

The Vermont mountain experience of the last century was perhaps best summed up in an 1883 article in *Harper's Magazine:* "Of the Green Mountains, one might probably say, they are more generally admired than visited. Poets sing without seeing them. They have furnished ready and familiar figures to orators who could hardly point them out on a map." In the author's pronouncement that "here, all is primitive, idyllic, Arcadian," lay the seeds of his complaint—the

Jerome Thompson painted The Belated Party on Mansfield Mountain *in 1858. The panoramic view of Lake Champlain on the distance shares the spotlight with the unusual geologic formation of the Chin.* Photo courtesy Metropolitan Museum of Art, New York, NY.

Green Mountains were too pastoral, too harmonious an environment to be really exciting.

The grand-hotel era and Mansfield's days as a summer destination never lived up to expectations and lasted less time than investors had hoped. By 1870, the summit-hotel company was facing financial difficulties, and the Mount Mansfield House at Stowe burned in 1889. Between then and 1920, the Summit House changed hands a number of times, finally being acquired by today's Mount Mansfield Company. It continued to operate through the 1920s and 1930s, luring hay-fever sufferers and assorted excursion groups, but in a rather diminished condition from its former glory. Guests often danced to phonograph records in the evenings, and parties still hiked up to the Nose before breakfast to view the sunrise. And when the hotel was overcrowded, some guests slept in cars, on benches, or even on the lobby floor.

A modified truck provided the first regular motorized passenger service up the carriage road to the Summit House. A capacity load consisted of eight people, plus six bales of hay for horses stabled at the hotel and for the cow whose milk the guests consumed. The road was rebuilt for automobiles in 1922, a mammoth undertaking in those days, and continued to get heavy use in the summers, mostly from day-trippers rather than overnight hotel guests.

Sadly, but predictably, the Summit House outlasted its public. Though plans for expansion were announced in 1949, they never materialized. Following the 100th-anniversary celebration in 1958, the hotel ceased operations. The building itself was used as a snack bar for a few more seasons, but in 1964, fearing the hazards of its dilapidated condition, its owners waited for the first snowfall and then burned it down.

On the Underhill side of the mountain, a parcel of about a thousand acres that contained the ruins of the old Halfway House was bought by Dr. W. G. E. Flanders in 1924. He attempted to reestablish the Underhill side of the mountain as a competitive tourist attraction, rebuilding the Halfway House Hotel, adding tents to accommodate twenty-four overnight campers, and cutting several new trails. The unorthodox hotel included an astronomical telescope, a sprinkler system to cool the roofs of the porch and dining room during hot spells, and a searchlight that was visible far off in the Champlain valley.

Recreation and Conservation

Other aspects of activity on Mansfield were picking up, too. In 1910 Vermont mountaineers organized the Green Mountain Club and began to create the Long Trail, a ridge-top footpath running north to south throughout the state. Volunteers cut the section of the Long Trail across Mount Mansfield by the next year, but two more decades were required for the completion of the entire 265-mile path.

When the Green Mountain Club went to work on Mansfield, the only trails were the Halfway House Trail on the west side, and the Judge Seneca Haselton Trail on the east side. Only a 400-acre strip along the summit ridge was protected, having been transferred by W. H. H. Bingham, builder of the Summit House, to the University of Vermont in 1859. The transaction carried important restrictions— the property was to be used for "scientific purposes" and there was to be no destruction of the trees or vegetation growing there.

Private owners controlled the remainder of the mountain until 1914, when the Vermont Forest Service bought 3,155 acres to initiate the Mount Mansfield State Forest. Over the years, other parcels have been added in Cambridge, Morristown, Johnson, Bolton, and Waterbury, until today the state owns 27,162 acres, including the land on which the ski area is built. Smuggler's Notch was incorporated into the state forest in 1940, ending sporadic attempts at commercialization there. The Green Mountain Club continues to work to achieve protected status for all the lands along the Long Trail today.

The C. E. & F. O. Burt Lumber Company began the era of skiing on Mount Mansfield. They had acquired much of the harvestable timber lands on Mansfield, and even into the twentieth century, as Burt Forests, Inc., they continued to produce lumber and manage the forests on the parts of the mountain not under state ownership. In 1970, the state purchased the last of the Burt-owned lands on the mountain and dismantled the familiar landmark that was their mill. But around the turn of the century, Burt's loggers used snowshoes in winter, and a few adventurous ones tried experiments with home-made skis. When three Swedish families arrived in Stowe in 1912, their familiarity with ski travel inspired Burt to further research and the eventual purchase of factory-made skis by mail, which many loggers found to be much more efficient than snowshoes.

From this humble beginning, after World War I, a group of local businessmen decided to start promoting the sport. They organized winter carnivals to draw people and dollars to Stowe. Ski jumps and toboggan runs were featured attractions, and throughout the 1920s there was snowshoeing, skating, and assorted dances and displays of winter merriment. Downhill skiing was conspicuously absent in those earliest years, though it was being practiced all around the area.

The honor for the first descent of Mansfield on skis goes to Dartmouth College's librarian, Nathaniel L. Goodrich, remembered today as one of New England's great hiking-trail builders. Accompanied by a friend on snowshoes, the two climbed to the Summit House in February 1914, then after lunch descended, each in his own fashion, along the route of the Toll Road.

Use of the toll road for the new sport caught on; Burt was persuaded to keep his logging camp open in winter to house and feed skiers, and in 1933 the Civilian Conservation Corps cut the new Bruce Trail specifically for skiing. Within the next few years, local enthusiasm, outside financing, and visionary leadership would make Mount Mansfield into one of the premier ski destinations in the East.

A New York businessman named Roland Palmedo was looking for the ideal mountain on which to plan a new ski development. Having hiked Mansfield in the summers, he recognized that it met all the necessary requirements, and he approached the Burt Lumber Company, which owned most of the mountain, with his idea. Before long, the expert Nose Dive Trail was built, the Mount Mansfield Ski Club was incorporated, and the mountain had the first ski patrol in the United States, formed in 1935.

In the early years, skiers walked the 4 1/2 miles up the Bruce Trail—one round trip per day was par for the course. On Nose Dive, the very athletic sometimes managed three runs. A revolution in downhill skiing came in the winter of 1934, when the first American ski tow was set up at Woodstock, Vermont. Stowe had a lift two years later, a thousand-foot, Cadillac-powered rope tow. Fifty cents bought an all-day ticket; a season pass sold for five dollars.

Ski trains from Boston and New York brought hundreds of eager skiers to Stowe and swelled the limits of local inns and guest houses. An Austrian ski instructor named Sepp Ruschp was hired to start a ski school and eventually ran the Mount Mansfield Company. The last-minute move of the Eastern Downhill Championship race from Greylock to Stowe in February of 1935 flooded the town with 10,000 visitors and gridlocked traffic on the main road leading into town.

The modern era of alpine skiing began on Mansfield in 1940, when the new owner of the mountain operation, C. V. Starr, added a 6,300-foot-long single chairlift to haul skiers up Mansfield all the way to the place where Bingham had first constructed the Summit House. Starr's philosophy was to expand slowly and do everything with elegance. By 1950, he had consolidated the many separate groups

Skiing began on Mansfield in the 1930s with a single Cadillac-powered second-hand tow and two CCC built trails. Photo courtesy Stowe Reporter, Stowe, VT.

involved on the mountain into his own single enterprise—the Mount Mansfield Company.

Stowe and Mount Mansfield were suddenly famous. Lowell Thomas, Sr., radio personality, avid skier, and local investor, made several broadcasts from Stowe and brought national renown to the tiny village at the foot of the mountain. Stowe itself blossomed from a provincial little town into a winter mecca where the wealthy came to ski and socialize. "For a land of forgotten cellar holes," mused Vermont historian Ralph Nading Hill in his *Yankee Kingdom*, "who could have forecast such a destiny? It is as if nature were making up for her failure to run veins of silver through the mountains, and was now tracing them on top."

The cachet of the area was further enhanced when the Kennedy family began skiing there in the 1960s. Equally well known is the Trapp Family Lodge, the home of Maria von Trapp, whose World War II autobiography, *The Sound of Music*, brought acclaim from millions. After the family's escape from Nazi-occupied Salzburg, they made their way to Stowe, where they began an inn that welcomed guests for music, worship, and regular hikes to the summit of Mansfield. Today, the third generation of the Trapp family operates a year-round, multimillion-dollar family resort, complete with Austrian-style main lodge and time-share condominiums.

Environmental Issues

Ever since Bingham's far-sighted restrictions in 1859 regarding preservation of the summit ridge, Mansfield has been at the center of struggles between those who might alter the mountain's environment to maximize its potential for human use, and those who might limit such intrusions. In 1947, for example, the University of Vermont permitted the state's Department of Public Safety to put up an antenna for radio transmission several hundred yards north of the Summit House. From there the state received its first commercial-television station as well as its first public-television transmission.

Later, the university allowed the construction of several other antennas and a 30 x 40-foot transmission building. But in recent decades the school's trustees have reevaluated their stewardship and adopted policies to reduce the technological presence on the mountaintop. The radio antennas have come to be considered a blemish on the natural face of the mountain, and they can be expected to disappear soon, especially since such towers are being rendered obsolete by stationary satellites.

As use of Mansfield has increased, so has concern over the effects of visitor traffic on the fragile alpine vegetation. Beginning in 1969, the Green Mountain Club took on the task of stationing rangers on Mansfield and Camel's Hump to enforce regulations, educate hikers about preservation of the plant communities, and lend assistance when problems arose. The Summit Caretaker Program, as it has been renamed, is supported jointly by the Green Mountain Club, Mount Mansfield Company, UVM, and the state Department of Forests, Parks, and Recreation. Today, a crew of three or four on Mansfield comprises an effective backcountry management team that mediates between the interests of recreation and protection.

Vermont's 265-mile Long Trail crosses the summit of Mansfield, where fragile alpine plants are at risk from the footsteps of thousands of hikers every season. Kurt Stier.

Other issues have surfaced related to the continued expansion of the ski area, especially since it is built almost entirely on state-owned lands for which the state receives a hefty sum in lease payments each year. Most recently, after a two-year trial period and hearings under Act 250, Vermont's strict environmental law, the Mount Mansfield Company received full approval to institute night skiing, placing bright lights over much of the mountain terrain. A planned 1995–96 expansion, with a new 50,000-square-foot base lodge/conference center, expanded parking lots, new waste-water treatment facility, and a new lift and ski trails crossing the historic Haselton Trail has also been approved, subject to minor compromises and concessions on environmental and scenic issues.

Intensive use in the twentieth century, destined to continue into the next, sets Mansfield apart from the other mountains in Vermont so far considered. As if to compensate for its lack of prosperity during the era of summit hotels and carriage roads, all the groups involved, from the Green Mountain Club to the state to the mountain company itself, are working hard to provide a satisfactory and rewarding experience of the place to the increasing and diverse audiences attracted to its slopes.

Suggestions for Visitors

With somewhere around forty thousand hikers and toll-road visitors each year, Mansfield ranks as the third most popular mountain summit in New England, behind Washington and Monadnock. Skier counts range well into the thousands, but Stowe's management concedes that today Killington, Stratton, and Mount Snow are all busier.

Hikers should obtain the Mansfield Region Trail Map from the Green Mountain Club or use the GMC *Guide Book to the Long Trail*, and choose a route suited to their abilities and interests. The GMC's *Guide Book* lists thirty different trails for Mansfield, adding up to well over 35 miles of trails on the mountain. The Long Trail parking area may be reached from Stowe Village by following Route 108 past the Stowe Mountain Resort.

Green Mountain Club headquarters are located on Route 100 between Interstate 89 and Stowe Village. Their mailing address is RR 1, Box 650, Waterbury Center, VT 05677; 802-244-7037.

The 4.5-mile toll road, operated by the Mount Mansfield Company, gives nonhikers access to the summit and to the 1.2-mile above-treeline walk through the arctic-alpine zone from the Nose to the Chin. Cave of the Winds and the Rock of Terror are notable summit features; the Subway and Wall Street trails pass through open joints on the path to the top.

Visitors to Mansfield's alpine zone encounter miniature spruce and fir trees, so dense in their growth they are almost impenetrable. Alden Partridge in 1818 complained about having to walk on them, but today there is a well-cleared path through these plants. Although they are less than two inches thick and are only a few feet high, they might be eighty-five years old. Here also are such rare alpine plants as Greenland sandwort, few-flowered sedge, Bigelow's sedge, grass-leafed fleabane, highland rush, hare's-tail cotton-grass, and the extremely rare Lapland diapensia. This little shrub blossoms toward the end of May or early in June. Visitors are cautioned that though these plants are hardy with respect to cold and wind, they are vulnerable to boots and weight. Ranger-naturalists do their best to enforce the regulations aimed at protecting all the delicate plants and educating the public as to the rationale for the strict "keep off the grass" policy.

In clear weather in winter, skilled cross-country skiers can take the chairlift to the Octagon, then ski up the toll road to the site of Summit House, go along the west side of the summit for the view of Lake Champlain and the Adirondacks, then descend the east side for a view of the White Mountains of New Hampshire.

From the village of Stowe, the Stowe Recreation Path extends 5.3 miles along the mountain road toward Mansfield. Paved and used by cyclists and rollerbladers as well as walkers, this off-road route was completed in 1989 with state, town, and private funds. It is a model of a well-planned community greenway and has won both local and national awards.

The entrance to the Mount Mansfield Toll Road. Kurt Stier.

Smuggler's Notch's steep walls and dark glades are worth seeing, and are accessible by following the Mountain Road (Route 108) past the Mansfield Ski Area. There are state-run picnic areas and campgrounds throughout the Mansfield/Smuggler's area. While no camping or fires are permitted within the state forest, the Green Mountain Club maintains the Taft and Butler lodges along the route of the Long Trail over the summit of Mansfield. The Smuggler's Notch Ski Area is on the other side of the notch in Jeffersonville and cannot be reached via this route in winter.

Ascutney

Ascutney is a beautiful mountain, rising in almost perfect symmetry from the banks of the Connecticut River in southeastern Vermont. It is not wild but looms directly over a well-settled land. This close proximity to civilization colors its unique history and character. From the nearby town of Windsor—Vermont's revolutionary capital and one of the state's most prosperous and important towns for two hundred years—Ascutney's attraction has been as much to those who would bask in its beauty from below as it has been to those who have sought the 360-degree panoramas from its 3,140-foot summit.

Over the years, Ascutney has known both attention and neglect. As with the other mountains in Vermont, entrepreneurs seeking profits here have not always been successful. Its granite quarries, and later its ski slopes, have been the scene of grand plans and hopes gone awry. Yet its place in New England's mountain history endures, and today its pleasant hiking trails reveal many of the attractions that have drawn explorers, speculators, artists, and lovers of high places to it through the years.

Early maps show the mountain's name as Ascutegnik, an Algonquin name that means "meeting of the waters." Other authorities believe the name is derived from the Indian word Cas-cad-nac, which means "mountain of the rocky summit" or "very steep slopes."

126

Both translations seem apt. Ascutney was also called Tri-mountain because of its three principal heights or ridges which radiate from the summit. The two lesser summits are now known as West Peak and North Peak.

Geography and Geology

Ascutney is not part of the Green Mountains or the New Hampshire hills to the east; it stands alone. And it has an almost perfectly symmetrical shape when viewed from above or seen as contour lines on a map. Its eighteen principal lobes, or scallops, according to one writer,

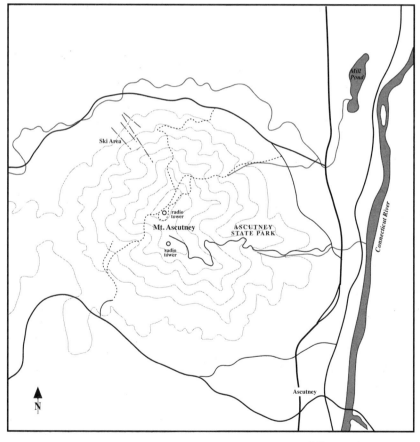

Mount Ascutney

"bear a striking resemblance to an inverted Vermont sugarcake." The technical term for these lobes is ring dikes. Sheer rock walls rising up around the base of the mountain are visible in many places, providing dramatic evidence of a great intrusion of molten rock. At Crystal Cascade on the Weathersfield Trail, Ascutney Brook falls eighty-four feet over such a rock face. Vertical walls loom above the hiker at several points along the Brownsville Trail, too, found on the opposite north side of the mountain.

Mount Ascutney is a relatively recent feature on the ancient New England landscape. Just 120 million years ago, a molten intrusion, or pluton, thrust up through a fault inside the earth. As the magma cooled, it hardened into igneous rocks called granite, syenite (a granitelike rock), and gabbro-diorite (an uncommon dark granite), distinguished from each other by the percentage of quartz they contain. All these rocks are quite resistant to erosion in comparison to the surrounding terrain, which has gradually worn away to expose this isolated cone rising nearly 2,000 feet above the surrounding plain.

The movement of the great ice sheets that began about one million years ago did little to change the hard igneous rock defining Mount Ascutney's contours. But chunks of rocks the glaciers split off provide geologists today with valuable clues about how the glacier actually moved. Ascutney's fan-shaped boulder train, one of the largest in New England, indicates that the glaciers advanced unevenly, not straight through valleys but spilling sideways along the margins. Millions of tons of Ascutney's distinctive boulders may be seen in stone walls and fields throughout southwestern New Hampshire, reaching as far as the Massachusetts border. Their origins can be determined by the presence of a rare greenish type of quartz-syenite called nordmarkite.

Early History

The earliest record of human activity around Ascutney is archeological. Investigations have unearthed traces of a western Abenaki campsite on the opposite bank of the Connecticut River at the mouth of the Sugar River. There, the remains of a long house were discovered, within which was evidence of a large ceremonial fireplace and six other cooking hearths. According to the *Mount Ascutney Guide*, published by the Ascutney Trails Association in 1992, "these Abenakis cultivated corn on the Connecticut River intervale, hunted the woods and fished the rivers. They apparently abandoned the site sometime before the arrival of Europeans whose diseases were to devastate their civilization." White historians have not recorded any ceremonial or religious traditions the native inhabitants of this region attached to Mount Ascutney.

As with many of New England's mountains, the record of European settlers' interaction with Ascutney commences around the time just preceding the American Revolution. After the close of the French and Indian Wars, land grants to veterans along the upper reaches of the Connecticut River hastened development. In scattered villages concentrated along the waterways, population began to grow rapidly and citizens began to form a sense of community based upon the unique character of the land they inhabited. By 1770, several towns were established at the base of Ascutney, with the river itself and the roads along its banks, affording the principal means of travel in the region.

Early settlers discovered that the hardness of Mount Ascutney's rock made it useful as a building material. By the early 1800s, there were granite quarries on the south and east sides of the mountain, where stone was cut for bridges, paving, millstones, and railroad abutments. On the north side of Ascutney, near Brownsville, two quarries mined a greenish variety of nordmarkite granite for building stone. This Norcross Quarry provided sixteen columns for Columbia University's library and thirty-four for the Bank of Montreal. Mower quarry stone was used for memorials—President William McKinley, assassinated in 1901 and buried in Canton, Ohio, rests in a sarcophagus of Mount Ascutney granite.

Ascutney's granite quarries, unlike the marble quarries in the Equinox area, were not destined for major success. Because the stone was not of the very best quality (it contained a high percentage of iron, which oxidized into rust as the stone weathered), owners decided not to invest in a railroad line to the quarry sites. Instead, roads were blasted and dug by hand. Cutting the stone involved more potentially dangerous blasting. Then the huge blocks were maneuvered by means of wooden poles, or derricks, onto low-wheeled wagons (or sleds in winter) and drawn down the mountain and out of the woods by horse or ox teams. Over particularly steep pitches, when the braking mechanisms on these conveyances were inadequate, a cable was attached to the load, looped around a tree, and eased out gradually by several strong men. The largest block of granite quarried here, some twenty tons, required a twenty-horse hitch to remove.

The poor overall quality of the granite ultimately forced some speculators into ruin and worse. In 1907, promoter Joseph Enright of Windsor, owner of the Enright Quarry, took his own life after losing

The hard granite of Ascutney was mined for building stone beginning in the early 1800s. Kurt Stier.

all his investor's money in a vain search for iron-free granite. Production continued to decline, and the last quarry, on what is now the Brownsville Trail, was closed by 1923. Today hikers on the trail will discover neatly cut blocks of stone, cables, and even a huge, well-preserved section of a derrick lying along the path, mute relics of the quarrying operation that was once the hope and livelihood for many on Ascutney's shoulders.

In its early years, Windsor was a prosperous commercial center, as the stately old homes lining her main street attest today. In Ascutneyville, just south of Windsor, a thriving enterprise developed to capitalize on the lime and soapstone deposits in the western section of the town. Quarrying and logging on the mountain, and precision-tool making in the town, all with ready access to water transportation routes, helped to build Windsor's reputation as the provincial capital.

An important event in the history of the colonies took place in the shadow of Mount Ascutney. Vermont declared itself a sovereign republic before the end of the Revolution, asserting its independence from New Hampshire and New York, which had previously claimed ownership of its territory. In July 1777, at the Old Constitution House in Windsor (now open as a museum), the first state constitution was signed and the name Vermont was officially adopted. Vermont did not relinquish its status as an independent republic until 1791, when it was admitted to the Union as the fourteenth state. Legislators continued to meet in Windsor until the state capital was established at Montpelier in 1805.

The people of Windsor felt a justifiable sense of pride in their mountain. In 1825, they responded to the honor of a planned visit from the Marquis de Lafayette on his tour through the United States by proposing to build a road up Ascutney by which they could transport their distinguished and rather elderly visitor to view the countryside from the summit. *The Vermont Republican & American Yeoman* on June 6, 1825, carried a notice for citizens to turn out to help build the road, advising those interested to bring their own tools, plus luncheon and spirits to last until sundown. Lafayette, unfortunately, was a day behind schedule when he reached Windsor, and the trip to the summit had to be canceled.

Lafayette may have found the view of Ascutney equally satisfying. The thriving little town of Windsor, nestled against the symmetrical mountain, presented an agreeable juxtaposition of picturesque nature and commercial enterprise, much like the view from Mount Holyoke farther south along the same river. Nicolino Calyo, an Italian artist famed for his paintings of Naples, traveled down the Connecticut River about 1848 on a specially constructed seventeen-foot raft, painting panoramic scenes of the river all along the way. Only one panel survives of his planned panorama of the river from Wells River, Vermont, to Hartford, Connecticut. In *View Along the Connecticut River Showing Windsor, Vermont and Mount Ascutney*, the artist is seen painting on the New Hampshire shore. The scene is bustling with activity; farmers at work in pastures along the river bank and up the mountainside, ships carrying goods on the river, and a locomotive steaming toward the proud capital of Windsor.

An unusual panoramic view of the town of Windsor and Mount Ascutney was painted around 1848 by Italian artist Nicolino Calyo, who floated down the river on a raft specially built to keep his equipment dry. Photo courtesy Shelburne Museum, Shelburne, VT.

Except for references to farming, logging, and quarrying, the historical record yields little new information about the mountain from 1825 until 1857. Then, in that year, a man named D. C. Linsley decided to build a trail up the mountain. (Perhaps he is the Burlington engineer who turns up at Mount Mansfield a few years later.) With volunteer help, Linsley surveyed and constructed a road over the overgrown route of what was believed to have been the Lafayette-inspired trail. Using rock cut from the site, he also built a 14 x 20-foot stone house on the summit, incorporating a stone fireplace into one end. The iron roof was covered with long poles to hold it securely to the foundation.

The opening of the Linsley Road was celebrated in high style, inaugurating a tradition of mountaintop festivities that has persisted to the present day. On September 4, 1858, the dedication of the trail took place at the new structure on the summit. It was later reported that "a heavy rain the night before kept many away, but...over 300 persons attended and enjoyed the dinner, the interesting speeches, and the music by the Windsor Cornet Band."

Despite the enthusiasm surrounding the opening of this new trail on Ascutney, maintenance was not considered a high priority. Natural deterioration was compounded by a prolonged forest fire in the summer of 1883 that burned much of the summit and most of the trail above the old logger's cabin at Half-Way Spring. Dead and partly burned trees had fallen across the path, and the Stone Hut itself sustained damage that prevented its offering any real shelter to overnight campers. Infrequent excursions to the summit and an occasional gala celebration there were not enough to sustain widespread interest in climbing the mountain thereafter.

Art and Artists

Yet there was much admiration of the mountain from below, or across the valley, in these years. Vermont embodied an agrarian ideal that remained strong, even as other regions were succumbing to urban growth, manufacturing, and commercial activity. This was the image of Vermont popularized by artists after about 1860, and the one that is still with us today, often in spite of the realities of rural poverty and depressed mill towns.

Albert Bierstadt's View of Mt. Ascutney, Vermont, from Claremont, New Hampshire *is the quintessential artistic expression of rural New England life: lofty mountain, white-spired villages along a wide river, and contented cows and sheep in well-tended fields.* Photo courtesy Fruitlands Museums, Harvard, MA.

When it came to finding a perfect pastoral image, Ascutney suited Albert Bierstadt exactly. Bierstadt, a German immigrant who grew up in New Bedford, Massachusetts, became one of the best-known artists in nineteenth-century America. He visited New Hampshire in the summer of 1863, painting *View of Mount Ascutney, Vermont, from Claremont, New Hampshire* that same year. It is the quintessential expression of rural New England life: a lofty mountain, white-spired villages along a wide river, and contented cows and sheep in well-tended fields. Bierstadt's paintings created a peaceful and optimistic sanctuary for a country torn by the Civil War and struggling to reconcile its earlier ideals with an industrialized reality.

Attracted by the same qualities as Bierstadt, an inspired group of artists, sculptors, and writers made this region a thriving summer arts community known as the Cornish Colony. For twenty-five years beginning in the early 1880s, a group of New York–based intellectuals spent their summers relaxing and socializing in the hills on the opposite bank of the Connecticut River from Windsor, turning to Ascutney for artistic inspiration and spiritual nourishment, finding in its presence on the horizon a reminder of all that was steadfast and good in nature.

Sculptor Augustus St. Gaudens was invited to Cornish by a wealthy New York lawyer and art patron, and soon such other artists as George DeForest Brush, Thomas Dewing, Henry O. Walker, Charles Platt, Kenyon Cox, Stephen Parrish, and his son Maxfield Parrish came and built homes of their own on the open hillsides. At the turn of the century, the community included dozens of artists, writers, musicians, dramatists, and public figures from Boston and New York. Percy MacKaye, well-known playwright and uncle of the Appalachian Trail's founder, Benton MacKaye, had a cabin in Cornish, as did writers Louis Shipman and Hamlin Garland. President Woodrow Wilson spent three summers here, from 1913 to 1915, and his rented quarters became known as the "summer White House."

In the New Hampshire hills, the Cornish Colony artists created a society patterned after a classical ideal. They produced dozens of outdoor "entertainments," with the mountain scenery part of the set. Ascutney appeared in many of the painters' works as well, recognizable in outline but lacking the specific sense of place that it had occupied in Bierstadt's work. This group preferred to be distant observers of the mountain, to be inspired by beauty in the landscape they could admire from afar. Not surprisingly, the heyday of the Cornish Colony, from 1880 to 1905, coincided with a period during which the trails on Ascutney were badly overgrown and completely unmaintained. Surviving records of the aesthetic group's activities contain scant evidence of hiking excursions to Ascutney during these years.

Conservation and Recreation

But a revival of interest in hiking the mountain was not far off. Within a few years of the turn of the century, both private citizens and the federal government would contribute to the growing usage and appeal of Ascutney. In 1898, the Brownsville Trail was cut on the northwest side of the mountain, along a route that leads through the present ski-area development. Then in 1903, two men named Wardner and Duncan revived the old Linsley trail from Windsor, rebuilt the Stone Hut, and went on to create an organization called the Ascutney

Mountain Association (AMA), dedicated to preserving the summit structure "and roads leading thereto."

The work of rebuilding trails and restoring the summit house breathed new life into recreational activity on the mountain. The revived Linsley Road, now known as the Windsor Trail, followed the old route but included a few new stretches near the summit. It was both a footpath and a bridle path, and remained the most popular approach to the mountain for many years. Burros named after the major players in the election of 1912—Wilson, Taft, and Roosevelt—could be rented at the trailhead near the Dudley farm: You took 'em up, and they found their own way back down to the farm.

The AMA was formed for the purpose of restoring the Stone Hut and relocating burned-out parts of the Windsor Trail. Its members included Frank Duncan, who is said to have carried up a new woodstove for the Stone Hut, piece by piece; Frank H. Clark, who authored the first guide to hiking on Mount Ascutney (published by the AMA in 1905); and Houghton Hoisington, Luther White, and Dr. Dean Richmond, all enthusiastic climbers.

The AMA held a well-publicized ceremony to rededicate the Stone Hut on September 5, 1904, attracting a crowd of 700—more than double the number who had hiked to the top for the earlier ceremony in 1858. After a luncheon, "there was a flag raising by fifteen young boys and girls, short speeches, the singing of patriotic songs, and a band concert by the Windsor Military Band." Newspaper accounts of this event took note of the presence of two elderly men who had also attended the ceremonies dedicating the Stone Hut in 1858. For the next dozen years, the AMA held an annual Labor Day picnic on the summit, building a big bonfire on Windsor Rock overlooking the town the night before to advertise the event. But the organization proved to be short-lived, perhaps another casualty of the coming of the automobile. By 1917, the AMA was gone.

A second new trail was added to Ascutney in 1906 when the Weathersfield Club, from the town in which the southern portion of the mountain is located, cut the appropriately named Weathersfield Trail. It ascends the mountain past Crystal Cascade, a high waterfall where the rock faces of the igneous pluton that forms the mountain

The summit cabin, most often called the Stone Hut, was built in 1858 by D.C. Linsley, who had cut a trail on the mountain the previous year.
Photo courtesy *The Vermonter*, June 1910/Kurt Stier.

can be clearly seen. The club also built a log cabin just below the summit that sheltered travelers until it burned in 1930.

Yet once again, trail maintenance suffered from a lack of sustained volunteer commitment. After the demise of the AMA, it would be fifty years before a new effort emerged to encourage and maintain hiking on Ascutney. In 1967, a new organization called the Ascutney Trails Association (ATA) was formed with Herbert Ogden, Sr., as charter director and chairman. In addition to their primary focus on the trails, members published a new *Guide to the Trails of Ascutney Mountain*, collecting the history and lore of the mountain into one small volume. They also revived the tradition of a summit picnic, holding their first on a rainy day in 1967. An annual picnic is now held every Labor Day; the ATA welcomes members and anyone else who happens to be on the mountain. One of the few celebrated peaks never to have any formal mountain hospitality, Ascutney has found an inventive substitute in this event.

James P. Taylor, the founder of the Long Trail, hiked on Ascutney during the turn-of-the-century revival of interest in its trails. Taylor was a devotee of Alden Partridge, the peripatetic captain from Norwich University who had climbed Ascutney nearly ten years before the first trail-building effort in 1825. As principal at Vermont Academy in nearby Saxtons River, Taylor frequently took his students on trips up Ascutney. There he noted the contrast of well-kept trails with the inadequate paths elsewhere in the state. In 1909 on Stratton Mountain, Taylor hit upon the idea of creating a state-long trail, and helped organize the Green Mountain Club to create it. The Long Trail, completed in 1930, may have partly inspired the establishment of the Appalachian Trail, and Ascutney may have partly inspired the Long Trail. Yet Ascutney, because of its isolation in the eastern part of the state, was bypassed by the routes of both.

Besides Taylor's students and their successors, groups of young people from other schools have adopted Ascutney as their own. Carved or painted names and dates in the rocks of the higher elevations hint at the numerous adventures had here by students from Kimball Union Academy in Meriden, New Hampshire, and Dartmouth College farther north. And for some local Windsor youth in the days before television, Ascutney provided a quick, midweek overnight getaway. As described in the *Mount Ascutney Guide*, "young people thought nothing of packing a bedroll with provisions and, after school, climbing the mountain, spending the night up top, then descending in time for school in the morning. A blazed trail, now gone, running down the ridge to the south of Mountain Brook was a favorite rough, but rapid, route home. Campers often lit fires on Windsor Rock to tell worried parents back home that they were safe up top."

This solitary peak could be approached a little differently by less athletic adventurers. As early as the post–Civil War era, many people took horse and buggy and drove around it. A patent-medicine advertising broadside, dated 1868, uses a view of the mountain from Claremont to help sell its "Green Mountain Balm of Gilead and Cedar Plaster," and, making an exaggerated claim in describing the peak, gives the potential visitor two options: "The view from its summit is very extensive in all directions," and, "A drive of 20 miles around its base cannot be surpassed for beauty and variety of scenery in the world." Later, in

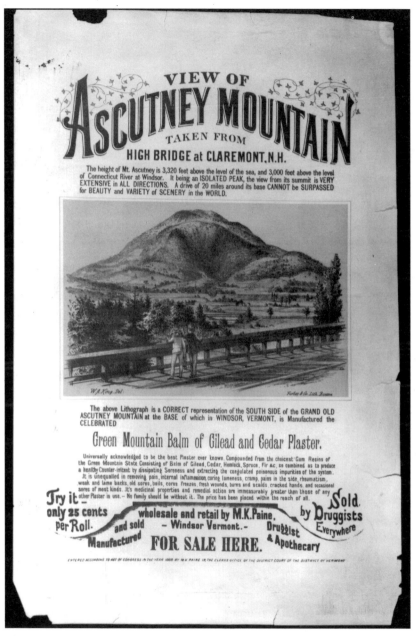

Centerpiece of an early advertising campaign, Ascutney was featured in an 1868 broadside selling "Green Mountain Balm of Gilead and Cedar Plaster."
Photo courtesy Vermont Historical Society, Montpelier, VT.

the 1930s, an article exalting the charms of the mountain featured the photographs of a man named Oscar S. Marshall, "who in making a summer's study of the mountain, took 30 negatives of it for enlarged pictures, and drove happily around it seven times."

In 1920, Ascutney's development began to accelerate. That year, the state constructed a fire-observation tower on Ascutney and, until 1947, maintained a fire warden living in a ranger's cabin at the summit. In the Great Depression, work programs for the unemployed brought the Civilian Conservation Corps (CCC) to Ascutney. Between 1935 and 1937, using only horses and hand labor, the CCC built a 3.8-mile scenic toll road up the east side of Ascutney. In addition to the Mount Ascutney Parkway, which made the summit easily accessible by car and considerably reduced foot traffic on the trails, the CCC also constructed campground facilities and a park ranger's cabin at the base of the mountain, built of Ascutney granite and local wood. Their report for 1935–36 indicates that a 1-mile ski trail and a thirty-meter ski jump on the western boundary of the park were also completed.

Federal Public Works Project funds, available after the depression, allowed the state of Vermont to purchase a total of 1,500 acres on Ascutney for a state park, which included the area where the CCC had developed the campground in 1935. The park has since expanded to about 2,000 acres. The state added a parking lot at the upper end of the toll road and now oversees, among other things, annual races by sports-car enthusiasts and bicyclists.

Ascutney's summit, as the highest in southeastern Vermont, has not escaped the pressure to construct communications towers. The first user was the state itself, one of the prime contributors to a serious problem recognized in recent years. The summit had become littered with unused communications equipment, including microwave dishes, shacks, cables, abandoned cement pads, and leaking fuel tanks. The Ascutney Trails Association initiated negotiations with the state, not only for a summit cleanup, but to have the old fire tower replaced with a viewing platform.

In 1987, after a ten-year effort and only modest progress, the ATA's desired goals were finally attained. A private cable-television company, applying to the state for rights to erect its own tower on the mountain, agreed to finance the cleanup and consolidation of buildings and equipment. In 1989, the cable company also funded removal of the fire tower and construction of a new observation platform 300 feet away from the two remaining communications towers on the summit. Up until a few years ago, the broadcast facilities on Ascutney were staffed twenty-four hours a day, all year long.

Additional trail work has included a fourth major trail, called the Futures Trail, cut in 1983. Named after the Vermont Futures Program, which provides work for unemployed state residents, this route ascends Ascutney's eastern side and lies entirely within Ascutney State Park. In the late 1980s, the upper portion of the Weathersfield Trail was relocated to join the 1906 route a half-mile above Crystal Cascade. And in 1992, the opening section of the Brownsville Trail was moved to eliminate its passage over private land, thus securing the trailhead. With the western part of the mountain designated as part of the West Windsor Town Forest, the State Park encompassing most of the northern and eastern part of the mountain, and the Ascutney Trails Association dedicated to trail maintenance and protection, the future of hiking on Ascutney seems to be relatively secure.

Skiing and Other Sports

Development of skiing on Ascutney has followed the rather typical cycles of expansion and decline. Ignoring the 1935 CCC trail, local enthusiasts calling themselves the Mount Ascutney Ski Club cut a single trail in a farmer's pasture land on the north side of the mountain in 1938. World War II cut short this venture, but skiing was revived after the war when the newly introduced sport was catching on all over the region. At Ascutney, the efforts of one woman, Kip Cushman, mobilized local support to clear more trails, install four rope tows, and open a simple base lodge by 1947.

Ascutney Ski Area hoped to capitalize on its easy accessibility from Boston, New York, and Albany, but never had enough capital to advance beyond a modest operation. Several snowless winters in a row put the area out of business. In the 1950s, two local businessmen bought the defunct ski area and expanded it again. These new owners added one significant feature—snow making. Some fruit growers in Lexington, Massachusetts had accidently discovered how to make snow while trying to develop a fog machine to protect their trees from frost. Ascutney's owners, partners in the Windsor Machine Products Company, fabricated their own equipment, and in 1957 installed hoses and pipes to make Ascutney the first ski area in Vermont to have snow making. Their success heralded the start of a whole new era in downhill skiing.

Ascutney's owners chose to retain the local flavor and family-oriented character of the area, rather than catering to a more sophisticated, upscale clientele as on Mount Mansfield. They made only modest upgrades to lifts and trails, until a new owner took over in 1972 and development on the mountain expanded significantly. Through the next eleven years, two other owners tried their hands at operating the ski area, the last forced into bankruptcy largely because of unpredictable snowfall (the partial snow-making efforts notwithstanding).

Summit Ventures, a new owner taking over in 1983, made big plans to turn the small-scale area into a four-season resort and "world-class conference facility." With a $65 million investment, they added slopeside condominiums and a hotel, increased snow making, and built swimming pools, tennis courts, and a complete fitness facility. They even extended the ski runs farther down Ascutney's slopes to create more beginner terrain, the upper part of the northwestern mountain face being surprisingly steep.

But their optimism about the potential of Ascutney proved again to be misplaced. As New England slid into a recession in the late 1980s, average winter snowfall was less than normal and sales of vacation homes throughout New England bottomed out. Mount Ascutney Resort shut down, the hotel and condos stood empty, and the owners declared bankruptcy. Only the day-care facility and the sports-fitness center remained in operation.

Mount Ascutney would wait several years, until the 1993–94 season, to have a new group of investors reopen the ski area and hotel at the base of the mountain. This time, the purchase price was a bargain $1.1 million at auction. Lifts ran again, more emphasis was placed on skiing itself, and there were high hopes that this latest venture would be able to sustain itself.

Skiing does not get the last word in recreational sport on Ascutney, however. Among a skilled and dedicated few, Ascutney is the premier mountain in New England for hang gliding. The bulky

From its modest beginnings in the 1940s the ski area on Mount Ascutney has experienced some of the same vicissitudes as the hiking trails. Expansion in the mid-1970s led to bankruptcy in the 1980s and eventual rebirth in the 1993–94 season. Kurt Stier.

equipment can be hauled conveniently by car or van up the toll road to the parking lot. And, as an isolated peak with wind currents swirling around its sides, Ascutney offers clear soaring in all directions. For twenty years, the mountain has offered challenge and reward to practitioners of this sport, and the state park has welcomed their presence. They fly routinely to landing sites at the hang-gliding school across the river in Charlestown, or to Claremont or Keene. They head toward Equinox or the Rutland area in Vermont, and sometimes these highly skilled pilots land as far away as Boston, with the distance record from Ascutney being 130 miles away in Providence, Rhode Island.

Suggestions for Visitors

Mount Ascutney is a great family hike. While its terrain can be challenging, it is perfect to break in young hikers and still reward the grownups. There are lots of distractions along the way to hold a

Hang gliders have claimed Ascutney as a favorite launch site, thanks to its free-standing location, strong wind currents, and an auto road to get equipment to the summit. Photo courtesy Morningstar Hang Gliding Center, Charlestown, NH.

child's interest—streams and waterfalls, great overlooks, trailside lean-tos, half-log bridges, and the newly rebuilt summit lookout tower rising above the trees for 360-degree viewing. With all the trail junctions near the summit, Ascutney is a perfect training ground for sharpening map-reading skills, too.

It is possible to make a circuit hike of the mountain, going up one trail and down another. The trailheads of the Brownsville and Windsor trails are about a mile apart along Route 44, one of the most convenient places for covering two routes. Several rocky lookouts along the way give views almost as rewarding as the summit, though the summit observation tower provides a chart showing the location of Equinox and Monadnock, and naming the major peaks of the Green Mountains and the White Mountains. Mount Washington is seventy-four miles away.

If you go on a nice breezy day, you may have the added thrill of seeing hang gliders soaring around the summit. For hikers, the voices overhead can come as a surprise if no one else has been seen along the trail. Favorite launch sites for these manned kites are off West Peak on the Weathersfield Trail and at Brown's Rock and Castle Rock overlooking the Brownsville and Windsor trails.

Ascutney is also popular with birders, harboring a great variety of species on its slopes and summit. Migrating hawks pass overhead in spring and fall. According to the *Mount Ascutney Trail Guide*, in July 1968 one observer counted thirty-one different species between the 2,000-foot mark and the summit. A noted ornithologist, George Nelson Gerry (1886–1931) is remembered with a bronze plaque at Gerry's Falls on the Windsor Trail, where his ashes were scattered after his death.

As with all mountains that have a road, the presence of non-hikers on the summit changes the atmosphere somewhat. Fortunately in Ascutney's case, the road ends in a parking lot well below the summit, and the top is no longer as cluttered as it used to be. The state of Vermont operates the road as well as the 2,000-acre park and campground, all easily reached from Route 5. Park and toll-road information, as well as hiking maps, can be obtained by calling 802-674-2060. Not all the trails on the mountain are on public land, however; hikers should be mindful of the privilege of crossing private lands on three of the four major trails on Ascutney.

The Ascutney Trails Association, a nonprofit organization, encourages membership to help support their work. Their address, from which copies of their *Mount Ascutney Guide* may be obtained, is P.O. Box 147, Windsor, VT 05089.

Several interesting side trips can be included with a day-hike of Ascutney. The Constitution House on Windsor's main street, where the independent Republic of Vermont was created in 1777, is now a museum. Crossing the river on a historic two-lane covered bridge, one enters Cornish, New Hampshire, the site of the St. Gaudens National Historic Park. Here one can learn more about the Cornish Art Colony and the artists who painted Ascutney into their landscapes. And just beyond the mountain to the west, in Plymouth, Vermont, is the birthplace of the state's only U. S. president, Calvin Coolidge.

Grand Monadnock

Monadnock rises 3,165 feet in the southwestern corner of New Hampshire, in the towns of Jaffrey and Dublin. Known officially as the Grand Monadnock, this mountain—an isolated mass of tough rock that resisted erosion while neighboring rock broke up and washed away—has become a generic name for all such distinctive geological formations. Because of its significance, it was designated a National Natural Landmark by the U. S. Park Service in 1987.

Its geology is not the only thing for which Monadnock is known. Monadnock was a landmark for early explorers of the area who used it as a lookout point for Indian encampments. By the mid-1800s, its hiking tradition was already firmly established, and, as the favorite mountain of Henry David Thoreau and Ralph Waldo Emerson, its reputation has become assured. Today, Mount Monadnock is wholly reserved in the public trust and boasts the distinction of being one of the most climbed mountains in the world.

Geography and Geology

The outline of Monadnock's base covers twenty square miles. Located near the exact center of New England, Monadnock's summit offers a unique opportunity on clear days—from there one can see all six

A long view of Monadnock from the northern side. Kurt Stier.

New England states. Mount Washington is sometimes visible 104 miles to the north. Grand Monadnock's immediate neighbors are Pack Monadnock in Peterborough and Temple, Little Monadnock in Fitzwilliam and Troy, and Gap Monadnock in Jaffrey and Troy, all so named because they are smaller examples of the same type of geological feature. The appellation "Grand" distinguishes the preeminent mountain from these, and also from Monadnock Mountain in Lemington, Vermont.

The rock of Monadnock is mica schist, a metamorphic rock characterized by strong layering. It began as sea-floor deposits of mud and sand that formed sedimentary rock. Tremendous geological pressures altered its chemical composition and at the same time folded the horizontal layers in the original rock. Visitors can observe evidence of this folding in the many rock outcroppings and barren summit of Monadnock. Elongated crystal deposits within the schists mark the presence of an unusual mineral called sillimanite, which was first discovered here.

History

The name Monadnock is derived from the Algonquin name meaning "the unexcelled mountain" or "the surpassing mountain." The Indians who lived in this area were part of the Abenaki tribe that ranged throughout southern and central present-day New Hampshire. In 1704, military accounts referred to it as Manadnuck Hill, and maps from the same period labeled it both Great Manadnuck and Grand Wanadnock.

Colonists did not venture to Monadnock's summit for more than a century after the settlement of Boston, even though the mountain was visible from the hilltops of Bay Colony towns. A New England map published in 1677, the year after the end of King Philip's War, indicates the presence of Monadnock but does not name it, a sure sign that this area had yet to see much exploration by whites. Even after the war, Indian attacks continued on scattered towns in the Connecticut River Valley, and in 1724, as a new round of hostilities was heating up, scouts were sent into the Monadnock area to provide advance warning of any imminent attacks.

Captain Samuel Willard of Lancaster led such a scouting expedition in 1725, when he made the first recorded ascent of Monadnock. Setting out from Lancaster, Willard and fourteen men made their way north through Ashburnham, then westward to Monadnock, where they "camped on the top...and discovered 26 ponds." Willard's account goes on to describe how they "found several old signs which the Indians had made the last year and where they camped when they killed the people at Rutland, as we imagine." Through the efforts of Willard and others, the Contoocook band lost control of the mountain it had named and was eventually driven out of the area altogether to resettle in Canada.

By the late 1730s, towns were springing up all around Monadnock. "A Plan of the Monadnock Townships" was drawn in 1749–52, and land grants attracted the first permanent settlers to Dublin and Jaffrey in 1759. That same year, when Roger's Rangers massacred the native refugees at St. Francis in Quebec, effectively marked the end of Indian domination in New England.

Here were no travel writers' picturesque accounts as with the Massachusetts mountains; instead a more scientific perspective held

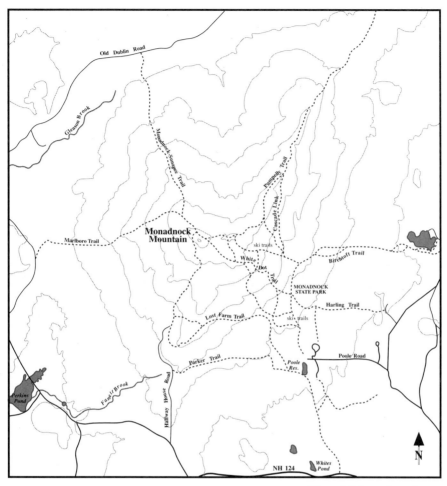

Grand Monadnock

sway. Jeremy Belknap, whose important *History of New Hampshire* was published in 1792, was the first to describe the physical characteristics of the Grand Monadnock: "Its summit is a bald rock; on some parts of it are large piles of broken rocks; and on the sides are some appearances of the explosion of subterraneous fires....Black lead is found in large quantities...(and) some small specimens of copper."

Belknap cited the barometric calculations of James Winthrop, Esq., in listing the height of the mountain as 3,254 feet, only 89 feet higher than the present determination. He noted some other curious facts related to the mountain: "People who live near them humorously style the mountains their almanack because, by the ascent and attraction of vapors, they can form a judgment of the weather....A storm is preceded for several hours by a roaring of the mountain, which may be heard ten or twelve miles. This is frequently observed by people who live near the Grand Monadnock."

Accounts of the "mountain roar" that Belknap first described persisted, and in *Annals of the Grand Monadnock,* published by Allen Chamberlain in 1936, they are given more credence.

> Many have heard of that peculiar phenomenon called the Monadnock "roar." For some reason it does not appear to be so commonly spoken of today as formerly, but the writer, who has never had the good fortune to hear the "roar" himself, has been assured by men in whom he has confidence that it does occasionally still manifest itself. Scott A. Smith, who spent his summers for many years at the Half Way House or in his cottage near by, first heard of the "roar" from Augustus P. Chamberlaine, also a long time summer resident on the mountain. After that Mr. Smith was ever on the alert in the hope that he might hear this singular sound, and listened for it days and nights. Not long before his death he wrote me that one day, while picking berries among the ledges..."there came a roar not describable, like the roar of a hundred bulls, and it was all over in fifteen seconds or less."....In olden time, so 'tis said, the "roar" has been heard as far away as Jaffrey village on a still winter day.

This phenomenon is not exclusively Monadnock's own, for it has been often noticed in other mountainous regions, specifically where the forest grows well up toward the summit, and where the crest lies athwart the courses of cyclonic storms. It has been explained that in such cases the winds, at a point during the onset of a storm, blow at right angles to the mountain's long axis, and as the upper air is moving more rapidly than that below, the sound waves, caused by the wind in the trees, are deflected downward so that they converge upon the place where the roar is heard.

Such meteorological or pseudoscientific observations remain among the more obscure aspects of the mountain's history. Most local inhabitants in the early days had more pressing concerns, like surviving the harsh climate and raising enough food to feed their families. Gradually they transformed the wooded terrain into cleared fields bordered with stone walls, and made it into sheep-raising country. The only problem was predatory wolves coming down from Monadnock's heights, and because much of the summit of the mountain was covered with uprooted trees and great bushy thickets, it was nearly impossible for hunters to track the wolves there.

Even after the state offered a bounty on wolves, the problem persisted. Finally, in desperation, the local farmers resorted to fire to drive the wolves from their mountaintop stronghold. On two different occasions, the summit of the mountain smoldered with intentional fires, reducing the wolf population significantly but burning the Monadnock summit bare in the process. Even though the peak is well below natural treeline, only a thin soil has accumulated in the years since glaciation. It was enough to support the growth of trees, but once the fire destroyed them and their roots no longer held the soil in place, the thin cover quickly washed off the summit. Today, the summit has only low-growing alpine vegetation on its rocky outcroppings.

The last wolf hunt in the Monadnock region is said to have taken place in the winter of 1819–20. A single wolf remained, eating sheep alternately between Monadnock and Mount Watatic. Hunters and hounds started off in pursuit, following the wolf day after day through Jaffrey, Fitzwilliam, Winchendon, and Rindge. While the hunters rested at night, the wolf always killed a sheep somewhere. For nine or ten stormy days this continued, with the wolf often being sighted and fired upon. Finally the people of Fitzwilliam Village turned out and formed lines along the roads to Rindge and Jaffrey. Their hounds ultimately drove the wolf into a meadow, where it was shot and killed.

With the elimination of wolves and the clearing of the summit ledges, there came a notable shift in local residents' perception of the mountain. Once the threatening and inhospitable domain of dreaded predators, Monadnock became a pleasant destination for those wanting a more elevated view. In 1801, a young lawyer named Samuel Dakin [some accounts read Eaking] moved from Concord to Jaffrey and spent some of his leisure time hiking up the mountain. Carrying a hammer and chisel, he carved his initials and the date into a rock at the summit, thus inaugurating a practice frequently employed on Monadnock for the rest of the nineteenth century.

Monadnock became a popular destination for those interested in mountains, and a primary source of that interest lay in the discoveries in geology, botany, and physics that could be made there. An illustrious group of scientists from Boston, on their way to Ascutney and the White Mountains, climbed Monadnock in 1815. Included in the party were Dr. Jacob Bigelow, Francis C. Gray, Dr. Francis Boott, Nathaniel Tucker, and Lemuel Shaw, several of whose names are now associated with features on other mountains. Professor Benjamin Silliman of Yale, a geologist, is remembered in the name of sillimanite, the peculiar rod-shaped crystal formations visible in much of the schist on Monadnock. Another geological formation, the Billings fold, is named for Katherine Fowler Billings, who studied Monadnock's geology intensively in the twentieth century.

Monadnock reputedly played a starring role in the dedication ceremonies for Boston's Bunker Hill Monument, although verification of the story has proved difficult. Commemorating one of the earliest American victories of the Revolution in 1775, the monument's cornerstone was laid by Lafayette in June 1825. It took seventeen years to build the 221-foot-high obelisk overlooking Boston Harbor from Breed's Hill, and a fittingly glorious celebration was planned for its completion. Daniel Webster gave the oration at the dedication ceremonies on June 17, 1843, and as a final spectacle, a beacon of flame on Monadnock was to be seen lighting up the distant horizon. A gigantic bonfire of empty tar barrels was consequently laid. Unfortunately, no record of the success of this pyrotechnic display survives. Today the city gives back the honor, for on fall days at sunset, from the summit of Monadnock, the light reflecting off the mirrored surface of Boston's John Hancock tower appears as a column of fire.

Mountain Hiking and Hospitality

One of Monadnock's first trails was created, so it is said, in the process of hauling all those tar barrels up to the summit. A man named Darling blazed the Old Dublin Trail, which still leads up the north side of the mountain. Alden Partridge, forefather of New England mountaineering and not one to be dissuaded by the lack of cleared pathways, climbed Monadnock in 1817. By 1824, Jaffrey town records show the granting of a liquor license to a John Fife, "near the path travelled in passing to the top."

Beginning with the Old Dublin Trail in 1843, trail-building efforts proliferated. Routes up all sides of the mountain gradually were cleared and marked, and various accommodations provided for the needs of a growing number of visitors. The opening in 1847 of the Cheshire Railroad, with service from Boston to nearby Troy and Peterborough, hastened the pace of development. The Monadnock area filled with summer homes, hotels, and other facilities catering to those who wished to escape the city and take in the mountain's natural and scenic beauty.

The earliest mountain hospitality dates from the 1820s. Several proprietors of small shanties on the mountain catered to day-hikers and may have, on occasion, provided a rudimentary overnight shelter. In one newspaper advertisement, "Monadnock Entertainment" was offered consisting of "tea and coffee, with suitable meats and drinks.... Spiritous liquors may at all times be had."

Joseph Fassett cut the White Arrow Trail, which ascends a basin on the southwest side of Monadnock, in 1854–55, and built a modest stone hut by the brook just north of where the Mountain House was later erected. In 1857, the lower half of Fassett's trail was expanded to a wagon road, leading to within a mile of the summit. Then in 1860, Moses Cudworth built a small establishment called the Mountain House, where he took in overnight guests who arrived by horseback. Taking care of tourists' horses, in fact, became an important part of Cudworth's business. For stabling and feed, Cudworth charged $.35 per horse, sometimes caring for as many as 75 or 100 head in one day.

The U. S. Coastal Survey used Monadnock as a geodetic and magnetic survey station during July and August of 1861. They pitched their camp on the southern slope about 2,500 feet from Cudworth's Mountain House, on a plateau very near the upper edge of the woods. Mr. McDonnell of the U. S. Coastal Survey extended the road from the Mountain House to the camp, so they could easily haul all their instruments and equipment. On the final stretch of trail from the camp to the summit, the members of that 1861 team laid stone steps for which the modern hiker can be grateful. All traces of the survey's cabin are now gone, but the geodetic station is marked by a copper bolt and triangle embedded in the rocks.

The era of comfortable mountain hospitality began in the 1860s. In 1866, the former Mountain House was enlarged into a three-story hotel by George D. Rice. For a short time, this hotel was the center of activity on the mountain. Here Ralph Waldo Emerson stayed in July of this year, while his son and daughter and their friends, including Nathaniel Hawthorne's daughter Una, camped out on the mountain.

Two other guests, Luther Richardson and Mrs. Rachel Tarbox, were written up in the newspapers in Keene for their mountaintop wedding in October 1866. But the hotel was fated to last less than a year. On the season's last day, October 11, as the weary owners trudged down the carriage path at the end of their summer on the mountain, they looked back to see their hotel in flames. It burned to the ground.

The Mountain House was replaced by a small building the next year. This structure was successively enlarged and then taken over by Mrs. Blair in 1919, who changed its name to the Half-Way House. Different architectural styles are reflected in the different sections of the house, from gable roof to mansard, chronicling the various stages of construction from 1867 to 1885. The Half-Way House operated until 1954, when it too succumbed to flames. Today the flat plateau, site of so much activity, is barren of any remains save for a stone bench. A plaque identifying the site was moved to park headquarters in the 1960s after suffering repeated vandalism.

Another of the mountain's venerable tourist hotels, the Ark, stood at the base of the southeastern side of the mountain. It had its

The Half-Way House evolved on the spot of an earlier structure called the Mountain House, about halfway up Monadnock's southern side along an old cart path. Note the photographer at left, set up to take pictures of vacationing guests. Photo courtesy New Hampshire Historical Society, Concord, NH.

origins in 1777, when a farmer named Joseph Cutter bought the land, built a modest house, and began to plant crops and make maple sugar. His son, Joseph Cutter, Jr., expanded the original house about 1808 into the structure that became known as Cutter's Ark.

In 1873 the Ark was bought by J. H. Poole, a grand nephew of the original builder. Poole was persuaded to rent part of the house to a Massachusetts physician, and before long, Poole found himself in the hotel business. The Ark was a popular summer retreat for many families from the Boston area. When Poole died in 1926, the Ark was purchased by Charles W. Bacon, whose family continued to run it as a hotel until 1965. The Bacon family has retained ownership of most of the land, and continues the production and sale of maple syrup, begun on this property more than two hundred years earlier. Today, the Monadnock Christian Conference Center, which holds retreats for young people, operates the buildings.

Many trails emanate from the Ark, summer home for many Monadnock devotees. The first trail to be completed up the southeastern side of Monadnock was the White Spot Trail, which was built by Dr. N. Emmons Paine, a Newton, Massachusetts, physician; his children; and William Royce, an employee of the Ark. Now called the White Dot Trail, it is the most popular route to the summit, with about half of all Monadnock hikers taking this direct and shortest (1.9 miles) route to the top.

A second trail from the vicinity of the Ark was laid out by a Harvard University zoologist who stayed at the Ark in 1897 and for years thereafter. Parker and Arthur Poole finished a trail up the valley of Meads Brook and blazed it with red crosses in September of 1909. The popularity of this approach, now known as the White Cross Trail, became assured after the senior Poole built an auto road across his property, completed in 1921, which he donated to the state in memory of his son. Called Poole Road, this is the access route off Dublin Road to get to the present Monadnock State Park.

Literature and the Arts

Perhaps the rapid rise and continued popularity of this mountain owed something to that most famous New England writer and naturalist, Henry David Thoreau. Monadnock was Thoreau's favorite mountain. He climbed here four times between 1844 and 1860, and camped a total of eleven days on the mountain. In his journal for Setember 6–7, 1852, Thoreau describes a visit by railroad (which he refers to as "the cars") from Concord to Peterborough.

He and his close friend Ellery Channing went "across lots" to follow the most direct route to Monadnock's summit, rather than taking roads, and by this method "were on the top of the mountain at 1:00 P.M. The cars left Troy, four or five miles off, at three. We reached the depot, by running at last, at the same instant the cars did, and reached Concord at a quarter after five, i.e. four hours from the time we were picking blueberries on the mountain, with the plants of the mountain fresh in my hat."

Thoreau's description of his mountain camp, in his journal for June 2, 1858, provides a detailed picture of how he, and others like him, passed nights out-of-doors on the mountain more than a hundred years ago.

We chose a sunken yard in a rocky plateau on the southeast side of the mountain (perhaps half a mile from the summit by the path) a rod and half wide by many more in length, with a mossy and bushy floor...where a dozen black spruce trees grew, though the surrounding rock was generally bare. There was a pretty good spring within a dozen rods, and the western wall shelved over a foot or two. We slanted two scraggy spruce trees, long since bleached, from the western wall, and cutting many spruce boughs with our knives, made a thick bed and walls on the two sides, to keep out the wind. Then, putting several poles transversely across our two rafters, we covered them with a thick roof of spruce twigs, like shingles. The spruce, though harsh for a bed, was close at hand, we cutting away one tree to make room. We crawled under the low eaves of this roof, about eighteen inches high, and our extremities projected about a foot.

Later that evening, he and his companion, Harrison Blake, went up to the summit to watch the sun go down. After a long passage about the snowbird, an alpine species nesting on the summit, Thoreau records how they lost the path coming back down over the summit rocks, and he muses at some length about those rocks.

Nothing is easier than to lose your way here, where so little trail is left upon the rocks, and the different rocks and ravines are so much alike.... Notwithstanding the newspaper and eggshell left by visitors, these parts of nature are still particularly unhandled and untracked. The natural terraces of the rock are the steps of this temple, and it is the same whether it rises above the desert or a New England village. Even the inscribed rocks are as solemn as most ancient gravestones, and nature reclaims them with bog and lichens.... One, who was probably a blacksmith, had sculpted the emblems of his craft, an anvil and hammer, beneath his name. Apparently a part of the regular outfit of mountain-climbers is a hammer and cold chisel.... Certainly you could not hire a stone-cutter to do so much engraving for less than several thousand dollars.... Some have carried up a paint pot, and painted their names on the rocks.

Thoreau's friend and mentor, Ralph Waldo Emerson, admired and appreciated Monadnock as well, and his writings helped popularize the mystical qualities the mountain seemed to possess:

Monadnock from Afar
Dark flower of Cheshire garden,
    Red evening duly dyes
Thy somber head with rosy hues
    To fix far-gazing eyes.
Well the Planter knew how strongly
    Works thy form on human thought;
I muse what secret purpose had he
    To draw all fancies to this spot.

If Monadnock was a spiritual magnet for the Transcendentalists, and full of fascinating discoveries for scientists and naturalists, it comes as a surprise to learn that it was completely overlooked by popular artistic taste of the pre–Civil War period. The rugged terrain and wild scenery of the White Mountains were much more in keeping with the prevailing trend in art, and it would not be until the 1870s, when preferred subjects were more contrived and aesthetic, that fine artists began to see in Monadnock a fitting subject for expressive visual art.

One of the earliest pictorial depictions of Monadnock, probably done between 1860 and 1870, is a lithographic view after a drawing by A. E. Dolbear. In the foreground is Stone Pond on the Dublin-Marlboro line, with the mountain in the west behind it. This spot is still one of the best vantage points for viewing the mountain from below. A representative image of the mountain, with its cleared pastures far up the sides and the deforested summit, this showed what it looked like, without arousing much emotion. That job was left to succeeding generations of professional painters.

Abbott Handerson Thayer (1849–1914), is perhaps the best known of the later group of artists that gathered around Monadnock and came to be known as the Dublin Art Colony. Like many members of the group, Thayer was a Bostonian. He earned acclaim as a painter while in Paris, and later, when his work entered prominent museum collections and was honored with numerous prizes, he main-

One of the earliest pictorial depictions of Monadnock, probably drawn between 1860 and 1870, is the lithographic view after a drawing by A.E. Dolbear. In the foreground is Stone Pond and the Dublin-Marlboro line, with the mountain in the west behind it. Photo courtesy New Hampshire Historical Society, Concord, NH.

tained studios in New York as well as in Dublin. His *Monadnock Angel* expresses a common religious theme in his art, bringing an otherworldly subject to a very specific physical place.

Thayer was not only a successful artist but also a naturalist and a conservationist. His studies of protective coloration in animals led to the development of camouflage in World War I. To him goes much of the credit for the preservation of Monadnock at a time when its natural state was seriously threatened. Thayer was an early member of the Society for the Protection of New Hampshire Forests and campaigned tirelessly to protect the mountain from logging and other private development. His wide circle of influential companions at Monadnock included Ralph Waldo Emerson, Mark Twain, and Louis Agassiz Fuertes, a prominent bird painter.

For all the artists, poets, writers, professors, and those of means and intellect who found Dublin and surrounding towns a perfect

Albert Handerson Thayer, the central figure in the Dublin Colony, was both an artist and preservationist who led the movement toward public ownership on Monadnock. His Monadnock Angel *(1920–21), expresses his spiritual connection to the place.* Photo Courtesy Addison Gallery of American Art, Andover, MA.

summer retreat from the discomforts of the city, the mountain loomed as an inspiration. In 1925, Helen Cushing Nutting gathered *The Records of Monadnock through Three Centuries* into an anthology of writings about the mountain. Well-known names share the pages with those who have now faded into obscurity. Besides Emerson, James Russell Lowell, and Oliver Wendell Holmes, there is a tribute poem by Edna Dean Proctor originally published in the *Atlantic Monthly*.

The book also contains excerpts from letters or journal entries by Colonel Thomas Wentworth Higginson, Edward W. Emerson (son of Ralph Waldo), and anecdotes of Rudyard Kipling's snow sculpture of a Buddha facing the mountain. Kipling, from his home in Dummerston, Vermont, could see Monadnock and knew it well. "Miles of paths thread through deep, quiet forests....Those who climb this mountain are the regulars who know its trails and scenic places well—they are on intimate terms with a benevolent nature here."

The popularity of Dublin remained well established into the twentieth century. Mark Twain summered here in 1905–06, and had great affection for the little colony around Monadnock:

> The summer homes are high-perched, as a rule, and have contenting outlooks. The house we occupy has one. Monadnock, a soaring double hump, rises into the sky at its left elbow—that is to say, it is close at hand. From the base of the long slant of the mountain the valley spreads away to the circling frame of the hills, and beyond the frame the billowy sweep of remote great ranges rises to view and flows, fold upon fold, wave upon wave, soft and blue and unworldly, to the horizon fifty miles away. In these October days Monadnock and the valley and its framing hills make an inspiring picture to look at, for they are sumptuously splashed and mottled and be-torched from sky-line to sky-line with the richest dyes the autumn can furnish; and when they lie flaming in the full drench of the mid-afternoon sun, the sight affects the spectator physically, it stirs his blood like military music.

Pulitzer Prize–winning novelist Willa Cather (1876–1947) spent summers for thirty years in Jaffrey, where she stayed at the Shattuck Inn and pitched a tent in the woods during the autumn. Parts of

My *Antonia* and *One of Ours* were composed here. After the 1938 hurricane destroyed the firs that stood around her tent site, she did not return except to be buried in the cemetery in Jaffrey. The simple marker reads: "The truth and charity of her great spirit will live on in the work which is her enduring gift to her country and all its people."

A strong literary and artistic tradition continues in the Monadnock area in the present day, fueled in part by the MacDowell Colony in Peterborough. A retreat for writers and composers, this large tract of unspoiled woods and fields is dotted with cabins and other quiet havens where many of today's foremost artists have created some of their best work. Within the shadow of the mountain, and looking toward it for inspiration, such luminaries as Leonard Bernstein, Aaron Copland, and Edwin Arlington Robinson have spent productive time away from the cares of everyday life to create masterworks in peace.

The mountain continues to inspire visual and performing artists alike. Art galleries in nearby Keene, Sharon, and Peterborough collect and exhibit the work of local artists, many of whom find their muse, either directly or indirectly, in the mountain's presence. Monadnock has even inspired a unique expression of dance. Dianne Eno, who grew up hiking Monadnock, has choreographed a special performance inspired by the mountain every year since 1985. Performed on the summit in mid-August and also at the state-run Gilsum Pond picnic area, Eno's work is set to music and combines personal expression with the theme of environmental awareness.

Public Ownership and Preservation

Such rich celebrations of the mountain might not have come about had there not been those who, from an early date, saw the need to protect Monadnock from commercial exploitation. Five thousand acres, most of the mountain, is now protected, thanks to a process that began in 1884 when the selectmen of the town of Jaffrey received a gift of summit lands. In 1904, when other landowners planned logging on the mountain, Abbott Thayer (artist and Dublin resident) formed the Monadnock Forestry Association to prevent the timber removal. The association petitioned the New Hampshire Forestry Commission to take by eminent domain the land that was to have been logged.

The landowners, some with reluctance, sold their property to the state, which then created the Monadnock State Reservation in 1904. That same year, the three-year old Society for the Protection of New Hampshire Forests was called in to assist with the conservation efforts, and by 1926 had obtained deeds to 1,100 remaining acres of the mountain. The deeds stipulated that the qualities that were most cherished in Monadnock be always preserved; that the land was to be held "in trust, to maintain forever its wild and primeval condition, where the forest and rock shall remain undisturbed in their wild state, and where birds and game shall find natural refuge."

Protecting their investments, and attempting to prevent the destructive forest fires that claimed so much White Mountain forest, the state developed a system of mountaintop fire lookouts early in the century. In 1914, the Forestry Department built a low stone-and-wood fire tower on Monadnock's summit and hired a warden who hiked up the mountain each day to man his post. After 1948, the practice was discontinued and the fire lookout tower was removed.

Other changes around the base of the mountain made these "wild lands" more accessible to visitors. In the 1930s, the Civilian Conservation Corps established state-park headquarters that included a campground, toilet facilities, and a few outbuildings. They even built a short-lived ski trail, now completely overgrown, up the mountain's east side in 1935. A ranger's cabin, built by the Pooles, was also added to the state park. The most recent park expansion, which took place in 1989, was to officially incorporate Jaffrey's summit holdings into the reservation.

The partnership between New Hampshire State Parks and the Society for the Protection of New Hampshire Forests has led to one of the most successful joint stewardship programs in America. The entire park system's maintenance and operations are funded solely through user fees and park-store revenues, and these funds are dedicated solely to the New Hampshire state park system. General funds (other state revenues) are sought only for major capital improvement projects.

The park and mountain are used year-round for hiking, cross-country skiing, and camping (at the base). Fall is perhaps the busiest time for Mount Monadnock, with thousands of foliage viewers making the trek to the summit for the brilliant fall displays at every point

At the state park headquarters, buildings constructed by the CCC in the 1930s afford a rustic welcome for the many visitors Monadnock attracts. Kurt Stier.

of the compass. Winter use of the mountain is growing rapidly, and Monadnock is notorious for its "regulars" in all seasons.

Hiking

Monadnock attracts a certain breed of "power hikers," those who climb the mountain regularly and repeatedly. It is not uncommon for people to challenge themselves with ever faster or greater numbers of ascents. Larry Davis has been hiking to the summit every day (with a four-month interruption) since 1990, showing up at state-park headquarters headed for the White Dot Trail, rain or shine, regular as clockwork, shortly after lunch every day.

Ken Peterson, another regular, averages 200 climbs a year and has climbed the mountain over a thousand times. He holds the record for the fastest climb of Monadnock: twenty-five minutes, forty-five seconds on the ascent and about fifteen minutes to get down. During the winter of 1986, he was the first to locate the crash site of a small plane known to have gone down on Monadnock. Both pilot and copilot had been killed when their plane failed to clear

Pumpelly Ridge by a mere fifty feet. The wreckage was eventually air-lifted off the mountain by helicopter.

It has often been claimed that people climb the Grand Monadnock more than any other mountain in the world. Park management discounts this boast, however, deferring to Japan's Mount Fuji. Still, about 125,000 people per year walk up Monadnock. Over Columbus Day weekend in October, if the weather is good, Monadnock will get 12,000 visitors.

The stresses on the mountain from such heavy use are considerable. And these numbers will not diminish, for tourism is now New Hampshire's number-one industry and state parks are part of the advertising strategy used to attract more tourists to the state. At Monadnock, dispersion is the key to successfully accommodating these ever-increasing numbers, and the wide choice of hiking trails means that only the parking lots and the summit will seem crowded on any given day.

Monadnock's rocky summit is often crowded with hikers, especially on summer weekends, when more than a thousand people make the trek to the top. Kurt Stier.

Tradition is a large part of Monadnock's popularity. Since the days of Thoreau and Emerson, those within easy range of the mountain have made a regular habit of coming to this peak, returning with children and grandchildren. While trends have changed and most of these visitors come just for the day, school trips, church groups, and camp outings have, over the last hundred years, introduced thousands to the mountain, forming a bond that often calls individuals back again. To add "attractions" for a wider market and encouraged by the building boom of the 1980s, a resort developer has built a golf course and may add 356 condominiums clustered around the old Shattuck Inn at the base of the mountain. The strength of tradition in how this mountain is to be appreciated may be altered significantly if other privately owned lands around the base of the mountain are similarly "enhanced" with development.

For now, whether they come to hike or to picnic, because of some historical association or to be closer to nature, Monadnock pilgrims experience a traditional mountain. Careful concessions have been made to accommodate crowds, but for the most part Monadnock seems relatively untouched by modern life. Although Monadnock cannot compete with the White Mountains farther to the north for height, wildness, or tourist attractions, this mountain, and the small villages that surround it, have their own quiet charm. Within a few hours' drive from the major metropolitan centers of the Northeast, Monadnock offers the perfect combination of accessibility, difficulty, and sense of escape to make it unsurpassed in popularity.

Suggestions for Visitors

Most people who climb Mount Monadnock approach the mountain from state-park headquarters; the park is open year-round for hiking, camping, and cross-country skiing. Access is west of the town of Jaffrey, off Route 124. Once on the mountain road, note the restored Shattuck Inn and the Monadnock Christian Conference Center, formerly the Ark. The state park charges a small fee for parking and provides an excellent trail map. Information can be obtained by calling 603-532-8862.

For a hike that covers more than just one side of the mountain, ascend the White Dot Trail (or the White Cross Trail) and, after exploring the summit, go down the White Arrow Trail to the site of the Halfway House (note the Moses Spring and plaque here). From there, follow the Old Toll Road to the Parker Trail and a long run-out back to park headquarters. This route covers about five and a half miles, with an elevation gain of 1,815 feet (about one and a half Empire State Buildings).

The Marlboro Trail offers a more challenging experience. It ascends the west side of the mountain from Shaker Road (unmaintained for the last half-mile), so named because the Shaker community in Shirley, Massachusetts, owned this property in the nineteenth century and annually drove their sheep to summer pasture here in New Hampshire. There is parking for only a few cars at the rough turnout for the trailhead, but this is a sure bet to avoid the crowds.

The most scenic route, and also the longest, is the Pumpelly Trail up from Dublin Lake. It was laid out by Professor Raphael Pumpelly, a noted geologist and summer resident of Dublin. The hike to the summit follows a long ridge, with views in both directions much of the way. An average round-trip hike on Monadnock takes about four hours; plan on more time to take the Pumpelly Trail or to linger and explore the local area.

Mount Monadnock is one of two New Hampshire mountains that prohibit dogs on its hiking trails. Park officials argue that dogs pose a sanitary nuisance, reduce other wildlife on the mountain, overrun the alpine bogs, and sometimes threaten to harm each other and even humans.

Moosilauke

Northern New Hampshire's mountains were everything the Vermont mountains were trying to be in the nineteenth century, and the Presidential Range was everything Mount Moosilauke aspired to. For although Mount Moosilauke had the requisite height and regional prominence to make it a celebrated and popular mountain, it was separated from the center of tourist activity around Mount Washington. It never developed as an important vacation center, and no communications towers, satellite dishes, or ski lifts have ever intruded on its slopes.

Instead, over the years its lands were bought up or given to Dartmouth College, which has held Moosilauke as something of a sacred trust for nearly a century and a half. Serving a constituency of students and alumni, Dartmouth has focused on preservation, scientific study, and quiet recreation above all else.

Geography and Geology

Moosilauke rises in the towns of Benton, Warren, and Woodstock, New Hampshire. The main summit (north peak) is 4,802 feet above sea level, an elevation that places it behind most of the Presidentials but well ahead of Mansfield's 4,393 feet. The highest of Moosilauke's subordinate peaks, running about a mile along a high crest to the south and north, are South Peak at 4,523 feet, and Mount Blue at 4,529 feet. To the east, separated from the main mass of the mountain by Jobildunc Ravine, stands the other four-thousand-footer in the range, Mount Jim at 4,172 feet.

Rivers linking this high mountain area with drainages to the east and west surround Moosilauke. To the northeast, between Moosilauke and the Kinsman Range, the wild Ammonoosuc begins its descent northwest to the Connecticut River. On the west, Tunnel Brook drains to the same watershed. On the other side of the mountain, the streams drain into the Merrimack, the great river of central

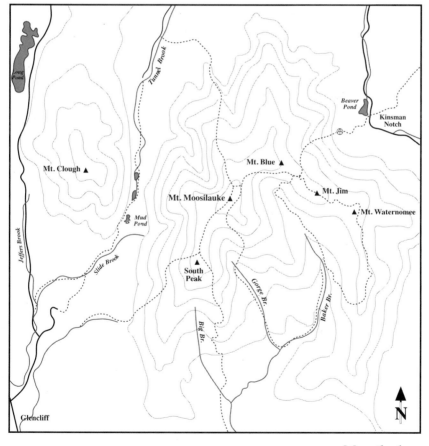

Moosilauke

New Hampshire. Across the northeast flank of the mountain flows the Lost River. Baker River collects the waters of the south side of the mountain through Jobildunc Ravine, then joins the Pemigewasset at Plymouth. These important rivers provided exploration routes, determined settlement patterns, and made possible large-scale commercial-logging activities.

Moosilauke's geological structure is similar to that of the Presidential Range, being part of the Littleton Formation that makes up Mount Washington. While most of the mountains of New England are granite, in this case the overlying granite has eroded and exposed highly metamorphosed schists and gneisses, light-and-dark banded coarse-grained rock. Specifically, Moosilauke's rocks are gray micaceous quartzite and gray coarse-grained mica schist that contain black micaceous biotite, red garnet, sillimanite, and local andalusite. These foliated crystalline schists are most exposed at the summit, where they intermingle with a small area of alpine vegetation.

Early scientists and naturalists found their way to Moosilauke because of its great height. They recorded their observations in such reports and publications as Charles T. Jackson's *Final Report of the Geology and Mineralogy of the State of New Hampshire*, published in 1844. Jackson carefully described Moosilauke's prominent geological features, such as Jobildunc Ravine, a glacially formed cirque on the southeast side of the mountain. Cirques are rare outside of the Presidentials—Katahdin has a famous exception. The ravine's name, which sounds somewhat like an Indian word, is supposed to have come from a combination of the names of three brothers, Joe, Bill, and Duncan, who were early loggers in the area.

Another feature, Lost River Gorge, just to the northeast of Moosilauke in Kinsman Notch, was formed in much the same way as Smuggler's Notch on Mount Mansfield. It was sculpted over a mere few centuries, not by moving ice but by waters draining from a glacial lake that occupied the Ammonoosuc Valley during the retreat of the least glacier.

The arctic-alpine vegetation covering the summit of Moosilauke drew much attention and appreciation from early scientists and observant naturalists. D. Q. Clement, a self-educated farmer and woodsman,

Aerial view of Mount Moosilauke from the east, showing Gorge Ravine at center, Jobildunc Ravine at extreme right, and the zig-zag of the Old Carriage Road running up the ridge. Photo courtesy Dartmouth College Library, Hanover, NH.

kept a diary of a memorable year he and his brother spent on the mountain around 1876 or 1877, and described the plants in detail:

> The crest and the peak are in bloom now for the warm days have come. A small white flower [greenland sandwort] grows thick down to the green fringe of dark fir. You crush a score of them each step you take. The mt. cranberry is rank among them, in red splashes like spots of blood. It is three inches tall and quite thick. Grey, red, blue, green, brown and black moss and all shades of these, are by the rocks that gleem [sic] with as many hues of the three score kinds of lichens that cling to them. How they shine when the dew is on. All these with the shrubs and vines make a carpet, thick, soft and rich with hues and tints that vie with the rainbow and the deep blue of the sky. No man can weave one so fine and grand as this that grows on our crest.

Early History

The mountain's name probably is taken directly from the original Algonquin designation, usually translated as meaning a bald place. The pronunciation can be either MOO-sil-ock or Moo-sil-OCK-ee, with locals generally preferring to include the fourth syllable. Early-nineteenth-century maps spell it Moosehillock, a corruption of this word, which historians adamantly insist has nothing to do with either moose or hillocks (low hills).

Native American relics discovered near Moosilauke were well known to early writers of the area. Storage mounds for supplies of corn, stone axes and arrowheads, and even pieces of simple pottery have turned up along the rivers around its base. It is believed that an old Indian trail from the Merrimack River Valley in central New Hampshire passed through here on its way to the upper Connecticut River Valley at Coös, the Indian name for Haverhill, New Hampshire, about fifteen miles to the west.

The aboriginal residents of the Mount Moosilauke area were Algonquins, with bands of Nipmuc, Coös, and Pemigewasset all present in the area. They believed that Gitche Manitou, the great divinity of the eastern tribes, resided on Moosilauke. According to legend, the Pemigewasset sachem Waternomee once cut across the top of Moosilauke while traveling from his central village on the Pemigewasset River to the Connecticut River (surely one of the worst short-cuts on record, to pass over such a summit). A great storm descended whenever anyone tried to climb to the god's domain, forcing Waternomee and his group down off the mountain to take shelter in the thick spruce woods.

Waternomee's people called their tributary of the Pemigewasset River the Asquamchumauke (now the Baker River), meaning "water of the mountain place." The first whites travelled through the area along this route. In 1712, Thomas Baker and thirty soldiers marched up the Connecticut River from Fort Number Four at Charlestown, then along the Asquamchumauke. They ambushed the Indian encampment there, and in the ensuing chase, there was a fight near Bridgewater in which Baker killed Chief Waternomee. The defeated and disheartened remainder of the tribe moved to Quebec, joining the Arosagunticooks at St. Francis.

In the 1750s, Captain Robert Rogers led his rangers up the Asquamchumauke and built a fort at the Coös intervale on the Connecticut River. His force gathered here as they returned from sacking St. Francis in late fall of 1759 and recorded the first known colonial fatalities on the mountain itself.

Two of Rogers's Rangers set out from Coös; some accounts say to hunt game, others that they were anxious to return home and were seeking the shortest route to the south. As they were climbing over Moosilauke, one of them, Robert Pomeroy, collapsed of exhaustion and starvation. He died at summit, where his remains were found years later. A trapper discovered the other ranger wandering in a deranged stupor at the foot of the Seven Cascades (or Pleiades) on Gorge Brook, and sustained him until he could regain his strength.

New Hampshire provincial governor Benning Wentworth started granting backcountry lands as soon as the French and Indian Wars were over. The town of Warren was chartered in 1763–64. As its proprietors surveyed the town boundaries in 1765, they reserved any pines fit for use as masts for the Royal Navy. Prime specimens were sought and marked with a broad arrow, designating them as the king's property. Some of these trees, in the valleys around Moosilauke, were the direct relatives of the great spruce forest that lasted until the late 1930s.

According to William Little's *History of the Town of Warren*, the first recorded ascent of Mount Moosilauke where the climber survived to tell the story happened by accident. Chase Whitcher was hunting moose in 1773 when his pursuit of an animal led him over the summit. His impression of the height he had attained was typically Yankee in its brevity: "A cold place."

Scientific exploration of Moosilauke commenced around 1800, with an expedition that included Dr. Ezra Bartlett and Samuel Knight. The pair were forced to leave the summit halfway through the night because of cold and wind that had prevented them from lighting a fire. A local historian, in recounting the facts of this expedition, tells a story that stretches the limits of the imagination—that they felled a tree and slid down from the summit via Jobildunc Ravine.

Alden Partridge, making the rounds of New England's premier peaks, climbed Moosilauke in 1817; his published newspaper article about the hike is considered the first printed account of a Moosilauke ascent. While on the summit, Partridge observed that the mountaintop had been burned over not long before his visit, not improbable because other historical accounts of the time indicate that locals did indeed climb the mountain.

The first real trail on Moosilauke, which ran along the route of the present Glencliff Trail, was cut about 1838 by a local man named William Little, author of Warren's town history. He induced his friends to help him by promising them all the grog they could drink in return for their labor on the "road." Little doubted that his trail would tempt others to make the climb, however; writing later, he said he and his group thought they would be the only ones for many years to stand on Moosilauke's crest.

They were proven wrong many times over. Notable among other early climbers was Mrs. Daniel Patch, probably the first woman to ascend Moosilauke (at a time when women interested in going up Washington were generally advised to "give up all thoughts" of climbing). Mrs. Patch was from nearby Rumney, confirming the popularity of Moosilauke with locals. In an amusing footnote to her accomplishment, historians note that Mrs. Patch brought along her teapot and, over a kindled fire at the summit, "made a good cup of tea."

With the advent of railroad service to Warren about 1850, Moosilauke was, for the first time, readily accessible to visitors from outside the area. Interest grew in seeing the view from the summit of Moosilauke. The peak got several new trails wide and smooth enough to be called bridle paths and to be climbed easily on horseback. A bridle path approaching the mountain from Breezy Point, site of the Moosilauke Inn on the south side, opened in 1858, and within a year or two was widened to accommodate teams and wagons that could transport large quantities of supplies to the summit. This route would eventually become the carriage road, and opened the way for the 1860 construction of a building on the summit. Another bridle path on the west side of the mountain opened in 1859, and is now known as the Benton Trail.

The summit hotel, variously known as Prospect House, Tip-Top House, and the Summit House, had stone walls three feet thick. Local men Daniel Quincy Clement, his brother Jim, and their cousin

William Little, all helped to build it, choosing a location just south of the summit where good building stones were plentiful. According to D. Q. Clement's recollections, "The men laid them up where they found them and had to draw but few. They are blocks with square faces and some are six feet long." The thirty-by-fifteen-foot, six-room structure opened for business July 4, 1860. As on Ascutney, a brass band came up to entertain a crowd of about a thousand; the festivities included speeches and a performance of Indian music and dance.

The opening of the carriage road and summit house inaugurated a wave of tourism and associated development on Moosilauke. In 1870, according to D. Q. Clement, the state "made an act for a turnpike to this crest," and he and his brother Jim helped build it, funded in part by an appropriation of $300 from the town of Warren. Incorporated as the Moosilauke Mountain Road Company, the toll road covered the same route as the old carriage road, and quickly reaped a profit for the investors. It proved a boon to the hotel, vastly simplifying the five-mile trip up and down to get mail and restock provisions.

Hotel business was so good that a one-and-a-half-story wood-frame ell was added to Prospect House in 1881. In 1901, the addition of a second story doubled the size of the original stone portion of the building. According to an 1884 guidebook, this comfortable establishment, renamed Tip Top House, could handle fifty guests at a time. The cost was $3 per day or $14 per week. Ticknor's *White Mountain Guide* lavished praise on Moosilauke's charms, devoting five pages to a peak-by-peak catalog of the mountains and ranges visible from its summit. It also noted the many streams and small waterfalls, including the "woodland beauties" of the Seven Cascades near Gorge Ravine on the carriage road. Guests on the summit often amused themselves by building cairns in various shapes as memorials of their visits—arch, obelisk, and chimney styles prevailed.

Winter Occupation

At the end of the 1860s, a leading geologist of the mountains, Joshua Henry Huntington, conceived of a plan to observe the weather atop Mount Washington during the winter. Huntington had been appointed to assist Charles Hitchcock (son of famed Massachusetts geologist Edward Hitchcock), who was conducting the coastal survey

In the winter of 1869–70, J.H. Huntington and the photographer A.F. Clough spent January to March in Moosilauke's Summit House. After their success, they repeated the experiment on Washington the next winter. Clough's photograph, "House in Frost," reveals his artistry as well as his technical abilities in frigid conditions. Photo courtesy Society for the Preservation of New England Antiquities, Boston, MA.

for the state of New Hampshire, and he had become a pioneer in winter research in the mountains. But he had a difficult time arranging for this newest investigation, for despite his serious purpose, the owners of the Tip Top House on Washington refused to let him use their building. Happily, Prospect House on Mount Moosilauke was offered to him instead.

In the fall of 1869, Huntington and Amos Clough, a photographer from Warren, New Hampshire, hauled ten cords of wood and a three-month food supply to Prospect House and moved in for the winter on New Year's Eve. The men could not have anticipated the severe weather conditions they would encounter. Just three days later they had reason to fear for their survival when a tremendous storm engulfed the mountain. Clough, who literally had to crawl across the rocks in a gale-force wind to take his anemometer readings, wrote:

> It blows a great gale, not in gusts, but a long pull and a strong pull.... We find that the wind blows at the rate of 97 1/2 miles an hour, a hurricane, the fastest wind yet known in this land. If it blows much harder it may sweep us, house and all off the crest.... The wind moans, whines, shrieks and yells like a thousand ghosts, the house shakes and rocks... and the roar makes us deaf. The rain comes in through each chink and crack. Our stove is out once more and the light of our lanterns too. The wind roars like the sea on a rock bound coast. I speak, but no one answers, I call loud, but hear no voice, I shout but no shout comes back, I shake with cold and wet and storm. The dark and the wild wind, if not fear, reign.

The pair survived that storm to measure winds in excess of 100 MPH in February—world-record speeds at the time. Having proved the feasibility of winter occupation at that altitude, and conducting one of the first serious studies of winter weather and related phenomena, they left the mountain February 26. Their success on Moosilauke enabled them to raise the necessary funds and support to spend the following winter on Mount Washington, the first to practice winter-weather observation there.

Legends and Lore

Prompted by Huntington's winter occupation, another pair shortly afterwards spent a full year living on Moosilauke. Jim and Daniel Clement, builders of the carriage road, spent a year living at Prospect House in the mid-1870s, not for serious scientific research but just for the challenge and fun of it. Both Daniel and Jim were well-known local guides, and Jim operated the Prospect House hostelry for many years. D. Q. Clement's journal record of their year on the mountain combines homespun lore, backwoods philosophy, and historical fact in a lively, unpretentious narrative.

> At night when it is clear, often a bright light, too large for a star, bursts on the sight far down in the Pemigewasset Vale. It comes to us swift as the wind; then like a flash it is gone. No sound; more than a score of miles off. It is the headlight of the fast night train bound for Montreal. What a world of life goes with it. But they have no thought of us two who on this high crest look out for them. . . . As I go around to the south side of the inn a brilliant meteor sails full 60 degrees down the sky....It has a trail of red light wide as your hand with tints of blue and green. Stars fall by the score and I watch them a long time.

Clement also repeated ghost stories he had heard from others or read in the town history:

> Daniel Welch came most up here in 1825. He was crazy and it is told how one day he went to the woods and was lost. He came far up the peak and died in the great gorge south of it. It is said his ghost haunts the place yet. Old hunters tell how no one stops in this dark glen at night but has cold sweats on his back and weird fear in his heart and some say they have heard the lost man just at dark call for help and saw his white ghost glide through the dark fir and black spruce.
>
> In ten minutes we stand at the top of the gorge and see the fresh track of the slide. . . . How still it is. I shout long and loud. The wild ghost-like echoes course back from the green wood mountain crests, from the right, from the left, and from front of us, then from far down in the depths, a long, weird, wild sweet sound. It is the cry of the lost Moogens, says Jim, that were last seen here in this gorge four score years ago. They were a strange wild race that dwelt on the Summit once. There are none of them there now. One night late in the fall like the Arabs they fold their tents and steal off still and dark. A lost hunter says he saw them in the first blush of the morn, wend their way up through the gap twixt Mount Clough and Moosilauke, down by

Beaver Pond and that they were all lost in this deep gorge. It is told that like Hudson and his men in the Catskill Mountains, their ghosts hold high mass here once in ten years. Says Jim, I can swear on the book that twice in the last score of years, when there were fierce storms on the crest, I have heard dread and awful sounds come up from far down in the Tunnel as though all the lost Moogens hold a grand rout or as a good man said, 'they seem to raise hell and turn up jack.'

Another local legend, undoubtedly retold for the amusement of guests around the hearth at the Prospect House, concerned an American who had studied in Europe and became interested in alchemy. Returning to New Hampshire, the odd young man settled in Benton just north of Moosilauke, where, it was said, he used his neighbor's pets for experiments. He was a gaunt and mysterious man, seldom seen about town. When a child disappeared mysteriously one day, the doctor was blamed, people suspecting he had finally claimed a human victim for his experimental potions. "The enraged citizenry went to investigate. They arrived at the farm house laboratory only to find no trace of either doctor or child. Such circumstances confirmed their suspicions and fanned their already kindled fury into a blaze beyond control. The house was promptly fired and a posse organized to track down the demon doctor."

Pursuit began under threatening December skies. A hunter had seen the doctor scurrying on the bank of Tunnel Brook, headed for the mountain. The posse followed this route, noting the doctor's strange agility—they glimpsed him but never caught him. The snow began to blow fiercely, and the pursuers were forced to turn back at the headwall. At the top they caught their final glimpse of the doctor as he drank from a mysterious vial. Then they left him to his presumed fate—execution by storm.

The doctor's body was never found, but his spirit keeps turning up around the Summit Hotel. Steps are heard, or a shadowy form glimpsed. His actions seem to be capricious or mischievous rather than jealous, however, and he is often blamed for any missing food or dirty dishes left in kitchen. When an instrument shelter apparently dropped over a precipice, the doctor's ghost was blamed. Many have glimpsed him, on a dark night, as he dodges in and out among the many cairns built by Summit House guests.

In contrast to the wraiths, much activity on the summit was well grounded in fact. The New Hampshire Coastal Survey, remeasuring all of the principal heights and revising maps of the state, set up a survey station on Moosilauke in the early 1870s. Clement comments on this, too, noting how their "old mast with its bright tin on top, put up for a far off sign, still stands. How the tin shines and it can be seen a long way. It was put there to help find the place on the map, and the height of the hills. The wires that bind the mast to the rocks creak in the light wind."

Another relic of the survey's work was a neat shaft of rocks marking the spot where the coast survey had its camp. D. Q. Clement proudly placed his own mark at this spot, a "white cap of quartz rocks" on the cairn, which remains to this day.

Logging and Tourism

During the first half of the nineteenth century, the area's farmers rotated occupations by season, working their farms during the warm months and turning to logging as a part-time winter activity before the late-winter maple-sugar making began. They cut and hauled logs using oxen, which were superior to horses in deep snow. Horses, with their faster gaits, were used for long hauls on sled roads. But the rivers surrounding Moosilauke were unsuited to the huge log drives that could take place only on wider waterways, and so relatively small quantities of spruce were cut before the century's midpoint.

The situation changed dramatically after the Boston, Concord, and Montreal Railroad arrived in Warren in 1851. The locomotives that pulled the trains were wood fired, thus creating a new market for hardwood. Softwood, mostly spruce and pine, was shipped for lumber. New mills appeared along the Baker River, and logging supplanted farming as the foundation of the local economy. The population of the village of Warren doubled. Spruce lumber was the major product before 1890; mills produced rough lumber, clapboards, spruce oil, shingles, barrels, sap buckets, and piano sounding boards. After 1890, when the paper industry shifted from cotton rags to wood pulp for

The lumber industry reached its peak of operation at Moosilauke around 1890. Here, the Baker River brims with spruce logs while the cleared slopes of the mountain are visible in the background. Photo courtesy Dartmouth College Library/Fred C. Gleason, Hanover, NH.

fibers, loggers attacked the spruce forests of northern New Hampshire with renewed vigor and increasingly sophisticated technology.

Tourists on Moosilauke saw mixed land use on the mountain in the second half of the nineteenth century. Sheep and cows grazed in open pastures on the upper slopes in the 1870s, and loggers worked the heavy forests of standing timber nearer to the valleys. Yet the urbanites who patronized the hotels preferred to focus on the inspirational view from the mountain's summit and the rustic local life that reminded them of pioneer days.

Poets and writers who flocked to the White Mountains sometimes ventured as far west as Moosilauke, some even proclaiming it their favorite mountain. Lucy Larcom, the Lowell mill worker whose poetry brought her a national reputation, composed more than a few sentimental odes on Moosilauke in the 1890s. She wrote one of her best-known poems on the summit mourning the death her close friend, John Greenleaf Whittier.

The Mountaineer's Prayer

Gird me with the strength of Thy steadfast hills,
    The speed of Thy streams give me!
In the spirit that calms, with the life that thrills,
    I would stand or run for Thee.
Let me be Thy voice, or Thy silent power,
    As the cataract, or the peak,—
An eternal thought, in my earthly hour,
    Of the living God to speak!

Clothe me in the rose-tints of Thy skies,
    Upon morning summits laid!
Robe me in the purple and gold that flies
    Through Thy shuttles of light and shade!
Let me rise and rejoice in Thy smile aright,
    As mountains and forests do!
Let me welcome Thy twilight and Thy night,
    And wait for Thy dawn anew!

Give me the brook's faith, joyously sung
    Under clank of its icy chain!
Give me of the patience that hides among
    The hill-tops, in mist and rain!
Lift me up from the cold, let me breathe Thy breath,
    Thy beauty and strength give me!
Let me lose both the name and the meaning of death,
    In the life that I share with Thee!

By the end of the century, small-time logging had all but disappeared, and the grip of the paper companies on Moosilauke's future had tightened. They bought up tracts of land to clearcut, the most profitable way to harvest trees. They even blasted the channel of the wild Ammonoosuc to float logs more efficiently from the north slope of Moosilauke down the Connecticut. The Fall Mountain Paper Company also installed dams to assure enough water to float the logs downstream.

French Canadian crews working between 1899 and 1914 took down nearly all of the mountain's old-growth spruce and fir. It is estimated that about 500 acres each year were clearcut. Where the slopes of Mount Moosilauke had no access to viable water courses, their timber was shipped away on logging railroads laid specifically to get out the timber. That job done, the tracks were taken up and moved elsewhere.

Conservation and Recreation

At the turn of the century, all over the White Mountain region, opposition to the paper companies was building. Tourists and influential writers could no longer ignore the devastated hillsides. A series of fires (commonly thought to have started by sparks from the locomotives hauling timber out of the woods) burned thousands of acres of slash and darkened the skies over the mountains for weeks. Clearcut mountainsides were even blamed for pollution in urban water sources downstream. And a growing back-to-nature movement that prized the pristine qualities of nature for moral and aesthetic renewal began to find its voice. All these factors combined to form a powerful opposition to logging.

The Weeks Act, passed by the federal government in 1911, effectively halted the destructive practices of the timber barons by appropriating funds for the purchase of White Mountain lands and their consolidation into the White Mountain National Forest (WMNF). Nearly a decade of intense lobbying by interests opposed to the paper companies had been required to pass the legislation. In 1914 the government made its first purchase in the Moosilauke region, about 7,000 acres. The United States Forest Service continued acquisitions throughout the ensuing decades, and today Moosilauke and surrounding lands form the westernmost boundary of the WMNF.

Dartmouth College is an equally important partner in the preservation of Moosilauke. It received an initial gift of land on the mountain in 1920 from two Dartmouth alumni, relatives of the wife of mountain writer D. Q. Clement. Charles Woodworth, class of 1907, and E. K. Woodworth, class of 1897, owners of the Tip-Top House and Moosilauke's summit in the early twentieth century, found that with the advent of automobiles, interest in the toll road's horse-and-wagon route to the summit was fading. The road had gradually declined, getting scant use in the 1910s even though the last official toll collection took place in 1919. With prospects for their own profits declining, the Woodworths gave to Dartmouth the summit, Tip-Top House, and a pie-shaped wedge of land leading from there down to the old logging camp at the foot of Jobildunc Ravine.

Moosilauke became Dartmouth's mountain, and it was a perfect match. The school had long emphasized the value of outdoor recreation in addition to scholastics. Dartmouth students, pioneers in the outdoors movement, had formed the earliest of the college outing clubs in 1909. Dartmouth students and faculty appear on every list of mountain firsts, playing important roles in the development of hiking, trail blazing, skiing, winter climbing, and every other activity in the ongoing history of New England's mountains. A group from the Dartmouth Outing Club (DOC) claimed the first Mount Washington ascent on skis in 1913, and shortly thereafter accomplished a winter climb of Moosilauke, making the round trip from Hanover to Moosilauke in three days, on skis all the way.

Already familiar users of Moosilauke's terrain when the Woodworths made their gift, the DOC took over the summit house and ran it much like the huts in the AMC system (see Mount Washington chapter). They also constructed a series of lean-to shelters along a hiking route that stretched directly from Hanover to Moosilauke.

Not surprisingly, Dartmouth introduced the sport of downhill skiing to Moosilauke. Originally skiing the carriage road, racers from all over New England congregated at what was then the first important downhill ski run in New England. A winter cabin was built near the summit, then other ski runs were added, including Hell's Highway and the Snapper Trail (which is still hikable). In 1933, the first National Downhill Championship was held at Moosilauke.

But always these skiers had to climb up before they gained the reward of a downhill run. Within a few short years, Moosilauke was all but abandoned for the easier ascents that mechanized lifts on other mountains could offer. A short-lived revival of skiing on Moosilauke took place after World War II, when a small ski tow, a few lights, and a 25-meter ski jump adequately served a much-diminished population of collegiate and prep-school skiers.

An abandoned logging cabin, known as Ravine Camp, found new service as a base lodge for skiers in the early 1930s. Although it was destroyed accidentally by fire, the Ravine Camp was rebuilt in 1937–38 as Ravine Lodge, using huge spruce logs cut in the adjacent Jobildunc Ravine area. Just after the completion of the lodge, in the fall of 1938, New England's greatest hurricane virtually destroyed all remaining old-growth forest on Moosilauke. Had the camp not been rebuilt when it was, there would never again have been an opportunity to use the virgin timber available on Mount Moosilauke.

Dartmouth's Ravine Lodge, at the foot of Jobildunc Ravine, was constructed of old-growth spruce logs just before the devastating hurricane of 1938. Photo courtesy Dartmouth College Library, Hanover, NH.

Other structures on the mountain have not survived as well as the ruggedly built Ravine Lodge. The Summit House, still popular with a regular hiking crowd, was apparently struck by lightning and burned in 1942. Dense fog completely hid the conflagration from observation down in the valley. In 1957, Dartmouth replaced the 1930s cabin near the summit with a new prefabricated structure; this was used for winter outings for a number of years but is now gone, too.

Dartmouth's acquisition of lands on the mountain has continued. Between 1965 and 1979, a far-sighted alumnus provided funds for the purchase of paper company–owned tracts adjacent to the college's earlier piece. The college acquired 930 acres from the Franconia Paper Company and 249 acres southwest of Gorge Brook. According to the *Forest History of Mount Moosilauke,* "this led to solid ownership by the College of 4,500 acres in the upper watershed. Dartmouth's holding is flanked on all sides by White Mountain National Forest…[making it] jointly with the Federal government, the dominant force in land ownership and management on the entire mountain."

An advisory committee was formed in 1974 to assist the college in planning for the future of its landholdings on the mountain. Along with the restoration of Ravine Lodge and scientific research that includes documentation of the spruce-fir forest and the effects of acid rain on it, strong emphasis is being placed on developing outdoor recreation uses. For instance, based on the research and recommendations of a student, Dartmouth has begun to implement a system of hiking and cross-country-ski trails following the routes of old logging roads that crisscrossed the mountain nearly a hundred years ago.

Moosilauke's lure for Dartmouth students and others is not only its great natural beauty and isolation, but the rich veil of history and legend that have grown up around it. Those stories are part of the orientation incoming freshmen receive as part of a three-day outing to the mountain held every September. And in downtown Hanover, where the Appalachian Trail crosses the Connecticut River from Vermont and enters New Hampshire, students are constantly reminded of the fun of hiking by the pack-laden, heavy-booted travelers who pass through the Dartmouth Outing Club's headquarters on their way northward to Moosilauke, over the Lafayette ridgeline and on to Mount Washington and the end of the line at Katahdin.

Dartmouth's many Moosilauke-centered activities include freshman weekend and a strong environmental-studies curriculum. Photo courtesy Nicolas Nobili/ *The Dartmouth Aegis*, 1988.

In the final analysis, it may be Moosilauke's isolation and elevation that have made it special, along with the stories of Indians and ghosts that abound in its past, but it is Dartmouth that has enshrined it as a celebrated peak.

Moosilauke, a quiet mountain always well appreciated, has reverted to unspoiled nature, remote and rewarding and far from the mainstream. Dartmouth cares for its prized possession well, and shares its riches generously with those who truly appreciate them.

Suggestions for Visitors

Moosilauke's incomparable view makes it a good hike for a clear day. The best approach is from Route 118 in Warren, where parking is available at Dartmouth Outing Club's Ravine Lodge (not open to the public). A loop of about nine miles begins by ascending the well-maintained Gorge Brook Trail (daylight will protect you from the ghost of Daniel Welch). At the outlooks, feast your eyes on the sight of Mount Lafayette and the Franconia Mountains.

For the descent, cross the crest to South Peak and follow the old carriage road, still a wide boulevard compared to other footpaths, which leads to the old ski run, the Snapper Trail, and back to Ravine Lodge. Having two cars makes possible a ridge hike from the Ravine Lodge to the summit, then around Jobildunc Ravine to Mount Blue on the Beaver Brook Trail, ending on Route 112 in Kinsman Notch.

Even a drive *around* Moosilauke takes in the beauty of the mountains, from Interstate 93 following the Lost River through Kinsman Notch, along the wild Ammonoosuc River in Benton, and back along the historic Baker River through Warren.

The most gradual route up the mountain is the old bridle path now known as the Benton Trail, reached from the northern town of Benton on Route 116. Most of Moosilauke's trails are scrupulously maintained by the DOC; others are under the jurisdiction of the White Mountain National Forest.

Mountain bikers tend to use the Blueberry Mountain Trail, which begins off Lime Kiln Road in East Haverhill. Logging roads of recent origin form the lower part of the trail, and even without regular maintenance by either DOC or WMNF, this trail still receives enough use to be followed without too much difficulty.

As the name of Beaver Brook suggests, these industrious rodents have made significant inroads into the landscape here. According to the current AMC guide, disruption to the Tunnel Brook Trail caused by beavers is not uncommon; good views of beaver ponds are available along this trail.

The advice of Daniel Clement, though a hundred years old, still seems appropriate for visitors to Moosilauke today: "One word to our friends who may go up to what was once our home on the crest. If you go, don't rush, go slow. See how many kinds of rocks you can find on the way, how many flowers, plants and trees, hark to the winds, list to the song of birds, the call of the wild beasts, the roar of the streams. Don't walk so fast as to make you puff and sweat and your heart beat too quick. Mind these things and you will like the trip a thousand times as well."

Lafayette ⋀⋀⋀

Mount Lafayette stands hard above a celebrated pass through the White Mountains. Franconia Notch, discovered by Europeans in the 1790s, provided an important north-south passageway through the seemingly impenetrable mountains of northern New Hampshire. Lumbering and tourism grew to be major industries here, while year-round settlement remained sparse. Today, the man-made attractions in the notch are as much a draw to outsiders as the mountains themselves. Accessibility and protection, both in the notch and on the mountain, form an uneasy alliance, for Lafayette is at once well protected and overused today.

Lafayette rises to a height of 5,249 feet on the east side of the notch and caps a row of high peaks here—Mount Flume at 4,328 feet; Liberty at 4,459 feet; and Lincoln at 5,089 feet. Another high peak, Garfield, stands 4,500 feet high to the northeast of Lafayette.

On the other side of the notch, the best-known peak is 4,100-foot Profile Mountain, so named because of the rock formation known as the Old Man of the Mountain on its upper ledges. Profile Mountain rises above two small glacial lakes, Echo Lake and Profile Lake. On the north-facing slope of Profile Mountain is Cannon Mountain ski area, an alternate name for the mountain that comes from a cannonlike outcropping of rock on its summit ridge. Two

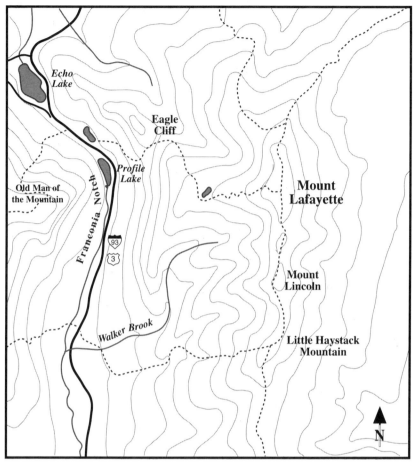

Lafayette

lower rounded summits to the west of the main peak are called the Cannon Balls.

Between the Old Man and the ski area towers a formidable rock cliff, 500 to 1,500 feet above the valley, which has offered an impressive challenge to rock climbers since 1928. Chunks of broken rock called talus, forced away from the bedrock by the action of frost in the cracks, have accumulated at the foot of this rock face, creating a serious hazard for climbers who lose their hold on the sheer wall.

The aspect of Lafayette has changed little since D. Q. Clement, introduced in the Moosilauke chapter, described its appearance in the mid-1870s: "Mt. Lafayette is...a true alp, with peaks and crags on which lightnings play, its sides brown with scars and deep with gorges down which the spring torrents plunge." Lafayette today borders the Pemigewasset Wilderness, a roadless, scenic area of rugged mountain terrain that forms the heart of the White Mountain National Forest. Beyond this region lie the better-known Crawford Notch and the more developed Mount Washington, but from the summit of Lafayette looking east, the hand of man is barely visible.

Lafayette's wild character contributes to its popularity as the second most-climbed peak (after Washington) in the White Mountains. It offers many of the same challenges as Washington without the commercial intrusions of summit buildings, auto road, and cog railway. Yet its very popularity affects its continued preservation, and serious environmentalists are working hard to prevent degradation from overuse.

Geology and Geography

The natural features of Lafayette are one of its greatest attractions. Growing along Lafayette's treeless crest is the second largest arctic-alpine area in New Hampshire (after the Presidentials), home to dwarf varieties of common trees stunted by extreme wind and weather and the rare ice-age relics diapensia and mountain avens.

The grinding forces of glacial ice have carved the Lafayette ridge into a dramatic pointed rampart—a very different aspect from the rounded Presidentials. Beginning about a million years ago, huge ice sheets worked their way through this preglacial valley, following the path of least resistance and carving out the distinctive U-shaped form of the notch today. Long horizontal scratches still visible on the valley walls and curiously shaped rock formations above treeline bear mute witness to the power of that ice.

The glacial basins of Profile Lake and Echo Lake, just below the Old Man of the Mountains, are also products of the Ice Age, created some 12,000 to 15,000 years ago when deep holes filled with meltwater. Another glacial basin, the secluded and charming

View of the western side of the Lafayette Range from Lonesome Lake. Maggie Stier.

Lonesome Lake, is tucked away behind Profile Mountain. Stream runoff from the mountains of the Franconia valley is divided much the same as on Moosilauke; the western and northern slopes drain into the Ammonoosuc and thence to the Connecticut River, and the southern and eastern slopes drain into central New Hampshire's Merrimack River.

The geology of the Franconia Ridge is complicated. Most of the underlying bedrock in the area is made up of Jurassic-period intrusions, about 150 million to 200 million years old. Lafayette and Garfield may be part of huge ring dikes, ten to twenty miles across, formed by molten rock intruding through nearly circular fractures.

Three distinct types of rock on the mountain reveal the successive layers of which the mountain is built. At Greenleaf Hut, the exposed bedrock is Kinsman quartz monzonite, about 300 million years old. Granite porphyry, found still higher on the mountain, is a lighter, gray-green rock, and closer to the summit a quartz syenite appears, the darkest color of all.

Early History

The earliest rough trail used by European settlers through Franconia Notch dates to 1793. Thomas Boise of Woodstock had the misfortune of getting caught in a swirling blizzard in the notch in those early days. As his horse stumbled along through the worsening storm, Boise realized neither of them would be able to make it through the notch in the deepening snow. Already half-frozen himself, Boise summoned the energy to kill his horse. In the blinding and drifting snow, he skinned the animal, crawled under an overhanging rock, wrapped himself in the still-warm hide, and waited out the storm. At his rescue the next day, the skin was so solidly frozen about him that he had to be cut out of it. The rock that is believed to have sheltered him still bears his name, about a half-mile south of Profile Lake.

This narrow footpath through the notch gradually widened until it could be used by teams. Beginning in the early 1800s, the state of New Hampshire assumed what was to be a pivotal role in advancing development in this area. It stepped in to construct a significantly improved road there in the early 1800s, at a time when the narrow cartpath through the notch was receiving more and more traffic. The new road was completed in 1813, opening new lands to settlement and trade and fostering improved communications between formerly disjointed parts of the state. Travel through the northern mountains of New Hampshire was expedited significantly, as important as the wonders of their craggy peaks, clear streams, and awe-inspiring scenery were to their eventual transformation into a vacation destination.

Perhaps the biggest single factor in the growth of interest in the Franconia region was the Old Man of the Mountain. Travelers related various versions of stories of its discovery, and after 1826, when the first known printed account of it appeared, more and more travelers sought out this marvel of nature.

Several stories of the discovery of the great stone face place the event in 1805, but most historians believe it may have been even earlier. One version relates that the profile was discovered accidentally by two men working on the new road as surveyors. One made his way to the edge of the nearby lake to get water, and when he looked up,

After the discovery of the Old Man of the Mountain in 1805, a short story by Hawthorne and dozens of paintings and photographs of the great stone face helped lure tourists to the area. The famous landmark is shown here in an early-twentieth-century postcard. Author's collection/Kurt Stier.

he thought he saw the face of then-President Jefferson staring at him high above on the mountainside.

Frederick Kilbourne, in his *Chronicles of the White Mountains*, offers another version of the story to which he gives equal credence. A Baptist preacher from Lisbon, New Hampshire, a town at the northern end of the notch, stopped to observe the progress of work on the road and happened to glance up at just the right angle. The strong and beautiful face gazing down on him he took to be the countenance of God.

Timothy Dwight, Yale president and backcountry publicist, made two trips to the White Mountains, the first of which, in 1806, included a mixed review of the Franconia Notch area. "Nothing," he wrote, "merits notice except the patience, enterprise, and hardihood of the settlers, which have induced them to venture and stay upon so forbidding a spot." Mitigating the austerity, however, was "a magnificent prospect of the White Mountains, and a splendid collection of other mountains in their neighborhood, particularly on the southwest....One, inferior only to Washington and Moosilauke, exhibits in its great elevation, elegance of form, and amplitude a very rare combination of beauty and grandeur. It is composed of three lofty conical summits accompanied by four vast, bold, circular sweeps, formed with a grace to which in objects of this nature I had hitherto been a stranger."

Dwight, perhaps not bothering to consult the locals about the names of the mountains, decided to name the highest himself. "I have taken the liberty to give the apellation of Mount Wentworth, from the respect which I have ever borne to John Wentworth, Esq., formerly Governor of New Hampshire." Notwithstanding Dwight's eagerness to honor his friend, the name did not stick, and later he made an equally sincere though unsuccessful attempt to rename Lake Winnipesaukee in honor of Wentworth. Wentworth, as the last colonial governor of the state during the Revolution, had chosen to side with the Crown, and among most citizens was not held in particularly high regard.

Maps of New Hampshire's mountains from the first two decades of the nineteenth century indicate that the mountain did already have a name. The highest peak in the Franconia range was Great Haystack, with the lesser summit being called Little Haystack. The

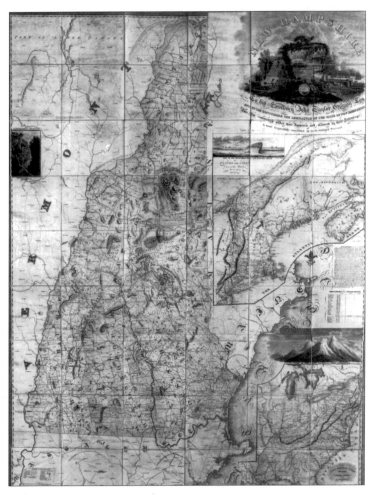

Carrigain's 1816 map of New Hampshire called the highest peak in the Franconia Range Great Haystack. The name was changed in 1824–25 to honor Lafayette's visit to the United States. Photo courtesy New Hampshire Historical Society, Concord, NH.

main summit was rechristened Lafayette in 1824–25 in honor of the great French war hero's visit to the United States.

Before touring the White Mountains evolved into a fashionable pastime, only a few hardy souls even thought to climb the steep peaks. In 1822, Alden Partridge marched his Norwich Academy cadets over here, following the Ammonoosuc River from Haverhill, New Hampshire. Spending the night in Franconia, Partridge noted the "seemingly inexhaustible" iron-ore beds there, which during their brief heyday in the 1830s yielded 600 tons of ore. The next day, Partridge and his charges climbed into the notch and up Lafayette: "a long and tedious ascent of this lofty pile of granite" where they went up "a blind footpath on the mountain's side."

Partridge had some problems on this trip from an undescribed accident that "injured" the barometer, and he had to rely on estimation to establish the height of Lafayette, which he generously put at 6,000 feet. Copying a custom originating on Mount Washington, each cadet wrote his own name on a slip of paper and put it in a tightly corked bottle that was then left in a specially built stone enclosure on the summit.

The president of Amherst College, Edward Hitchcock, made a visit to Mount Washington and the Great Haystack (as some were still calling it) in 1841. He published a series of articles in a Boston newspaper that explained the geology of the mountains and a decidedly unscientific regard for the uplifting character of the mountain scenery.

More visitors came to investigate these mountains and they, in turn, published accounts that spawned an even greater curiosity about the place. The trickle of summer visitors that began arriving in the 1820s prompted the construction of the first hotel in the notch, which opened in 1835. It catered to a steadily increasing clientele anxious to escape the summer heat of the cities and refresh their minds and spirits with the mountain scenery. Known as the Lafayette House and located at Echo Lake near the site of the future Profile House, this establishment grew into an elegant destination.

By midcentury, the notch in summer was full of genteel men and women, mostly from New York and Philadelphia, amusing themselves in the outdoors or enjoying the views from the porches of tasteful new hotels. The Flume House was built in 1849. In 1853, its owners opened the grand, 100-room Profile House, moving the old Lafayette House behind the new hotel to become servants' quarters.

Profile House, according to a guidebook, was considered "one of the best summer hotels in the United States" after it was enlarged

The Profile House was the most elegant of the summer hotels in the Franconia Region. From here, guests were offered day trips up the mountain on horseback, or pleasure boat rides on nearby Echo Lake. Author's collection/ Kurt Stier.

in 1866, and accommodated more than 500 guests at a time. Guests could choose among billiards, tennis, bowling alleys, rowboats for hire, and even a small steamboat named *Ida* touring Echo Lake. There were fireworks displays and rafts set afire on Echo Lake. One season, the great impresario P. T. Barnum presented a unique circus at the Profile House with his employees dressed as the animals.

A forerunner of today's man-made attractions in the mountains, an eighteen-foot-high wooden panther perched on the edge of Eagle Cliff facing the hotel. Profile House's panther was such a drawing card that a twenty-foot-high wooden Indian in pursuit of the panther was erected on the same cliff.

The highlight of the summer season, for most visitors, was making an ascent of the mountains around the notch. The first footpath up Lafayette probably dates to the mid-1820s, but not everyone had the courage or stamina for that. Most people preferred a now-obliterated series of trails emanating from the hotels to such easily reached destinations as Eagle Cliff, Artist's Bluff, Boise (or Boyce) Rock, and

Echo Lake. But for those who were hardy and determined, Lafayette offered rewards equal to Mount Washington, its higher and more celebrated neighbor to the east. The view of Franconia Notch and the cliffs of Cannon were well worth the trouble.

By 1845, tourists could spend the night at the summit in a small hotel, having ascended on horseback by means of a bridle path built some five years earlier. The trail was famous for a difficult, steep stretch known as the Three Agonies, which was circumvented shortly by an alternate path. In the 1880s, the bridle path became a toll route. Those who wished to walk up paid fifty cents; to take a "surefooted horse with guide" cost $3.50. But the mountain enterprise was perhaps too ambitious. The summit house appears either to have burned or fallen apart some time between the early 1860s and 1876. Its old stone foundation still remains, often providing slight shelter from the wind for chilly hikers, but it is definitely not a place of refuge during electric storms or severe weather.

Hikers try to find some shelter from the wind within the old summit building foundation on Lafayette. Maggie Stier.

Meanwhile, in 1858, an entrepreneur named Sylvester Marsh received charters from the state legislature for steam railways to go up both Lafayette and Washington. Due to the difficulties of the Civil War and the lack of adequate financial backing, Marsh's plans came to nothing on Lafayette. On Washington, of course, he originated what was to become the world-famous cog railway.

Lumbering

Making a living in the northern mountains meant adapting to the short growing season and rocky soils by finding other sources of income besides farming. The thick evergreen forests began to fall to the saw and ax as soon as settlers entered this area, and by the 1840s cutting timber had become an organized business here. The towns of Lincoln and Woodstock, along the Pemigewasset River, emerged as centers of lumbering activity and N.G. Norcross as their Timber King. An 1846 *New York Tribune* story described the log drives on the river: "The Pemigewasset is alive with them now, for miles and miles, and Norcross and his red shirters are after 'em down the river like so many hounds. It is a sight to see 'em ride these mill logs down the rapids."

Railroads built in the 1840s pushed loggers farther into the mountain valleys around Lafayette, especially to the east along the Pemigewasset's East Branch. For a time, tourism and logging seemed to coexist without conflict, but a clash was inevitable.

Following the Civil War, the state suddenly threw open the doors to widespread logging in much of the White Mountain territory. Influenced by pressure from lumber interests, the legislature voted in 1867 to sell 172,000 acres of White Mountain holdings. The "scandalously" low sum the state received went into a special fund to support literary education, and private commercial interests moved quickly to maximize profits in lumber production.

The logging industry's negative aspects could not be ignored. Incompatibility with the tourist trade and the increasing popularity of outdoor recreation in the 1870s were major influences in the growing opposition to the lumber companies. The state of New Hampshire formed its own Forestry Commission in the 1880s, in response to charges that, among other things, clearcutting practices washed silt and debris into the streams and rivers and threatened to pollute the water sources for some of the major cities in the state.

Despite strong pressure from hotel and tourist interests, the commission was unable to halt the extension of railroad lines through Franconia Notch. The landscape of Lafayette and the Franconia ridge was completely denuded in places after the 1890s, when a voracious market for paper pulp began consuming the standing timber on these lands at an even faster rate than before.

The visual intrusion of logging trains and clearcut slopes was not the only problem. Where loggers went, fires inevitably followed. Whether a spark from a passing engine ignited some brush along the tracks, or an untended woodstove or careless smoking got out of control in one of the many logging camps, fires were a hazard to be reckoned with. Logged woods full of dry slash burned quickly and often destroyed even the topsoil.

Near Lafayette raged one of the most serious fires in the history of the White Mountains. It lasted for more than a week in the month of August 1907, and burned perhaps as much as 35,000 acres. Fanned by high winds, it spread northeastward from Lafayette to Garfield and the Twin Mountain Range, areas that had not yet been cut over. Estimates at the time predicted that the forest growth would be retarded for thirty years; indeed, some said it might never recover.

According to C. Francis Belcher in his thorough study, *Logging Railroads of the White Mountains*, "the great conflagration was given almost daily coverage through August 29th, as the summer paper followed the progress of the fire almost as it might a favorite baseball team." One article noted that "the glow of the great fire in the Lincoln valley near Mount Lafayette reflected on the clouds above attracted the attention of Summit Visitors last evening," and another that "Thursday afternoon the fire in Lincoln was seen to advance northerly until the smoke rose along the whole eastern side of Lafayette."

Hotel interests, concerned in the meantime about their declining profits, had caved in to the timber barons' insatiable demand and had begun to allow lumbering on the 6,000 acres they controlled in the notch. The public protested. A far-sighted Philip Ayres, head forester for the Society for the Protection of New Hampshire Forests from 1902–36, spearheaded a nationwide campaign to save Franconia Notch from complete clearcutting. In 1925 he organized an effort to make it a state reservation and raised a combination of state money and private contributions for its purchase. On September 15, 1928, Franconia Notch became a forest reservation and state park.

Ayres had been instrumental in the creation of the White Mountain National Forest, too, whose lands now abut the state park along the Lafayette ridgeline. He argued that the White Mountains were a resource for the entire region, not just the state, envisioning a federal forest reservation to complement the state reserve. The Weeks Act, which became law in 1911, authorized the creation of the White Mountain National Forest and appropriated funds for land purchases.

Arts and Literature

Artists and writers of the nineteenth century played a key role in the popularization of Lafayette and the Franconia region. The veil of romanticism and nature-worship espoused by Ruskin and Wordsworth permeated their perceptions. Thomas Cole, who walked through the notch in 1828 and went on to pioneer a new artistic vision of the American landscape, reflected this sensibility in a journal entry describing the place: "Unbroken silence reigning through the whole region made the scene particularly impressive and sublime—an awfulness in the deep solitude, pent up within great precipices, that was painful. A childish fear came over me, the bold and horrid features that bend their severe expression upon me were too dreadful to look upon in my loneliness." While Cole ultimately found the region around Mount Washington more suited to his tastes, many of his followers developed a thorough appreciation for both areas.

Credit for much of the popularity of the mountains goes to a writer of midcentury, Thomas Starr King. A Massachusetts-raised Unitarian minister, King summered in the White Mountains for ten years beginning in 1850. *The Boston Transcript* began running his articles in 1853, and these later formed the basis of his best-selling book, *The White Hills, Their Legends, Landscape and Poetry*, published in 1859. A ground-breaking work that combined legends, poetry, personal observation, and a healthy dash of Transcendental philosophy, it was an immediate success.

In this influential book, King called Lafayette "the Duke of Western Coos," and asserted that "the view from its upper shoulders and summit has an entirely different character from that which Mount Washington commands. It is the lowlands that are the glory of the spectacle which Lafayette shows his guests."

> The narrow district thus enclosed contains more objects of interest to the mass of travellers than any other region of equal extent within the usual compass of the White Mt. tour. In the way of rock-sculpture and waterfalls, it is a huge museum of curiosities. There is no spot usually visited in any of the valleys where the senses are at once impressed so strongly and so pleasantly with the wildness and freshness which a stranger instinctively associates with mountain scenery in New Hampshire. There is no other spot where the visitor is domesticated amid the most savage and startling forms in which cliffs and forests are combined. And yet there is beauty enough intermixed with the sublimity and the wildness to make this scenery permanently attractive, as well as grand and exciting.

King, staunch abolitionist and persuasive lecturer, sympathized deeply with the Transcendentalist attitudes of these decades. His writing about the White Mountains expressed attitudes akin to those his compatriot, Henry David Thoreau, felt about Wachusett, Monadnock, and Greylock. Thoreau was out of his element in the White Mountains, and seems to have found less spiritual nourishment and more physical trial in his two visits to this area. On his first trip to the area, he walked from Woodstock northward through the notch and observed the Old Man of the Mountain, the Flume, and the Basin along the way. On the second trip, in 1858, Thoreau climbed Washington, then walked westward and camped "half a mile up the side of Lafayette, which peak was ascended, a good view being had of near points." One suspects that, after the length and difficulty of the climb (and knowing of his disastrous experience spraining an ankle and starting a brush fire on Washington), he could find little more to appreciate.

Indeed, many found a long-distance view of Lafayette's jagged ridge more inspiring than the prospect from its summit. Artists most often depicted the mountain from afar, either from north or south of the notch, with a foreground filled by a winding river or the reflecting waters of a small pond. Their broad views of the mountains, set off by heavy gilt frames, decorated drawing rooms and parlors in cities all along the East Coast, remembrances of summer idylls and memorials to the ideal of the mountain's Edenlike landscape.

Photographers after the Civil War found this area fertile ground for their profession, too. The White Mountains were surpassed only by Niagara Falls as a favored American subject. A modern study has found that in the twenty-five years from 1860 to 1885 more than forty-five publishing companies issued White Mountain stereographic views. These were side-by-side images that, when placed in a special viewer, gave the illusion of depth in one image. Stereo cards were a favorite souvenir of visits to the mountains.

Albert Bierstadt, whose greatest fame would come from his large-scale oil paintings of Yosemite and the West, got his start taking stereo views that were published in New Bedford, Massachusetts. (See his painting of Ascutney, p. 134.) Working with his two brothers, he produced a series of now-scarce prints of this locale, as well as other areas in the White Mountains. Kilburn Brothers of Littleton, New Hampshire, the most prolific stereograph firm specializing in White Mountain images, circulated their popular images worldwide. More than 2,000 different views of northern New Hampshire were listed in their catalog, and in their best years they turned out about 3,000 stereo cards a day. These turn up frequently in antique dealers' shops and are still relatively inexpensive for collectors today.

A flowering of literary efforts, complementing the visual products, planted the Franconia region firmly in the American consciousness. The Old Man, reliable and remarkable, was the focus of many of these. Ethan Allen Crawford, the first innkeeper and mountain guide in Crawford Notch, summed up the fascination of the Old Man in his *History of the White Mountains*. It had the ability to "present the perfect outlines of the human face to the beholder," yet "a few steps either way destroys the features, one by one, until nothing but a mass of ragged cliffs meets the eye."

The surprise emergence of the finely outlined features, where once there was simply a jagged rock cliff, elevated the landmark to almost sacred status. Furthermore, as Crawford noted, "the storms of ages seem not to disturb the resting place of the stern old man, or cause a wrinkle to be furrowed upon his brow." Here was a natural feature so worthy of appreciation that Americans eagerly seized the opportunity to prove their landscape held equal stature with the ruins of ancient civilizations in Europe.

Nineteenth-century American writers immortalized the Profile and used it as a vehicle for reaffirming a widely held belief in the Deity's presence in the mountains. Nathaniel Hawthorne visited Franconia in 1850 and wrote a short story called "The Great Stone Face" as an allegory about Daniel Webster. Hawthorne continued to visit the area literally to the end of his life: on an 1864 trip to the notch with former President Franklin Pierce, he was taken ill in Plymouth and died there during the night.

Daniel Webster, the great statesman and New Hampshire native, is credited with a description of the Old Man that has become so well known it is referenced in *Bartlett's Familiar Quotations*. "Men hang out their signs indicative of their respective trades: shoemakers hang out a giant shoe; jewelers a monster watch; and the dentist hangs out a gold tooth; but up in the mountains of New Hampshire, God Almighty has hung out a sign to show that there He makes men."

Poets, too, found their muse in this region. In 1865, John Greenleaf Whittier visited his friend and publisher, James T. Fields, in Campton, and there he composed the first of his "mountain pictures." In "Franconia from the Pemigewasset," part of the second stanza reveals Whittier's warm affection for the landscape of the Lafayette Range.

> I almost pause the wind in the pines to hear,
> The loose rock's fall, the steps of browsing deer.
> The clouds that shattered on yon slide-worn walls
>   And splintered on the rocks their spears of rain
>
> Have set in play a thousand waterfalls,
> Making the dusk and silence of the woods
> Glad with the laughter of the chasing floods,
> And luminous with blown spray and silver gleams,
>   Sing to the freshened meadow-lands again.

A different kind of Yankee poet came to these hills in the early twentieth century, one whose spare language and direct experience captured the essence of simple outdoor life and individual resourcefulness. Robert Frost (1874–1963) lived on a farm in Franconia from 1915 to 1920. According to one of his biographers, "the Franconia period was one of the most productive for Frost. Here, in a simple, eight-room, white frame farmhouse, on a hillside overlooking the mountains, he wrote his third book of poems, *Mountain Interval,* and most of his fourth collection, *New Hampshire,* which won a Pulitzer Prize. Three of Frost's most celebrated poems appeared in these books: "The Road Not Taken," "Birches," and "Stopping by Woods on a Snowy Evening."

Like so many New England farmers, Frost had little interest in recreational use of the mountains; yet as a farmer he went far beyond the typical working relationship with the land and expressed an understanding of the rhythms of nature and human existence in a unique way. His musings on life, in a long poem called simply "New Hampshire," provided some quotable lines about the topographical differences of the two states that lay yoked together.

> Anything I can say about New Hampshire
> Will serve almost as well about Vermont,
> Excepting that they differ in their mountains,
> The Vermont mountains stretch extended straight;
> New Hampshire mountains curl up in a coil.

Modern painters, equally reclusive, sought the quiet beauty of the Franconia region in the 1920s and 1930s. More comfortable with abstract modes of expression, and rejecting urban subjects, these artists expressed something quite different from the romantic realists of a century before. In the work of John Marin and Marsden Hartley (whose canvases of Katahdin are among his boldest), the mountains become organic, elemental forces within nature. Marin's watercolor of Lafayette, done in the late twenties, is a tribute not only to the place but to the dynamic forces of nature. Brilliantly colored, simply drawn, such pictures provide an alternative expression in the popular field of White Mountain art.

Modern artists revived painterly interest in Lafayette in the 1920s. John Marin, an architect by training, combined brilliant colors and almost mystical symbolism in his Franconia Range, White Mountains, No. 1 *of 1927.* Photo courtesy Phillips Collection, Washington, D.C.

Recreation and Preservation

The groundswell of interest in hiking and nature appreciation that helped create the Franconia Notch State Reservation and the White Mountain National Forest was part of a much larger back-to-nature movement of the same time. The Appalachian Mountain Club, founded in 1876, not only promoted outdoor recreation in the mountains, but also maintained for many years a Department of Art to support artistic and literary efforts. Its first councillor, Charles E. Fay, urged "all the fraternity to betake themselves as early as may be to the hill-country with eyes open to receive every inspiration of beauty and grandeur that can elevate the soul and make man himself grander and more beautiful."

Local residents claimed an active role in clearing, marking, maintaining, and using the trail systems in the notch. As the large hotels succumbed to fire, such as the Profile House in 1923, they were not rebuilt. A new breed of mountain enthusiasts enjoyed roughing it—exploring the backcountry on foot and sleeping on the ground or in rustic shelters. In the late 1920s, Colonel C. H. Greenleaf, one of the owners of the Profile House, contributed funds to the AMC for the construction of a hut on Lafayette (on land that is now part of the White Mountain National Forest). Located at Eagle Lakes (mountain tarns on a knoll below the summit), the new hut was sited where the sturdy forest gives way to the lower vegetation of the alpine zone. A sphagnum bog at Eagle Lakes provides unusual botanical habitat and opportunities for nature observation.

Greenleaf Hut, as it was called, differed from the typical construction of the other AMC huts in the Presidentials. It was a wood-frame structure rather than stone, making it considerably less damp. Immediately it became a popular way station for circuit hikes of

Colonel C.H. Greenleaf, one of the owners of the Profile House, gave the money to build Greenleaf Hut. Photo courtesy Appalachian Mountain Club/Paul Mozell.

Lafayette or for traverses from Lafayette to Garfield, where the Galehead Hut was later erected.

Winter recreation consisted mostly of snowshoe hikes until the downhill skiing craze hit in the 1930s. The Taft Trail on Cannon Mountain attracted the best ski racers in the country. Alexander Bright, 1936 Olympic team member and Boston businessman, brought an innovative European form of uphill transportation to Cannon's ski slopes: The nation's first aerial tramway opened at Cannon in 1938, sanctioned by the New Hampshire legislature, owner of Franconia Notch.

In 1980, a second tram replaced the well-worn original, a lift that had carried nearly 7 million passengers, both summer and winter, to the top of the ridge on the west side of the notch overlooking Echo Lake. The state still operates this ski area, a no-frills, steep-slopes kind of place that takes its skiing seriously. The state shows its conscience in balancing many interests for the notch, walking a thin tightrope between accommodating increasing numbers of visitors and trying to limit commercialization of the area's natural assets.

The centerpiece of the notch, the Old Man, has demanded a fair share of the state's attention, too. Early in the twentieth century, observers began to express concern for the future stability of Franconia's landmark. The Reverend Guy Roberts, who is honored by a plaque at the base viewing station, was the first to warn of slippage in the five ledges that make up the signature profile. The 1,200-foot-high cliff was first descended by ropes (the only way to reach the Old Man was from above) and the profile inspected about 1916. Recognizing that any alteration in the position of the ledges might mean the Old Man would eventually be lost, the state authorized major repairs in the 1920s. Steel cables, turnbuckles, and rods were installed to secure the five separate granite ledges in place, and cracks were filled with epoxy to prevent the expansion of ice that could force them farther apart.

More shoring up was necessary in the 1950s. On a regular basis thereafter, state highway crews have peformed whatever work is necessary to hold fast the profile. One member of those crews from the 1960s, Niels F. Nielsen, received the honorary title of official caretaker of the profile in 1987. When Nielsen retired in 1991, his son

David took over his father's duties, which in recent years have included application of a sealant to the rocks to prevent erosion from acid rain, the biggest present threat to the continuing preservation of the features of the state's symbol. The Old Man became the official emblem of New Hampshire in 1945, and is now used on everything from highway signs and tokens to commemorative liquor bottles.

Franconia Notch Parkway

Meanwhile a controversy—the likes of which the notch had not seen since the battles that led to the creation of the Franconia Notch State Park—erupted over the legislature's approval in 1959 for a north-south interstate highway that would run from the Massachusetts border all the way through the notch. It took until 1966 for the state to propose a specific route alignment for the northern segment, and then the pitched battle began. Environmental groups, led by the Appalachian Mountain Club, were outraged that an interstate highway would penetrate this natural scenic area, arguing that it would irreparably damage a unique environment and that a new highway simply was not needed in the face of the important historic and natural character of the notch.

Furthermore, there were fears that the blasting required to widen the roadbed might substantially alter the arrangement of rocks that made up the Old Man of the Mountain. In 1970, U.S. Secretary of Transportation (and former Massachusetts governor) John Volpe postponed indefinitely any intrusion of Interstate 93 through the notch, though construction continued on sections both north and south of it.

Then followed seven more years of wrangling, during which the White Mountain Environment Committee (WMEC)—a coalition of the AMC, SPNHF, and others—got a federal injunction to stop the construction. A compromise was finally reached. Congress passed a special amendment to the legislation that regulated the federal interstate system. In place of a full-fledged four-lane divided highway through Franconia Notch, eight miles of parkway could be substituted. Planning and designing this new solution took another six years, during which time the WMEC remained intimately involved.

Controversy surrounded the state's plan to extend the interstate highway through Franconia Notch in the 1960s. Kurt Stier.

When the Franconia Notch Parkway opened officially in 1988, it was one of only two substandard stretches in the entire federal highway system of 42,000 miles. But it was large enough to handle the traffic volume, and amenities abounded. The Flume got a new visitor's center; the Old Man got a new parking area; Lafayette Place was redesigned with a campground, a parking lot for hikers, and a ten-mile bike path. The road widening forced the relocation of several trailheads, but these are well marked, too.

For all its diversity, Franconia Notch's supreme feature is still the mountains. Leaving behind the controversy, the tourism, the changes that time has wrought, one can ascend Lafayette's long sides to gain a timeless freedom and a long view above it all.

Suggestions for Visitors

Franconia Notch and the eight-mile stretch of roadway between the Franconia and Kinsman ranges is part of a 6,441-acre state park that extends from North Woodstock, New Hampshire, to the town of Franconia itself. The White Mountain National Forest begins at the higher altitudes of the Lafayette Ridge. It is one of the prime summer tourist destinations in the state, by some estimates receiving 50 percent of the total attendance in all state parks. In winter, the prevalent storms that gather around the mountains and blow down through the notch make it somewhat less hospitable, but Cannon Mountain, one of two state-owned ski areas, continues to attract skiers, and the Lafayette Ridge its share of winter climbers.

As testimony to the importance of Cannon in the development of alpine skiing in New England, it is now home to the New England Ski Museum, founded in the 1970s. Its collections cover the origins of the sport, its earliest advocates, skiers, and entrepreneurs; the 10th Mountain Division of World War II; and equipment, photographs, films, posters, and books. This newly relocated museum is becoming a comprehensive study resource and a complementary feature of the other so-called "attractions" in the notch.

Within the park, the two main attractions are the Old Man of the Mountain, towering 1,500 feet above the roadway, and the Flume, a deep gorge cut during the Ice Age. At the southern end of the notch, the Flume offers another scenic attraction popular with sightseers in the past century as well as now. The Flume, a word meaning a narrow gorge, is an unusual formation of vertical rock walls, 10 to 20 feet apart, rising about 60 to 70 feet above the riverbed that runs through this passage for approximately 700 feet. Until a great flood washed it away, a large boulder was wedged high between these clifffs. Entrepreneurs built boardwalks and charged admission to this attraction in the nineteenth century; today the state has taken over and provides guided tours, bus service, a snack bar, and souvenir stands. The Pool, a deep glacial basin a half-mile from the Flume, is said to have been discovered by a ninety-three-year-old-woman, "Aunt Jess" Guernsey, while fishing the streams of Franconia Notch.

The house where Robert Frost lived, on the Easton road in Franconia, was purchased by a public trust for the town of Franconia in 1976. Now restored as a memorial to him, it offers summer concerts, lectures, and readings, as well as tours of the house and the barn where Frost kept a cow and a horse.

For hikers, the state maintains parking lots on both sides of the limited-access notch road at Lafayette Place, where there is also a campground. From there, trails start up Lafayette to the east and to Lonesome Lake and the Kinsmans to the west.

Eagle Cliff juts out from the western flank of Mount Lafayette, high above the road. This was a well-publicized attraction in the notch in the last century when a golden eagle's nest was located there. At the top of this inaccessible crag is the only virgin forest left in Franconia Notch, a small stand of spruce and fir. Looking up toward the mountain, one can see a rock slab known as Shining Rock. Underground springs wash the face of the rock with water, making its shiny surface reflect the light.

In one of the west-facing ravines of the mountain, when heavy winter snows have lingered into the spring, the snow sometimes collects in gullies in a crosslike formation. This phenomenon delighted tourists of an earlier era, who cited the existence of the Lafayette snow cross as indisputable proof of the presence of a transcendent God near at hand in the mountains. It mimicked an earlier discovery of a snow cross on the Mount of the Holy Cross in Colorado, familiar to easterners through the widely acclaimed photographs of William H. Jackson.

The snow cross of Lafayette, enhanced for better effect in this early-twentieth-century postcard, symbolized the sublime presence of the Almighty to the faithful. Author's collection/Kurt Stier.

A climb that takes in the famous knife-edge of Lafayette and the historic routes of the last century begins and ends at the Lafayette Place parking area, near where the famous Profile House once stood. The Falling Waters Trail ascends past beautiful cascades and over some steep stretches, then emerges on the ridge at the summit of Little Haystack. From there, across the ridgeline over Lincoln to Lafayette, one is above treeline in the realm of the rare plants of the arctic zone and the strange geological formations of the glaciers. Views in all directions are superb. There will be no summit caretakers or ranger-naturalists, but the need to educate hikers about the fragility of the environment they are crossing is no less real. Walk only on the rocks; do not disturb any plants. Descend via the Old Bridle Path, past the Greenleaf Hut and Eagle Lakes, and along a spur of the mountain back to the original starting point.

For reservations in the AMC huts—Greenleaf, Galehead, or Lonesome Lake—write or call AMC Reservations, Pinkham Notch Visitor Center, Gorham, NH 03581; 800-262-4455. The huts fill up fast on weekends and during peak weeks in the summer and fall, so it is best to reserve well in advance.

Chocorua

Chocorua's treeless granite pyramid is perhaps New England's most recognizable mountain. Reflected in the lake to its south, Chocorua is so picturesque that many claim it is the most-photographed mountain in America. The mountain resonates with a rich melodramatic legend—the Indian Chocorua jumping to his death from the summit cliffs as he cursed the white man and his encroaching civilization. Around its base lie peaceful farm communities and the unpretentious summer homes of many of the mountain's most loyal supporters. Today, as for decades, Chocorua's rocky sides challenge thousands of summer hikers and campers, and reward them with beautiful views over the varied lake and mountain scenery below.

Geography and History

At 3,475 feet, Chocorua stands far beneath it northern neighbors, Mount Washington and the Presidentials. It is not even the highest in its own range of the Sandwich Mountains, where it anchors the eastern end of a range running westward over Mount Paugus, Flat Mountain, Wonalancet, Passaconaway, Whiteface, and Tripyramid to Sandwich Mountain. To the south rises the circular mass of the Ossipee Mountains, and beyond shines the twenty-two-mile-long glacial lake, Winnipesaukee. Since the land around the base of

Some say Chocorua is the most photographed mountain in America. Its image, reflected in the still waters of the lake of the same name, adorns countless calendars and postcards. Kurt Stier.

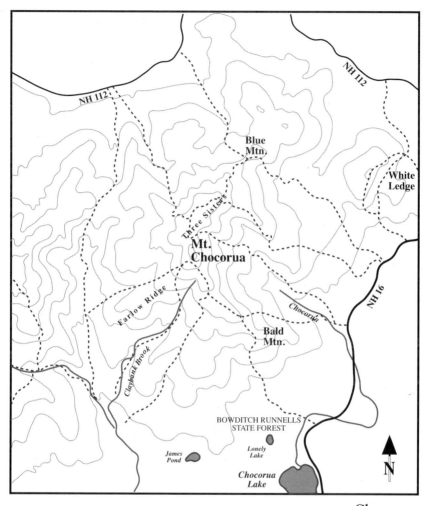

Chocorua

Chocorua is relatively low, the elevation gain for hikers is more than one might expect, and makes the climb seem more strenuous than many taller peaks.

Chocorua is in the township of Albany, settled in 1766. An old Indian trail probably led along its eastern side; this evolved into the main route to the White Mountains from the south. Thousands of travelers who visited that region as summer tourists all passed and admired the mountain. Many still do. Lake Chocorua, in the town of Tamworth and just south of the mountain, has a history entwined with that of the mountain itself. A summer colony here developed hiking trails on the mountain and worked to assure its ultimate protection as part of the White Mountain National Forest.

Historical references to the name of the peak indicate that several variations were in common usage. Jeremy Belknap, in his 1784 *Journal of a Tour to the White Mountains,* referred to the peak as Corua, perhaps the first printed association of the Indian chief's name with the mountain. By 1791, for a map in his *History of New Hampshire,* Belknap clarified the name to read Chocorua, the only mountain he identified in the Sandwich Range. Several early-nineteenth-century landscape painters hybridized the Indian name with that of the town farther north, Conway, in the variant Corway Peak. And on the railroad map used by Thoreau on his 1858 trip to the White Mountains, this mountain is clearly identified as Conway Peak.

Native Americans

Many of the other place names in this region are Native American words too, most often remembering leaders who played important roles during the century of volatile Indian-white relations here. First with equanimity and later with hostility, the Abenaki peoples of the Chocorua area faced the encroachment of white settlement beginning in the mid-1600s and ultimately yielded after 1725.

Passaconaway, Kancamagus, Wonalancet, and Paugus were successive leaders of the Penacook tribe. Passaconaway, whose name meant "child of the bear," ruled for many years. In 1660, reputedly at the age of 100, he abdicated, making a dramatic farewell speech to his devoted followers at the Pawtucket Falls of the Merrimack River. Although he had excelled in battles with Indian enemies, Passaconaway had been converted to Christianity by the apostle John Eliot, and so he urged his followers to accept the white settlers peacefully.

That policy was continued under his son, Wonalancet, who refused to lead his people into the conflict known as King Philip's War (1675–76), believing instead that a peaceful coexistence was possible. When the war ended in a failure to drive the English out,

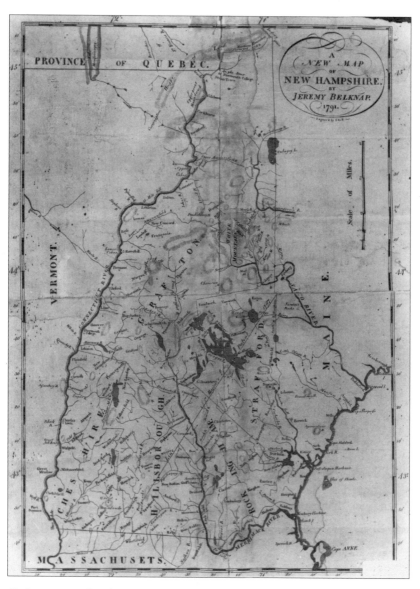

Only one named peak appears in the Sandwich Range on Jeremy Belknap's 1791 map of New Hampshire, the distinctive pyramidal Mount Chocorua (center, near junction of the map's folds). Photo courtesy New Hampshire Historical Society, Concord, NH.

the Indians of northern New England knew they, too, would eventually be overcome by the white settlers.

In 1685, Wonalancet resigned as chief and retreated to St. Francis, Quebec, leaving his son Kancamagus as tribal leader. Kancamagus, wise and respected, followed his father's example and counseled peace with the colonists. But after four years of neglect, insults, and persecution, Kancamagus could stand no more. When he learned the English had recruited the Mohawks to kill New Hampshire Indians, whether friend or foe, he decided the time to strike back had finally come. In 1689, Kancamagus led a surprise attack on Major Waldron's garrison in Dover, killing fifty-two people. Conflict between Indians and whites raged on into the eighteenth century.

One of the most famous battles in the north country region was the attack by Captain John Lovewell against a Pequawket (Pigwacket) encampment near the present town of Fryeburg, Maine, in 1725. Without roads or maps to guide him, Lovewell followed a stream northward from Ossipee Pond, past a mountain he called Pigwacket Hill (probably Chocorua), then eastward along the Saco River. His attack came by surprise. Casualties on both sides were heavy and included both Captain Lovewell and Paugus, father of Chocorua. The bloody battle afterward became known as the Pigwacket Fight, or the battle of Lovewell's Pond. After this defeat, the remaining Indians withdrew from New England altogether and went to live in Canada.

The Legend of Chocorua

The heroism and tragedy of these Indian encounters lingered in the region, striking a chord with the literary and artistically minded and giving rise to many variations of the "Legend of Chocorua." A youthful Henry Wadsworth Longfellow attended a memorial celebration of Lovewell's battle in Fryeburg, Maine, and composed "The Battle of Lovewell's Pond" while still a teenager. He published three more poems with Indian subjects by 1825, foreshadowing the later success of his narrative poem "Hiawatha."

Longfellow published "Jeckoyva" while still a student at Bowdoin. Considered the first version of the Chocorua legend to appear in print, the poem concerned a lost Penacook hunter. An author's explanatory note prefaced the poem: "The Indian chief, Jeckoyva, as tradition says, perished alone on the mountain which now bears his name. Night overtook him whilst hunting among the cliffs, and he was not heard of till after a long time, when his half-decayed corpse was found at the foot of a high rock, over which he must have fallen. Mount Jeckoyva is in the White Hills." Longfellow's portrayal was sympathetic:

Where was the warrior's foot when night
Veiled in thick cloud the mountain height?
None heard the loud and sudden crash—
None saw the fallen warrior dash
Down the bare rock so high and white!
But he that drooped not in the chase
Made on the hills his burial place.

When the young painter Thomas Cole ventured into the White Mountains and climbed Chocorua on October 3, 1828, he heard a slightly different version of the story. Cole's diary relates a more embellished tale that not only blames white settlers for Chocorua's death, but explains the devastation of a barren landscape as the direct result of the dying Indian's curse on the land's fertility.

Cole wrote: "We set out to climb the Chocorua Peak.... On the path through the wood, we came to many windfalls...where every tree is laid prostrate. We came out at length, to a lonely and deserted clearing, just at the foot of the mountain. The cause of this abandonment is, they say, the poisonous effects of the water upon the cattle; the result, according to tradition, of the curse of Chocorua, an Indian, from whom the peak, upon which he was killed by the whites, takes its name."

Like Longfellow, Cole found the story an appropriately romantic subject for artistic expression, and the mountain itself a dramatic symbol of wilderness. The next winter in his New York studio, Cole painted *The Death of Chocorua* from pencil sketches he had made during his trip.

A young Boston writer named Lydia Maria Child heard about the Chocorua story and added her own fictionalized touches to enhance its appeal to a popular audience. Child's "Chocorua's Curse," illustrated with a steel engraving of Cole's painting as its frontispiece,

An engraving of Thomas Cole's famous painting, The Death of Chocorua, *illustrated Lydia Maria Child's enduring version of the Chocorua legend.* Photo courtesy Dartmouth College Library, Hanover, NH.

appeared in the 1830 issue of *The Token*, an annual literary magazine published in Boston. Child was a masterful storyteller and left nothing to the imagination of her readers. She added many new elements to the traditional tale, including the white settler Cornelius Campbell and his family, the fox poison that killed the Indian's son, and the language of Chocorua's curse.

In Child's story, the Indians and the lone white settler's family coexisted peacefully. Chocorua's son often played with the Campbell children. During one of these visits, the curious young Indian mistakenly drank some poison that had been left out for a marauding fox. The stricken father refused to believe the death was accidental. In his grief and fury, Chocorua massacred Campbell's wife and children and set fire to their house. When Campbell returned home from the fields that evening, he went wild with rage. He rallied several men and they began the fatal pursuit of Chocorua, chasing him up the mountain and closing in on him at an isolated precipice near the top. As Campbell fired, Chocorua hurled himself off the cliff, uttering a bitter curse:

A curse upon ye, white man! May the Great Spirit curse ye when he speaks in the clouds, and his words are fire! Chocorua had a son, and ye killed him while the sky looked bright! Lightning blast your crops! Winds and fire destroy your dwellings! The Evil Spirit breathe death upon your cattle! Your graves lie in the warpath of the Indian! Panthers howl and wolves fatten upon your bones! Chocorua goes to the Great Spirit—but his curse stays with the white men!

Child created such an unforgettable tale that her version replaced most of the earlier accounts, eclipsing what Cole or Longfellow had heard and recorded. The 1870s guidebook writer Moses Sweetser claimed to have heard the Chocorua story from an old inhabitant of Tamworth, and through his published accounts, legions of summer tourists took what was actually Lydia Maria Child's tale to be ancient tradition. Adding truth to the tale, cattle did not prosper in the town of Albany during the early years of settlement.

The Chocorua story entered the realm of colorful local lore, and there it has persisted, lending a special flavor to the mountain that no other peak in New England can boast, despite some very obviously improbable details. In fact, Marjory Gane Harkness, writing in *The Tamworth Narrative* in 1958, urged her readers "not to listen to the voice of reason which reminds us that an Indian, so much more a creature of the woods than they, could hardly be chased to a mountaintop by white men." And when a Dartmouth professor announced that excessive amounts of muriate of lime in the ground water were responsible for the cattle deaths, it did little to diminish the spine-tingling power of a near-perfect frontier tale.

Art and Artists

The widespread familiarity with the legend of Chocorua added drama and mystery to a region that was already becoming a mecca for artists, writers, and adventurous tourists. The wild scenery, even as it changed from trackless forest to well-settled agricultural villages, expressed deeply held ideals in America. The Enlightenment concepts of the Sublime and the Beautiful invested landscapes with significant philosphical attributes. Mountains were perfect places from which to draw moral encouragement and spiritual uplift.

Sublime, as defined by the great British philosopher Edmund Burke in 1756, meant something terrible and emotionally arousing:

> Whatever is fitten in any sort to excite the ideas of pain and danger, that is to say, whatever is in any sort terrible, or is conversant about terrible objects, or operates in a manner analogous to terror, is a source of the sublime; that is, it is productive of the strongest emotion which the mind is capable of feeling.

For artists in pre–Civil War America, wild mountain scenery was the ultimate expression of the Sublime. Twisted and gnarled trees, crags and cliffs, landslides, swirling clouds and the attendant thunder and lightning, were all visual elements of the Sublime and part of the standard repertoire of artistic expression.

King's best seller *The White Hills* echoed aspects of the Sublime in describing Chocorua in 1860: "How rich and sonorous that word Chocorua is!...Does not its rhythm suggest the wilderness and loneliness of the great hills? To our ears it always brings with it the sigh of the winds through mountain pines....It is everything a mountain should be. It bears the name of an Indian chief. It is invested with traditional and poetic interest. In form it is massive and symmetrical. The forests of its lower slopes are crowned with rock that is sculptured into a peak with lines full of haughty energy, in whose gorges huge shadows are entrapped, and whose cliffs blaze with morning gold."

The poet John Greenleaf Whittier added a different kind of literary luster to the Chocorua area when, at the zenith of his celebrity and success, he came to the Bearcamp River House in West Ossipee. From 1867 until the end of his life, Whittier spent his summers in Ossipee. Here, with the peak of Chocorua dominating the view, he composed part of the poem "Among the Hills," a companion piece to "Snow-bound," perhaps his most famous composition.

To Whittier, Chocorua was the most beautiful of the New Hampshire mountains. The poet Lucy Larcom was a special friend of Whittier's, and with her he compiled "Songs of Three Centuries" in 1875. Though he himself did no climbing, he entertained many friends and relatives who did, and enjoyed the tales of their adventures around the fireside in the evenings. One of his more playful poems describes "How They Climbed Chocorua:"

> One sharp tall peak above them all
> Clear into sunlight sprang,
> I saw the river of my dreams,
> The mountain that I sang.
>
> O full long shall they remember
> That wild nightfall of September,
> When aweary of their tramp
> They set up their canvas camp
> In the hemlocks of Chocorua!
>
> There the mountain winds were howling,
> There the mountain bears were prowling!
> And through rain showers falling drizzly
> Glared upon them, grim and grisly,
> The ghost of old Chocorua!

Arts and Artists

The first real art colony in America developed around 1850 in the area just north of Chocorua, the broad intervale of the Saco River where long views of Mount Washington and the symbolic peak of Chocorua offered endless possibilities for subject matter. It has been estimated that about forty artists were coming to the North Conway region in the 1850s, their white umbrellas dotting the landscape as they sketched by day, and their congenial company filling the local inns at night. Most of the important members of the Hudson River school visited the White Mountains—John F. Kensett, Jasper Cropsey, Asher B. Durand, and Albert Bierstadt. Their preference was for the open fields, small villages, and the grand view of the towering mountains in the distance. If they climbed the higher peaks, it was more for inspiration than to find new subject matter.

The Boston painter Benjamin Champney (1817–1907), was one of the first to visit here, arriving in 1850. He returned for several summers and in 1853 bought a home in North Conway, where, until the end of the century, he formed the nucleus of a thriving art community. A typical painting was his *Mount Chocorua, New Hampshire*. The distant view showed few traces of the Sublime aesthetic which so intrigued Thomas Cole—no blasted trees, swirling clouds, or jagged cliffs. Instead, Champney celebrated the beautiful form of the symmetrical peak soaring above a well-ordered foreground of river and fields. This mode of representation, though it was destined to lose widespread national appeal by the end of the 1860s, continued to bring Champney attention from the many tourists in the mountains.

Other artists associated themelves with the larger hotels, spending summers painting for the amusement of guests and selling dozens of pictures to the middle-class summer trade. Their work represented the basically reactionary ideals of the White Mountain school, idealizing a version of country life as contrived as it was simplistic. After 1865, photographers produced thousands of inexpensive stereo views as mementos of a summer's vacation, and these often

Benjamin Champney, who founded a long-lived artist's colony in North Conway, depicted a benign and regal peak in his 1858 painting, Mount Chocorua, New Hampshire. *Photo courtesy Museum of Fine Arts, Boston, MA.*

replaced paintings as remembrances of a pleasant summer. Inevitable changes in artistic preference changed styles toward more intimate subjects and heightened atmospheric effects, where grand mountain vistas were no longer requisite elements of the composition.

The legacy of the White Mountain school, besides hundreds of paintings of the mountains, may be found today in place names that the artists left behind. Champney Falls, on Champney Brook in Albany, was named for Benjamin Champney. In Crawford Notch, the high railroad bridge known as the Frankenstein Trestle recalls not Shelley's incautious doctor but the painter Godfrey N. Frankenstein. Shapleigh Falls and Church Pond are two other sites invested with the names of former habitues who found them favorite subjects for the pencil and brush, and Artists Falls in North Conway commemorates them all.

Mountain Development

On Chocorua itself, hiking was concentrated on a few footpaths. Most of these ascended the south and east sides of the mountain. Joshua Piper, an Albany stage driver, cut the Piper Trail from his property up the eastern slope of the mountain and acted as guide for parties ascending that route.

In 1887, Jim Liberty (1835–1916) of Tamworth improved an old path on the southwestern side of the mountain that became known as the Liberty Trail. An old logging camp partway up this route was turned into the Halfway House where visitors could stable their horses and walk the remaining distance to the peak. Just below the summit cone, Jim Liberty also built a simple stone foundation anchoring a tentlike canvas roof. This arrangement for accommodating overnight guests didn't last long in the high winds of the mountaintop, so Liberty simply pitched a couple of tents inside the foundation and offered slightly less commodious quarters. He himself was considered something of a character, always drinking green tea and puffing on a pipe. For entertainment, he often sang French Canadian songs and accompanied himself on the accordion.

David Knowles of Silver Lake and a partner, Newell Forrest, bought the Halfway House and the trail leading to it from Jim Liberty in 1891. Hoping to create their own profitable business patterned after the successful carriage road and summit house on Mount Washington, they applied to the state of New Hampshire for a charter in 1892. Work on the Chocorua Mountain Road began once they had their approval. Parts of it were blasted out of rock ledge to make a level pathway. The hotel component, the three-story Peak House, was sited high on the mountain just below the summit cone in the flat clearing where Jim Liberty's camp had stood. Oxen hauled up the building materials by sled in the winter. The furnished house even had an organ in the parlor, which Knowles, a talented musician, often played.

Besides a kitchen, dining room, and parlor, the Peak House had a special "bridal suite" on the first floor. Bedrooms occupied the second floor, and the third floor's accommodations were dormitory style, popular with groups of young campers who regularly climbed the mountain. Water came from a spring located not far away at the junction of the Liberty and Brook trails, where a fire warden's station also

Chocorua's Peak House, perched just below the summit, blew off the mountain in a fierce storm just after the close of its 1915 season. Photo courtesy Cook Memorial Library, Tamworth, N.H./Kurt Stier.

stood. The remains of the warden's steel lookout tower that once stood on the mountain are still visible today.

One of the most distinctive features of the Peak House was the flights of narrow wooden stairs that Knowles constructed across the summit rocks for the convenience of his guests. The stairs, which had iron handrails, ran along the traverse up the last steep stretch of trail to the summit, presumably because the ledge rocks became very slippery when wet. Several reports suggest that, as the years passed, the footing seemed safer on the rocks than on the wooden steps, and they were finally removed by the end of the 1920s. Remnants of these iron railings, drilled into holes in the rocks, are still in place.

In 1896, Knowles bought out his partner's interest and ran the hotel during the summer with his wife. Life was pleasant on the mountain. A telephone line connected the hotel with the world below so that the horse, named Gypsy, could be sent down the mountain alone to pick up a called-in grocery order at the nearby store in Silver Lake. Blueberries were gathered from the nearby ledges where they thrived, and the hotel became famous for Mrs. Knowles's hot blueberry pie. Wild low-bush blueberries still cover the open rocky ledges near the summit.

The Knowles House, as it came to be called, also sold postcards and Indian souvenirs, baskets and other trinkets made by descendants of the peoples that once roamed free in the area. Up until the 1950s, St. Francis Indians returned every summer to their ancestral homeland on the intervale in North Conway, where they sold their handcrafted items, and Knowles probably obtained his stock of items directly from them.

Hurricane-force winds completely destroyed the Peak House on September 26, 1915, despite the chains that held it to the mountain. By then, it was closed for the season, and its loss was first reported by residents who noticed something missing from the mountain as they looked up at it from below. It had literally blown away, fortunately at a time when it was unoccupied. Rubble from the building itself, along with remnants of the wooden beds and tables, was later found strewn all over the mountainside.

But that was not the end of a building for hikers and campers on the summit of Chocorua. Though there was nothing left of

The Jim Liberty Cabin, constructed on the site of the Halfway House, has evolved through more than a century of use. Kurt Stier

Knowles's Peak House, the stone shelter that Jim Liberty had built was still standing, having been pressed into service as a stable during the Peak House years. In 1924, the Chocorua Mountain Club built a new structure on top of the old Jim Liberty cabin foundation, renaming it the Jim Liberty Shelter. Once again, high winds blew the roof off, this time in 1932. The entire structure was replaced by a more substantial building called the Jim Liberty Cabin in 1934.

The Mountain and the Lake

During the years, roughly 1891 to 1915, that Knowles was attracting tourists and turning a profit from his road and mountaintop hostelry, many of the local people, augmented by an influx of summer cottagers, staked their own claim to the mountain. After the Liberty Trail became a toll road, locals resented having to pay to climb their mountain. They cut the Brook Trail to avoid paying the charge.

The Wonalancet Outdoor Club, formed in 1898, devoted itself to opening up and maintaining more woodland paths and trails throughout the Sandwich Range. Their efforts at trail blazing and maintenance were so zealous that a reactionary movement set in, protesting the myriad bright blazes, cleared swaths, and fancy signs. In 1908, this splinter protest group organized as the Chocorua Mountain Club.

Leadership of these clubs was drawn largely from a sociable community of summer cottagers that gathered around Chocorua in the last two decades of the nineteenth century, heavily favoring professors and intellectuals connected with Harvard University and other East Coast institutions. Their motives were simple, and they stood in the vanguard of the trend toward the sale of old New Hampshire farmsteads for summer homes. As William James related to a friend:

> New England farms are now dirt cheap—the natives going west, the Irish coming in and making a better living than the Yankees could. Here were seventy-five acres of land, two thirds of it oak and pine timber, one third hay, a splendid spring of water, fair little house and large barn, close to a beautiful lake and under a mountain 3,500 feet high, four and a half hours from Boston, for 900 dollars!

Such writers as Horace Scudder, editor of the *Atlantic Monthly*; William James; Frank Bolles, secretary of Harvard University; and even President Grover Cleveland settled themselves for the summer on a network of country roads in Tamworth and Albany. Many congregated on the shores of, or overlooking, Lake Chocorua. In Tamworth, every child was "told how the Indians thought that the Great Spirit who lived on the mountaintop wished silence on the lake below, and that a word spoken aloud in a canoe would cause it to sink immediately."

Frank Bolles would write four books (published by Houghton Mifflin) about this place he loved best. Two of these, *At the North of Bearcamp Water* and *Chocorua's Tenants*, were celebrations of the rich natural environment of Chocorua. His prose and poetry celebrated, through his personal experience, the restorative and rejuvenating powers of country life and nature observation. Physical challenge, pioneer hardships, and appreciation of the Sublime were not within Bolles's repertoire. Instead, he tended toward the rhapsodic and picturesque—a harmonious summer idyll.

The original owners of the Tamworth and Albany farms bought up by the summer people tolerated with good humor the new residents and their determined attempts to live the rustic, simple life, perhaps because they were able to succeed in keeping out twentieth-century progress better than the old farmers themselves. The Bowditch and Runnells families cooperated in creating the Bowditch-Runnells State Forest to preserve from clearcutting forest lands opposite Chocorua along the highway.

The Lake Chocorua Association accomplished something even more impressive—getting all shore front property owners to agree that no one should construct any building that would be visible from the water, and that no motorboats ever be allowed on the lake's pristine waters. It is these two principles that create the serenity of lake vistas and the air of quiet calm which pervades the public swimming area.

Along the shores of Lake Chocorua are the well-built yet unobstrusive camps of the Boston intellectuals who favored this spot as a summer retreat around the turn of the century. Kurt Stier.

The Chocorua group celebrated all of nature, not just mountains, showing a decided preference for the picturesque viewpoint over the Sublime. Julius Ward, an 1890s White Mountain guidebook writer, declared that Chocorua "appeals to the feeling for the graceful and the beautiful." A well-known saying about Chocorua, that "it may not be as big as the Matterhorn but the principle is the same," is credited to Samuel McChord Crothers, a Unitarian minister from Cambridge. Rev. Edward Cummings, from Boston's South Church, and his son e.e. cummings were part of the group, too.

One of the second generation summer regulars, LeGrand Cannon, Jr., produced a historical novel about this area, set in the fictional town of Kettleford, but with the unmistakable pyramid of Chocorua watching over his pioneer homestead. *Look to the Mountain* made the best-seller list in the 1940s and is still in print.

John Albee, another writer, published a long narrative poem called "Lake Chocorua" in 1910. Its first stanza captures perfectly the essence of this bucolic period:

> Weary of ocean's restless tides,
> I climbed Chocorua's rugged sides
> Where all is fixed and motionless,
> And solemn calm the senses bless
> There on his lofty pyramid
> Heaven is near and earth more hid;
> There slowly comes the summer night,
> And shine the stars with brighter light;
> While on Chocorua Lake below
> As in another sky they glow.

Recreation

The trails on Chocorua are well marked and maintained. Since the division of the Wonalancet Outdoor Club and the birth of the Chocorua Mountain Club in 1908, both groups have taken responsibility for the clearing and upkeep of trails, and have participated actively in the New England Trail Conference, a consortium of hiking groups. The White Mountain National Forest (WMNF) after

1911 added the north slope of Chocorua and attendant peaks to the lands under federal jurisdiction. Today, WMNF shares responsibility for trail maintenance, keeps up the two shelters (Jim Liberty and Penacook Camp), and handles search-and-rescue efforts.

Chocorua remains a heavily climbed mountain, especially during the summer months when the many boys' and girls' camps throughout the Lakes region regularly organize day-climbs for their members. One ranger in the 1960s reported that he never patrolled the mountain during the day on weekends, saving his strength for after dark when he would invariably be called to go out and hunt for some straggler or unaccounted-for member of a church or camp hiking group.

Suggestions for Visitors

Route 16, the main highway from the south to the White Mountains and the Presidentials, is the best route for views of Chocorua and access to hiking there. The road swings along the shore of Lake Chocorua, where a public bathing beach is almost always busy during warm weather. From here, Fowler's Mill Road heads west to the trailheads of the Brook Trail and Liberty Trail, the favored approaches to the south side of the mountain and a nice combination for a loop hike.

The most heavily used trail on the east side of the mountain starts at the side of Route 16, where a parking fee at Piper Trail Cabins is charged. The Piper Trail covers some steep terrain just below the shoulder, where it converges with other trails for the last half-mile stretch over exposed ledge to the summit plateau.

On the north side of Chocorua, the Champney Falls Trail falls into the heavily used category also, but is recommended nevertheless. It is reached via the Kancamagus Highway, a relatively new and extraordinarily scenic route along old logging roads that was opened for traffic when it was still unpaved in 1959. The Champney Falls Trail leaves the Kancamagus Highway three miles east of the Passaconaway Information Center.

Not far up the trail is a waterfall named after Benjamin Champney, the North Conway artist who was largely responsible for the popularity of this region among nineteenth-century painters. Sabbaday

Falls, a short distance farther along the highway, is even more spectacular and always crowded with tourists. Its name, a corruption of the words Sabbath day, derives from the popularity of this spot as a favorite destination for a carriage ride on a pleasant Sunday afternoon.

The latest incarnation of the Jim Liberty Cabin is just below the summit on the Liberty Trail. A second shelter is located in the woods below the summit just off the Piper Trail, a lean-to called Penacook Camp, from where the lights of the Route 16 valley seem to twinkle all night long. Because Chocorua is so popular, the White Mountain National Forest has declared most of it a Restricted Use Area. No fires or camping are permitted within these zones, so the shelters are often full during busy weekends.

Besides waterfalls and the blueberries for which Chocorua is justly famous, there is a rare wild rhododendron colony found on Mount Chocorua. Growing at the northern limit of its range, the rosebay rhododendron resembles the garden variety, with pale pink flowers that bloom in July.

Washington

M ount Washington, the "Crown of New England," presides majestically over a ridge of nine barren peaks on the treeless heights of New Hampshire's Presidential Range. It is by far the best-known mountain in the Northeast. At 6,288 feet, more than a mile above sea level, Washington's summit is also the highest point north of North Carolina's Great Smokies and east of the Black Hills of South Dakota. This mountain's celebrated status derives as much from its physical presence as it does from its long social and cultural history.

Mount Washington can lay claim to a long list of mountain firsts—the site of America's first cog railway; the first auto road up a mountain in the East; the only mountain to have a newspaper published on its summit; the highest wind speed ever recorded; and a daredevil skier named Toni Matt who in 1939 skied straight down the face of the famed Tuckerman Ravine headwall and into skiing history. The place Washington occupies in the mind is as preeminent as the myriad accomplishments that have taken place on its slopes.

None of the other mountain summits in this book is so full of contrasts. Today, in the service of thousands of tourists, recreational users, scientists, and commercial interests, the mountain encompasses an infrastructure of trails, huts, and shelters. Automobiles and railway cars each year bring a quarter of a million people to the summit in the summer with relative ease. The state operates a spacious new handicapped-accessible summit facility that leases space to the year-round weather observatory and contains a snack bar and gift shop.

With the tourists are the sweaty and determined hikers, most on day-hikes; others making the long traverse of the Presidential Range; and about 150 each year completing the entire 2,100 miles of the Appalachian Trail from Springer Mountain, Georgia, to Katahdin in Maine. Chunks of broken rock and fantastic frost formations surround gas and water tanks and a parking lot. In winter, skiers and climbers brave the often fierce conditions to test their limits against Washington's ever-present and potentially fatal challenges.

And all these users invest a part of themselves in this place—whether their accomplishment is announced in a "This car climbed Mount Washington" bumper sticker, written in a book, charted on a graph, or retold after hours on the trail—and in some small or great way, each can claim a victory and feel part of an elite fraternity.

John Frederick Kensett's The White Mountains—Mount Washington, *1869, captures the picturesque beauty of New England's highest peak from the hills of North Conway, a mecca for artists and tourists.* Photo courtesy Davis Museum and Cultural Center, Wellesley College, Wellesley, MA.

Geography, Geology, and Natural History

Mount Washington is the anchor of a north-running crescent of high, treeless peaks known as the Presidential Range. The thirteen miles along the crest comprise the largest alpine area in the Northeast, where the stunted trees give way to rock-bound vegetation receiving rain or snow nine out of every ten days, year-round. From the mountain's shoulders, rivers flow into the Gulf of Maine and to Long Island Sound. Valleys surround the mountain on all four sides and along these lowland routes run the famous Saco, Androscoggin, and Ammonoosuc rivers.

The rocks of Mount Washington once lay as mud and sand at the bottom of a long-departed inland sea. As ages passed, other layers were deposited until these materials were buried under seven miles of sediment. About 390 million years ago, the heat and pressure of the

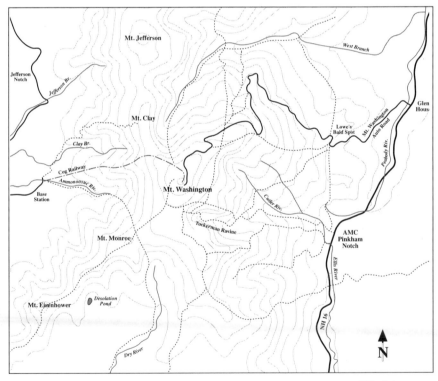

Washington

overburden softened the underlying rocks, folding these layers into what geologists call the Littleton Formation: gneiss, schist, and quartzite. In the deepest part of the formation, temperatures reached about 1,250° F and the rock became partially liquefied, allowing migration of contrasting minerals and resulting in pronounced banding. Folding took place on many different scales, from the intricate crumples visible in exposures of the rock to the great fold that is Mount Washington itself.

The lower section of the Littleton Formation is gneiss, in which inch-thick layers of dark mica and feldspar alternate with lighter bands of quartz and feldspar. The upper part of the Littleton Formation makes up the summits of Mount Washington and the other Presidential peaks and is composed of the sturdiest rocks the region has to offer: quartzite and mica schist. Here, as at Monadnock and Moosilauke, the mica schist contains crystals of sillimanite and garnet, but because the minerals occur in different proportions, the rock looks different from place to place.

After the great upheaval and folding of the earth's crust, the process of erosion began, and the rock of today's mountain was revealed. The ancient mountains might have been no higher than the modern ones. The miles-thick overburden washed away to a plain that had some hills on it—hills that are now the Presidential peaks. Later uplift raised the plain thousands of feet, forming plateaus, or fell-fields, named by botanists who explored these areas for rare plants in the early 1800s. Bigelow Lawn, the Alpine Garden, and Monticello Lawn on Mount Jefferson are the best-known examples.

In the series of great ice ages that lasted until about 12,000 to 15,000 years ago, huge glaciers reached from the polar icecap down across all of northern New England. These blankets of snow and ice could be more than a mile thick, and as they moved across the mountains, they carried thousands of tons of rocks with them. Glacial scratches, made by the transported rocks, are visible on exposed ledges within the ravines. Cut at cross-angles to the flow of the valley glaciers, they indicate that the valley glaciers preceded the ice sheet.

As the icecap gradually retreated, packs of snow and ice remained in the valleys. The valley glaciers that once flowed from the flanks of Mount Washington carved out huge chunks from the mountainside. Called cirques, or ravines, the largest of these is the wilderness area of the Great Gulf, a precipitous drop on the mountain's north side. On its eastern flank, two smaller bowl-shaped cirques take their names from early explorers of the mountains—Tuckerman and Huntington ravines. The glacier also gouged small basins on a plateau just south of Washington's summit; now the Lakes of the Clouds, these are the highest bodies of water in the state.

The glaciers left other clues to their forceful presence as well. Granite boulders were carried along by the flow, sometimes for miles from the bedrock of which they were once a part. These "erratics" are found in many locations on the mountain and throughout the Mount Washington valley. A truly monumental one ended up in the town of Madison as the Madison Boulder. Another glacial erratic, the Glen Boulder, perches on the lower cliffs of the eastern side of Washington, in clear view of travelers through Pinkham Notch and providing a familiar lookout point for hikers ascending that side of the mountain.

Talus covers the upper parts of the mountain, the result of the breaking-up action of frost since the Ice Age. When water penetrates joints in the bedrock and expands as it freezes, it splits rock from the intact ledge. The talus lies in curious patterns that vary depending upon the steepness of the slope. Where the slope is steep, gravity usually pulls talus into jumbled piles. On milder inclines the blocks are arranged with some subtlety. If the grade is less than 3 percent, the boulders often form net-shaped patterns, as on the gradual slope of the Alpine Garden area. When the grade is slightly steeper, between 3 percent and 7 percent, the rocks fall into striped patterns, and on even steeper ground, horseshoe-shaped lobes are formed, sometimes one above another in terraces.

The unusual plants that grow in the frigid climate above tree-line are one of the greatest attractions of the Presidential Range. Within the eight square miles of alpine zone, the vegetation never grows taller than a few feet. The plants and lichens that have a fragile hold here are species native to Labrador, hundreds of miles north. These are relic colonies, plants that followed glacial retreat from south to north, pioneering revegetation of the frigid land in the wake of the ice sheet. More than one hundred species of arctic plants grow

Potentilla robbinsiana, *the rarest alpine flower in the Presidentials, grows in only one spot, on the slope of Mount Monroe beyond the Lakes of the Clouds.* Photo courtesy Appalachian Mountain Club/Ron Paula.

here, including one found nowhere else in the world. *Potentilla robbinsiana*, a small yellow-flowering cinquefoil named for a fellow botanist by the man who first identified the tiny plant, is now carefully protected in a restricted area on Monroe Flats.

The cause of Washington's alpine zone is not completely understood, though a century and a half of study has helped to explain why the forest trees diminish, then fail altogether, near the mountaintop. The stunted woody growth near the treeline is called krummholz, gnarled brushy specimens of spruce and fir that look like bonsai—and are often as old. Snow cover keeps their profiles low; growth projecting over this protective layer is sheared off by wind and ice.

Cold does not necessarily cause treelessness—more-frigid climates than Mount Washington's are wooded. But several factors have been identified that contribute to this unique ecosystem. Wind places two pressures on plant growth: the passage of so much air has a desiccating, or dehydrating, effect, and strong gusts often snap off branches and foliage that are dry and brittle or ice covered.

Ice is the second big factor in retarding plant growth. The cold rocky mountaintops condense atmospheric moisture, resulting in fog and the deposit of frozen fog, called rime ice, on plants for much of the year. This in turn affects plants by obstructing the passage of oxygen and carbon dioxide through the pores in their foliage. Another factor may be the greater intensity of solar radiation at these altitudes as well.

Treeline, or the point at which natural growth is severely inhibited, occurs at about 4,800 feet on Washington's north-facing slopes and at 5,200 feet on grades that face south. Timberline is twice as high at the same latitude in western North America, suggesting that exposure and wind direction have at least as much influence as altitude.

Mammals are scarce on the upper reaches of Mount Washington. There is little food and little natural protection in the vegetation. Insect populations are much reduced from lower altitudes, but there is a surprising abundance of butterflies here in the summer season. The White Mountain fritillary, also called the Mount Washington butterfly, is a small brown species that blends so well with the rocks it is usually noticed only when in flight.

Because of the scarcity of insects, bird life is limited, too. Species found on Washington include the myrtle warbler, black-poll warbler, American goldfinch, red-breasted nuthatch, white-throated sparrow, sharp-shinned hawk, raven, and kestrel. Several kinds of thrush nest in the krummholz, too, but the only bird regularly present above treeline is the slate-colored junco, nicknamed "snowbird."

Edward Howe Forbush, one of the best-known ornithologists of the early twentieth century, described Mount Washington's natural environment in his landmark study, *Birds of Massachusetts and Other New England States*, published in 1929. Besides his listing of birds, many of which he identified by their calls, he described the natural environment:

On the 5th of August, 1926, I climbed, with a party of camp boys, up the rugged Tuckerman Ravine trail from Pinkham Notch to the top of Mt. Washington. On the way up the trail, we heard at frequent intervals the ecstatic song of the Winter Wren, the silver notes of the Hermit Thrush, the lisping calls of Golden-crowned Kinglets, and the songs of various forest-loving warblers, among which we distinguished the Myrtle, Magnolia and Black-throated Blue Warbler....About Hermit Lake, we were greeted by several small groups of Slate-colored Juncoes, busily engaged in searching for food among the dense evergreens....

Just below the rocky headwall of Tuckerman's, we came to the snowfields, at that late date still covering several acres....Last year's grasses lay brown and dead; a few feet away the alder catkins and pussy willows were just coming into blossom and violets were nodding in the cold wind; beyond these we found the yellow mountain avens and the tall white bog orchid, *Habenaria dilatata*, in bloom, and a little farther still, great showy sprays of mountain goldenrod waved in the breeze or bowed beneath the dainty weight of a silver and brown mountain fritillary butterfly.

Besides the birds, the blooming flowers of Washington are justifiably famous, attracting wildflower lovers as if on a pilgrimage early in June every year. Carpets of lapland rosebay, diapensia, alpine azalea, and moss campion bring bright color to the Alpine Garden, along with dozens of other species (including sedges and lichens) that add touches of color and interest to the mountain's gray rocks.

The beauties of spring on Washington contrast sharply with the long, frigid winter. Mount Washington is often said to have the worst weather in the world, and conditions can turn life threatening even on beautiful summer days. The high altitude, atmospheric disturbances from the Great Lakes colliding with moisture from the Gulf of Mexico, and the energy of coastal storms all combine to produce Washington's dramatic weather.

Because of its extreme conditions, Washington's summit has attracted weather observers since the mid-1870s. Since 1932, there has been a permanent weather station there, the Mount Washington Observatory. An average of more than 99 inches of moisture, mostly snow, falls each year, with one spectacular accumulation of ninety-eight inches of snow during a single three-day storm in 1969. The average year-round temperature is 27° F, with a daily high averaging 15° F in winter and 52° F in summer. The record low temperature is –46° F. The wind is relentless, averaging 40 MPH for much of the year and blowing at hurricane force on two out of three winter days. Wind

Rime ice, created by frozen fog, coats the old Mount Washington Observatory building and antennas on Washington's summit. Photo courtesy Mount Washington Observatory.

speeds of more than 100 miles per hour are not unusual. Staff meteorologists working in week-long shifts transmit data to New England and national weather centers, and broadcast daily weather forecasts from the summit on local radio and television stations.

Early History

Early explorers to the North American coast were quick to note the distant sight of Mount Washington's snow-covered summit from the ocean, but it was far enough inland that it would not actually be approached for more than a hundred years. The record of a voyage by Giovanni da Verrazano in 1524 is believed to hold the earliest reference to the White Mountains. Later, in Casco Bay during the 1604 voyage in which he named Mount Desert Island, Samuel de Champlain described their appearance from his ship.

The mountains were called White Hills or Crystal Hills for most of the seventeenth century; the first use of the name White Mountains appeared in 1677 on a map of New England engraved by John Foster of Boston. Still almost completely unexplored by Europeans, they were drawn as little more than a few unnamed bumps immediately north of a vaguely defined large lake that was probably Winnipesaukee.

Though archeological evidence of Indian presence in the mountains is sparse, there seems little doubt of their occupation here. The Penacook branch of the Abenaki lived in the river valleys where they could catch fish and hunt game. The flat, open grasslands along the river, called intervales, were probably cultivated with corn. The highest mountain they called Agiochook (or Agiocochook), and, according to Europeans, they venerated it as the sacred home of their great spirit.

Exposure to the teachings of John Eliot, the Puritan missionary, lent a biblical flavor to one of the native legends regarding Mount Washington. Abenaki tradition holds that, upon the death of the revered sachem Passaconaway, who was credited with supernatural powers, a sleigh drawn by wolves pulled the body up to the summit of Mount Washington, where it ascended to heaven in a chariot of fire.

The first white person to climb Mount Washington is generally believed to be an Englishman named Darby Field, the exploits of his

1642 ascent having been recorded in the journal of the governor of Massachusetts Bay, John Winthrop. According to that account, the curious and independent Field recruited some Indians to assist him in exploring Agiochook. Two of these guides actually climbed the mountain with Field, the others being too afraid. Perhaps motivated by the promise of riches, Field filled his pockets with crystals (hoping they were diamonds) that turned out to be quartz.

Historians could not agree on Field's route up the mountain, some saying it was through Pinkham Notch and over Boott Spur to the top, others asserting he followed a more southerly route along the Montalban Ridge. Winthrop's record simply did not contain enough description of the terrain to be positive about the route Field and his group took, and today some even dispute that the date of 1642 is accurate. That they saw black-watered lakes near the summit provides convincing proof they did make it to the summit.

A second account of Field's historic ascent came to light in 1984, in the correspondence of the deputy governor of Maine, Thomas Gorges, to his brother (the governor) back in England. References to crossing several lesser peaks before attaining the summit of the highest seemed to point to one path above all others—one that had not yet been considered. Today, it is widely believed that Field ascended from Crawford Notch over the southern Presidentials, roughly the same route that Abel and Ethan Allen Crawford would make so popular in the early 1800s.

If Field climbed as much for the adventure as for the possibility of wealth or individual recognition, he was certainly ahead of his time. In the years that followed, John Josselyn, author of the popular seventeenth-century *Account of Two Voyages to New England*, helped discourage potential exploration or settlement: "The Country beyond these Hills Northward is daunting terrible, being full of rocky Hills, as thick as Mole-hills in a Meadow, and cloathed with infinite thick Woods." Josselyn referred to the summit cone as the Sugar Loaf, and guessed that the mountains were hollow.

A further deterrent to exploration was the presence of native peoples who did not yield their lands to white settlers willingly. King Philip's War (1675) demolished what little trust had existed between the natives and English colonists, and from then until the end of the

French and Indian Wars (1763), none of the territory in northern New England was considered safe for white settlement. When the concluding Treaty of Paris finally established the North American boundary between French and English territory, most of the tribes had already retreated to relative safety in Quebec.

Soon after the peace, settlers and farmers moved into the fertile river meadows of the northern Connecticut Valley near Haverhill, and eastward toward the mountains. Lancaster, New Hampshire, was settled in 1764. Settlement from the coastal towns around Portsmouth spread northward to the Lakes region and beyond. Yet these two areas of north-country towns were cut off from each other by the intervening White Mountains, through which there was no passable route.

The discovery of a way through the White Mountains brought a major boost to the economy and prosperity of the state. According to one legend, it happened quite by accident in 1771, when a Lancastrian named Timothy Nash was tracking a moose. Having lost his prey, he climbed a nearby tall tree, and looking out, saw an unexpected break in the ridge of land before him. He had discovered what would become known as Crawford Notch.

Nash was so excited by his find that he hurried to Portsmouth to inform provincial officials. Governor John Wentworth liked the prospect of linking the northerly towns and promised Nash a generous grant of land if he could bring a horse through the notch. With the assistance of a rope and tackle to lower the horse over a particularly steep precipice, Nash and his friend Benjamin Sawyer succeeded. In return, the pair was awarded 2,184 acres in the notch on the west side of Mount Washington, land that still bears their names as the unincorporated town of Nash and Sawyer's Location.

Washington attracted serious scientific interest for the first time in 1784, when Jeremy Belknap, an eminent scholar who was writing a history of New Hampshire, led the first official exploration of the mountain. Belknap assembled a group of intellectuals to accompany him to the mountain, including Rev. Manasseh Cutler, a botanist; Rev. Daniel Little; and Dr. Joshua Fisher, president of the Massachusetts Medical Society. All were members of the newly founded American Academy of Arts and Sciences and intensely devoted to their chosen fields of study.

These four, and some younger men, set out from Belknap's home in Dover, New Hampshire, in July of 1784. At North Conway, they added local men to their party, and proceeded up the eastern side of the mountain to Pinkham Notch, where they camped near the present Appalachian Mountain Club facility. The next day, the group made their way up the mountain without a trail, most likely through Huntington Ravine. Belknap himself was turned back by the grade—the frontispiece portrait in his *History* indicated a tendency toward corpulence—but the rest of his party reached the top. They christened Agiochook with a new name in honor of George Washington. Cutler (after whom a river in Pinkham Notch was named) gathered specimens and recorded the mountain's unique vegetation, becoming Mount Washington's first serious botanist.

The Crawfords

Permanent settlement was not far behind. In 1791, a family of hardy pioneers from Guildhall, Vermont, decided to make the western flank of Mount Washington their home. Abel and Hannah Crawford and their sons, Erastus and Ethan Allen, built a cabin at the southern end of the notch on the Saco River. They were soon followed by Hannah's parents, Eleazar and Hannah Rosebrook, who occupied Nash and Sawyer's Location at the upper end. Both families endured terrible hardships in the extreme weather and isolation of the notch.

In 1803, a state-funded road through the notch opened a passage for goods between Portland, Maine, and towns north of the mountains. Gradually, more and more teamsters carried butter, rum, or molasses to northern New Hampshire and Vermont country towns. The Crawfords earned a little money as tavernkeepers, and passing teamsters chipped away at the loneliness of the long winters. Rosebrook, too, ran an inn, at the other end of the notch twelve miles by the road from Abel Crawford's.

When Rosebrook died in 1817, he left his property to his grandson Ethan Allen Crawford. Nick-named the Giant of the Mountains, Crawford stood six feet two and one-half inches tall, and it was said he was strong as a bear. He married his cousin, Lucy Howe, and together they operated Fabyan's Inn and later the Crawford House, whence hundreds of curious travelers toured Mount Washington.

In every way he could, Ethan Allen Crawford promoted tourism. He and his father cut the first trail up Mount Washington, the Crawford Path, in 1819. At the trailhead he built a cabin in which his guests could spend the night before their climb, and he carried a sheet of lead to the summit so that visitors could inscribe their names upon it. He improved and maintained the road through the notch, and to entertain his visitors with the echo from the mountainsides, he sounded a great horn, and later a small cannon. Crawford's flair for showmanship included collecting wild animals—such as deer and bear—to keep as penned exhibits at his hotel.

Ethan Allen Crawford hired out as guide on more than one important expedition to Washington. He guided a lively group of prominent citizens from Lancaster to the summit in 1820. The participants on this outing included Philip Carrigain, who had produced the first really accurate map of New Hampshire four years earlier. The cartographer stimulated the party's interest in geographic nomenclature and after much debate and liberal swigs of Crawford's "O-Be-Joyful," they named Mounts Adams, Jefferson, Madison, Monroe, Franklin, and Pleasant.

The expectations of this group heavily taxed Crawford's legendary fortitude. Lucy Crawford described the start of their expedition in her *History of the White Mountains*, which she told in the voice of her husband as narrator:

> I was accordingly fitted out, and when ready, my pack weighed eighty pounds. I carried it to the Notch on horseback, and when I arrived there the sun was setting, and the party had taken the path and gone along and left their cloaks by the way for me. I piled them on top of my load and budged on as fast as possible, and when I arrived at the camp it was dusk; there was no fire; wood was to be chopped, and supper to prepare, and when all this was done, I was tired enough to sleep without being rocked in a cradle.

Ethan Allen Crawford is the hero of Lucy's tale, and she tells his marvelous stories of early adventures on the mountain with humor, sympathy, and more than a touch of braggadocio. Crawford, for instance, guided the three young women who, in 1821, sought and attained the distinction of being the first females known to have climbed Mount Washington. These Austin sisters, plus their brother and a fiancee, made an expedition which lasted five days and three nights, with Ethan Allen Crawford assisting them for the final leg of their climb.

The Crawfords also accommodated and guided many of the scientists who visited Mount Washington early in the nineteenth century. In 1804, Manasseh Cutler returned with fellow botanists William Peck and Nathaniel Bowditch for another look at the alpine plants. As part of their climb, they estimated the mountain's height to be 7,055 feet, a much more accurate figure than the 10,000 feet Jeremy Belknap had guessed. Another party of scientists from Boston, Jacob Bigelow, Dr. Francis Boott, Lemuel Shaw, and Francis Grey, climbed the mountain in the summer of 1816 and took their own barometer readings. They got an altitude of 6,225 feet—reasonably close to the modern figure of 6,288 feet, and the most accurate until the Coastal Survey of 1869. Boott Spur and Bigelow Lawn are named for members of this party.

William Oakes, who probably spent more time on Mount Washington than any other botanist of his era, was also a Crawford guest. He began his work in the White Mountains in 1825 and wrote the first book about this celebrated landscape, *Scenery of the White Mountains*, which was beautifully illustrated with lithographs of the mountains drawn by Isaac Sprague. Oakes is credited with having named Mounts Clay and Jackson, and Oakes Gulf is named for him.

Professor Benjamin Silliman, a distinguished chemist and geologist, made two trips to the White Mountains to name and classify mineral specimens. The elongated white crystals found in Mount Washington's (and Moosilauke's and Monadnock's) mica schist are now known as sillimanite after him. Edward Tuckerman of Amherst College, whose name was given to the spectacular cirque on the mountain's east side, commenced a long career of scientific work on Mount Washington and its environs in 1837. Tuckerman made a lifelong study of the mountains and wrote many scholarly articles about his findings. He also contributed a chapter to Thomas Starr King's best seller, *The White Hills, Their Legends, Landscape, and Poetry*.

Thanks to the Crawfords' hospitality, a flood of books, articles, travel accounts, engravings, and paintings turned Mount Washington into more than just an exotic location. People wanted to come and see for themselves, to experience the extreme weather on the high peaks, to consider the vast territory of the unknown, to be challenged by the curiosities of nature, and to confront the Creator in all His mysteries.

The Willey Tragedy

The strange and tragic deaths of the Willey family in a landslide took place during the night of August 28, 1826. There were no survivors to tell the story precisely—perhaps this allowed more embroidering of the facts later on—and the Willey slide became so celebrated by writers, artists, and poets that it has maintained its hold on the public's imagination ever since. Certainly at the time, it made notch residents fearful and travelers melancholy with excitment.

The facts are these: In the twelve miles between the Crawfords and the Rosebrooks at either end of the notch, the Willey family built a small cabin to provide a way station for travelers. Samuel J. Willey, his wife and five children, and two hired men lived there. A particularly wet spring had set loose a slide of mud and rocks on the slope of Mount Willard near their farm in June of that year, and the family was unnerved enough to consider leaving the notch for a time. But their fears subsided, and they stayed through the hot, dry summer.

On the fateful day, Monday, August 28, a monstrous storm descended upon the White Mountains. Sometime during the night, the family must have heard a tremendous roar coming down the mountain, and they ran from their house in fright. A large boulder just above their house blocked the path of the slide and prevented it from hitting the house, but the entire family was carried away. The flow of debris knocked over the barn and rushed on into the valley, leaving the little cabin untouched. The flood that ensued washed out roads and bridges, drowned livestock, and overran fields full of ripening grain.

Not until Wednesday was the disaster discovered. John Barker, the first man to penetrate the ruins of the road through Crawford Notch, saw the huge slide that had stripped bare the mountain above and behind the Willeys. He saw the debris covering the land on both sides of the house, but found no one at home except the dog. Assuming that the Willeys had gone to the village below, Barker made himself comfortable for the night, but a low moaning disturbed him. His dawn search revealed the source of the noise—an ox trapped in the wrecked stable. Barker freed the animal, completed his passage through the notch, and reported the slide and the circumstances to people in the town.

Friends and relatives rushed to the scene and began to search for the missing family. Hours later the bodies of Mr. and Mrs. Willey and one of the hired men were discovered—that was on Thursday. The youngest child was found on Friday. The bodies of the oldest girl and the other hired man were located on Saturday. Three other children were never found.

The story ignited the artistic imaginations of writers and painters everywhere. Those who had known the notch on previous visits came back again to paint the scene or describe its devastation. Fictional accounts of the family's last days confirmed for the public the ironies of their fatal mistake—leaving the house—and the difficult lessons of the Almighty. Nathaniel Hawthorne's version of the story, "The Ambitious Guest," is perhaps the most eloquent. He tells the story through the eyes of an innocent traveler who had stopped at the Willeys for the night. Other literary and pictorial representations of the horrendous landslide and the pathetic surviving cabin kept the tragedy in the public consciousness for decades.

Arts and Literature

The arrival of the artistic legions in the North Conway area commenced shortly after the Willey tragedy, with the 1828 explorations of Thomas Cole. Before long, he convinced others to come and investigate the scenery and make sketches. By 1850, the little town had swelled to a summer haven for artists, hotels brimming and coaches running daily to all the natural landmarks. The view of Mount Washington across the flood plain of the Saco River intervale surpassed all others in popularity with this group. Artists made it so famous that the renowned firm of Currier & Ives even chose it for one of their mass-produced lithographs. Besides the perfectly framed view of Washington the intervale offered, there were spectacular sunset views directly west over the Moat Range, and, the artists claimed, this location was remarkably free of black flies.

Local Indian legends fascinated writers and artists. One of the best concerned the "great carbuncle," a mythical red gem. Since garnets occur naturally at Mount Washington, perhaps the discovery of an unusually large one gave rise to the tale. According to the story, a wonderful carbuncle that not only reflected but actually produced light was placed for safekeeping under a shelf of rock on the south side of Mount Washington, in the valley of the Dry River (also known as Oakes Gulf). To safeguard the treasure, the Indians sacrificed one of their men, intending that his bitter spirit would stay there to ward off intruders.

The carbuncle's light was reported to have flashed out over the country at times, and many groups tried to find it, sometimes guided by Abel Crawford. In Nathaniel Hawthorne's popular story "The Great Carbuncle," seekers of the gem who are not worthy characters are destroyed. An innocent young newlywed couple are the successful ones; they find the carbuncle high on the slopes of the mountain. But having witnessed the others punished for their greed in an obsessive search for the gem, they consider the corruption such a jewel might bring to their lives. In the end, they decide to leave the carbuncle where it is, and watch as a catastrophic landslide buries it forever.

Railroads and Tourism

The White Mountains were about to become a mecca for sightseers and summer vacationers. The romantic outpouring of prose, poetry, and painting set the stage to encourage even more tourists. Then in 1851, the Atlantic & St. Lawrence Railroad, connecting Portland, Maine, with Gorham, New Hampshire, brought the White Mountains from remote distance into easy accessibility. No longer did travelers have to make an uncomfortable wagon or stagecoach journey over dirt roads to reach the mountains. They could now take a steamboat from any of the major East Coast cities to Portland, board the train there, and disembark literally at the foot of New England's most majestic peak.

Hotels and the railroads cooperated in attracting tourists to the mountains, jointly promoting the sights and pleasures of the region through a variety of broadsides, pamphlets, and guidebooks. The success of these efforts ushered in the era of commercial development on

Mount Washington itself, helped dozens of innkeepers on both sides of the mountain to prosper, and brought more full-time settlement to the area.

The story of how Pinkham Notch was changed by the railroad is typical of the transformation the trains brought to the north country. In 1790, Captain Joseph Pinkham moved to what is now Jackson, driving a sled that was said to have been pulled by a pig. He occupied a remote valley that saw little traffic or growth. After 1851, Jackson found itself on a direct route between the train terminus at Gorham and the center of artistic activity at North Conway, and the town grew rapidly.

The first hotel in Pinkham Notch went up at the glen as soon as travelers could reach Gorham by train. J. M. "Landlord" Thompson ran it with a flair for showmanship that made the Glen House a popular and fashionable retreat. Thompson's stagecoaches were drawn by eight matching white horses, which drivers galloped around the circular drive at the train station in Gorham just in time to catch the attention of passengers stepping from the cars.

A story from the Glen House in the 1850s centers around the challenge of climbing Mount Washington in those days. A woman known to history only as Branch was bet a thousand dollars by a fellow guest that she could not walk to the top of Mount Washington and back in one day. The next day Branch, who weighed 230 pounds, gained the title of "the heaviest lady ever to have visited Tip-Top," and that night, so the story goes, she danced at the Glen House, a thousand dollars richer.

Throughout the nineteenth century, tourist hotels grew and prospered. On the Crawford side of the mountain, the last of the summer hotels to be built was also the most magnificent. The Mount Washington Hotel, constructed on a glacial ridge in what became known as Bretton Woods, opened in 1902, touted as "the finest hotel in the country." It was huge, sitting on a 2,600-acre estate and containing 235 rooms, two five-story octagonal towers, and a 900-foot-long wraparound veranda. Its red roof and white stucco exterior were spectacularly set off by the towering ridge of Mount Washington immediately behind it.

The Mount Washington Hotel in Bretton Woods is the last survivor of the grand hotels that made the White Mountains a renowned tourist destination in the nineteenth century. Photo courtesy Mount Washington Hotel, Bretton Woods, NH.

Though fire has claimed the Crawford House, Fabyan's, and all the other big hotels, the grand Mount Washington Hotel has endured. Today, it is surrounded by a golf course, tennis courts, and a pool, and it has been completely refurbished for year-round operation. Downhill skiing is available on a smaller hill across the valley, and, as in eras past, the guests here generally prefer to look up at Washington admiringly rather than test themselves by the challenges of clmbing or skiing on it.

The influx of tourists following the arrival of the railroad naturally warranted more amenities for them on the peak they had all come to see. Several of the original footpaths, including the one from the Crawford House, were improved as bridle paths for horses. A new path was cut up the east side of the mountain from the Glen House. In 1852, a small stone summit house was erected atop Mount Washington, with a wooden roof carried up board by board on pack horses from the glen. The proprietors, Joseph Hall and Lucius Rosebrook, served about 100 dinners per day during the summer season, by all accounts a successful enterprise. Most guests arrived on horseback and left their mounts at the stables located just below the summit.

The next year a second stone summit building was added, called the Tip-Top House. Today, with its slanted stone walls, it is the oldest building still standing at the summit. Beds in the Tip-Top House were stacked one above another and stuffed with moss. The bar served alcoholic beverages that were considered necessary for adjustment to the rarefied air—the density of air atop Mount Washington is only three-quarters that at sea level. Many famous visitors dined or stayed at the Tip-Top House, including Jefferson Davis, future leader of the Confederacy; Louisa May Alcott; and President Franklin Pierce.

One of two far-reaching midcentury changes to the mountain was General David O. Macomber's carriage road to Mount Washington's summit. The route was surveyed in 1854, taking advantage of the scenery on the eastern side of the mountain and incorporating many switchbacks to keep the slope gradual. The average grade of the carriage road was a gentle 12 percent. The first two miles were completed in 1856 and a halfway house was built at about 3,840 feet of elevation. Two more miles were finished before Macomber's company went bankrupt, well short of completing the eight-mile goal.

Another company was chartered in 1859, and the road was finally finished and opened to the public in 1861. For the rest of the premotor era, White Mountain hotels took their guests up the famous route in "mountain wagons," every visitor taking the thrilling ride to the summit at least once a season. Today, rechristened the Mount Washington Auto Road, this same route is privately owned and operated and still thrills with its hairpin turns and breathtaking views.

Henry David Thoreau was among those who came to Washington during its golden age, making his second visit in 1858. With his friend Edward Hoar, he arrived at Pinkham Notch, spent the night at the Glen House, and hiked up the carriage road the following day. Thoreau was dismayed to find so many buildings and so much activity on the summit, and he and his guide made their way back down to camp in relative solitude at the base of Tuckerman Ravine. Here, for some reason, their campfire accidentally got out of control, burning quite a bit of the mountain before it was luckily quenched by a sudden rain shower. To make things even worse, Thoreau sprained his ankle while collecting botanical specimens on the Alpine Garden. Needless to say, this sojourn to Washington was not his favorite excursion.

The second big change in the 1850s was a railroad on Mount Washington. During the construction of the carriage road, the state legislature granted inventor and businessman Sylvester Marsh permission to build a cog railway to the summit. Although there were doubts about the feasibility of this project—one skeptic suggested that the railroad might as well be continued to the moon—Marsh was able to succeed with his unprecedented venture.

The railway's nearly straight route ascended a western spur of the mountain, on which the average grade would be 25 percent. The first quarter-mile of track was laid in 1866, and after a successful demonstration on that initial stretch, Marsh had no trouble raising capital to complete the cog railway. To keep the tracks at a smooth angle, they were laid on wooden trestles or bridges. The highest trestle crossed at a crag called Jacob's Ladder that was completed in 1868. The first train reached the summit July 3, 1869, and the next month President Ulysses S. Grant rode the cog railway. Marsh built a little base station that he called Marshfield, partly after himself and partly after Darby Field.

Two kinds of conveyances carried passengers on the railway. Cars similar to conventional railroad coaches were nosed up the mountain by a coal-fired locomotive, pushing on the ascent, and braking from in front of the passenger car on the descent. The safety record of the railroad cars was impeccable. Not so for the other form of transportation on the center-cog tracks. Generally used only by workmen on the railway, "slideboards" were nothing more than a tiny sled with a hand brake that could bring a workman down off the mountain in blistering time—the record for the three-mile track was two minutes and forty-five seconds. Several deaths finally forced the retirement of these sleds about 1930.

Summit Business

With well-built and reliable access to the mountain from both the carriage road and the cog railway, more development at the summit was inevitable. Ushering in an era of year-round occupation of the

Slide boards offered a harrowing but efficient means of descent for cog railway workers. The use of these open sleds was prohibited after several fatal crashes. Photo courtesy Society for the Preservation of New England Antiquities, Boston, MA.

summit were Dr. Charles H. Hitchcock and J. H. Huntington, who spent the winter of 1870–71 there (following Huntington's previous winter atop Mount Moosilauke). Their group included two photographers and a representative of the army's Signal Service, which was interested in using weather observation from the mountain to predict storms that might damage coastal shipping. Telegraph lines connected to Hitchcock's office at Dartmouth College enabled messages to be sent and received.

Data obtained from Hitchcock and Huntington's winter on the summit proved so valuable that the Signal Service, the part of the army responsible for meteorological observation (preceding the formation of the U. S. Weather Bureau) decided to continue their work. They built their own headquarters and occupied the summit in winter until 1887, and summers thereafter until 1892. College and other scientific groups conducted short-term winter experiments on the summit until the end of the century.

In another small building on Washington, a totally different kind of enterprise flourished. Newspaperman Henry M. Burt commenced publishing a summertime daily, *Among the Clouds*, in 1877, covering the news of the summit, the comings and goings of visitors, and essays and articles of interest to mountain travelers. Thanks to the traffic generated by the cog railway and the carriage road, the paper gained a loyal following. Tourists were recruited to turn the wheel of the press, and visiting printers were welcomed to help set type. Special editions were sometimes speedily transported down the cog-railway tracks on the gravity-powered slideboards for distribution from the Marshfield base station. The paper lasted until World War I.

The look of the summit changed almost from one year to the next. A big new hotel called the Mount Washington Summit House opened in 1874; the stone Summit House and Tip-Top House were relegated to staff lodgings. Besides the newspaper office (built in 1884), the hotel, and Tip-Top House, a forty-foot-high wooden tower was erected behind the Summit House in 1880, positioned so that an instrument called a theodolite was precisely over the mountain's apex. The theodolite, a surveying instrument for measuring angles, was used by the United States Coast and Geodetic Survey to calculate the positions of other mountaintops, from which sunlight was flashed by means of a device called a heliograph.

A thirty-six-inch searchlight, which could be seen from western Massachusetts to the Maine coast, was later placed on the wooden tower. Although the light could be used for Morse-code signals, it functioned principally as a diversion for tourists. Filters were used to color the brilliant light on summer evenings.

The gradual decline of the tourist era was hastened by a devastating fire on the summit of Mount Washington in June 1908. Fanned by high winds, the fire claimed most of the summit buildings, including the second Summit House, the printing office, and the old signal station, while sparing the stone-walled Tip-Top House and the stables. Within a few years, the summit colony was back in operation, and new schemes to conquer the mountain reflected the changing times that increased automobile travel and new technology were bringing.

Construction of an electric railroad was proposed shortly after the fire of 1908; it was to have climbed the mountain by mild grades and circle the summit cone three times as it spiraled to the three-story hotel to be built at the top. This scheme was proposed at a time when conservation pulled more votes than tourism, and ultimately it was dropped. The third Summit House was completed in 1915, in appearance much like the second.

Mountain Tragedies

Not all tourists to Mount Washington spent their evenings in luxury and delightful diversion. Far too many perished on the mountain, whether from unfortunate accidents, foolhardy decisions, or simple bad luck. Visitors now are cautioned repeatedly that the mountain weather can turn fierce at any time, and that anyone attempting a climb should be well provisioned with food, water, warm clothing, and a healthy dose of humility. The early stories of Strickland, Bourne, and Dr. Ball are three oft-repeated tales of tragedy and survival.

The first known person to lose his life on the mountain was a twenty-nine-year-old Englishman named Frederick Strickland. Accompanied by a guide, Strickland set out on horseback in the fall of 1851 to climb the Crawford Path. When the weather worsened, the guide halted the expedition at Mount Pleasant (now called Mount Eisenhower). Strickland, however, was determined to reach his goal and stubbornly insisted on going forward alone and on foot. The guide, whose counsel was ignored, assumed that the young man would soon realize his mistake and turn back toward the notch. But searchers the next day followed Strickland's trail all the way to the summit—he had reached his goal, then apparently fallen over several precipices before completely succumbing to the cold. Beside a brook, his battered and lifeless body was finally found.

One of the best-known Mount Washington fatalities was that of Lizzie Bourne, perhaps because she was a woman, perhaps because she died so close to the Tip-Top House's warm hearth. On the afternoon of

September 15, 1855, twenty-three-year-old Lizzie set out in sunshine with her uncle and cousin to walk from the Glen House to the summit. About two miles from the top the weather changed and the three were soaked to the skin by rain. Unable to find their way down, they were soon lost in darkness and wandered through most of the night as temperatures dropped below freezing. At daybreak, when Lizzie's relatives rapped feebly at the door of the Tip-Top House, their clothes were covered with frost. During the night Lizzie had fallen to hypothermia; she lay only five hundred feet from the safety of the summit building, which had been invisible to them in the darkness and fog. Her relatives marked the spot where she died with a painted wooden sign, maintained for many years alongside the cog-railway tracks.

An amazing story of survival amid brutal winter conditions took place just a month later in October 1855. Dr. Benjamin Ball, a Boston physician and experienced climber, managed to survive sixty hours of exposure with only an umbrella for shelter. Starting out from the Glen House in rain that turned to freezing rain, Ball spent the night at the

The Lizzie Bourne monument marks the post where one of the most famous of the mountain's 115 fatalities occurred. She perished but a few yards from the warm hearth of the summit house. Photo courtesy Dartmouth College Library, Hanover, NH.

Halfway House, where he learned of the recent Lizzie Bourne tragedy. Nevertheless, he started out again the next morning, determined to reach the summit. Enveloped in a sudden snowstorm and strong winds, he wandered lost and dangerously close to succumbing to hypothermia. As darkness fell, he found a niche between a rock and some dwarf firs. Ball opened his umbrella, tied its handle to a root, added brush and slabs of crusted snow, and waited out the stormy night, keeping himself awake by assuming uncomfortable positions.

In the morning Ball tried to find the summit or a trail, but visibility was still poor, and he was breaking the snow's crust with every wearying step. Barely missing contact with a rescue party, Ball returned to his camp for a second long, snowy night. Miraculously, he survived through a second day without food. On the morning of the third day, he was working his way down the mountain when he met searchers looking for his body. Ball's recovery was slow and painful— it was six months before he regained the use of his hands and feet— but he lived to tell his tale in print.

The lessons of history are not always heeded. On a brutally cold January weekend in 1994, two students from the University of New Hampshire decided to attempt a traverse of the Presidential Range. Jeremy Haas and Derek Tinkham, though well equipped and experienced, lacked one crucial attribute, the willingness to admit defeat. Spending their first night on Madison, they pushed on toward Jefferson as Tinkham slowly became disoriented and clumsy from hypothermia. In the gathering dark, with temperatures of -32° F, and winds of seventy to nintey miles per hour, Haas helped his friend into a sleeping bag, marked its location by a bright yellow stuff sack lashed to a rock, and headed off alone toward Washington in blowing snow and fog. He reached the observatory at 8:00 that night, severely frostbitten and concerned that rescuers go out to find his friend.

Search and rescue on Mount Washington consists of a highly sophisticated network of skilled professionals and volunteers willing to risk their own lives to save others. A group of eleven rescuers snowshoed up Jefferson the day after Haas's arrival on Mount Washington, hoping against hope that Tinkham might still be alive. Amid conditions that one rescuer described as worse than Everest, they found Tinkham's body, half out of his sleeping bag and frozen solid.

Hiking and the Appalachian Mountain Club

Mountain climbing as a form of outdoor recreation and personal challenge gained a following throughout the 1870s and 1880s that rivaled the more comfortable approach offered by the carriage road or cog railway. Men and women braved the weather, the steep rocky slopes, and their own personal fears for the fun of conquering the mountain on foot. They constantly searched for new routes, cut new trails, built shelters, and camped in rustic fashion—the farther from civilization the better.

The Appalachian Mountain Club, the first organization of hikers in America, was founded in 1876 to promote hiking and conservation. The Boston-based club built the first of its "huts" on Mount Madison in 1888, partly to provide shelter on the far end of the Presidential traverse, and partly as a base for scientific exploration. Just a few years later the tragic deaths of two experienced members of the AMC indicated that more shelters were clearly needed, especially above treeline on the ridge of the southern Presidentials, over which ran one of Washington's most popular hiking routes, the Crawford Path.

On the last day of June 1900, William Curtis and Allen Ormsbee decided to hike up the Crawford Path to attend a summit meeting of the AMC. The weather was cold and rainy, but both men were veteran hikers in excellent physical condition. Along the exposed ridge near Mount Monroe, however, the weather turned suddenly worse, with fierce rain and high winds. Before long, the rain turned to sleet and the winds whipped up to gale force. Curtis, age sixty-two, was the first to falter. He tried to find shelter for himself in the rocks near the Lakes of the Clouds, hoping to be able to wait out the storm. The twenty-eight-year-old Ormsbee pressed on, struggling half-frozen over the ice-coated rocks in a desperate but doomed attempt to reach the summit, where he knew rescuers awaited. Tragically, the severity of the storm prevented rescue efforts, and the two bodies were not recovered until the next day. Ormsbee's was found just a few hundred yards below the summit building.

The loss of these two highly respected and experienced hikers mobilized the AMC to try to prevent further tragedies. Within two years a wooden shelter was built near where Curtis's body had been found. Though at first the club tried to restrict its use to emergency situations only, the hut's location was appealing for campers, and they eventually acquiesced to the demand. In 1915 a new structure was constructed that had bunks for thirty-six people and housed a caretaker to manage the facility and cook meals. From that small start, the Lakes of the Clouds Hut has grown into the busiest in the entire AMC system.

In 1920 the AMC decided to take over some old logging-camp buildings for a hut in Pinkham Notch. In 1922 they hired twenty-three-year-old Joseph Dodge as hutmaster. For more than thirty years Dodge was a towering figure, literally and figuratively, in Mount Washington's hiking community. Under his leadership, the club developed a fifty-mile chain of seven staffed high huts (Mizpah has since been added to make eight that the AMC runs today). Not only did Dodge supervise construction of the huts, but he helped establish the Mount Washington Observatory, helped organize the famous

The Lakes of the Clouds Hut, on a knoll southwest of Washington's summit, was constructed after two experienced climbers perished near this spot in a sudden, violent storm in June 1900. Appalachian Mountain Club/Lou Lainey.

"Inferno" ski race, and piled up a record of such extraordinary service that he is still memorialized today.

Dodge's energy and efficiency were legendary. So was his stubborn independence. Legions of young men who signed on as hut crews for the summer months revered him as a father figure, friend, and exacting boss. One night when the state police came to Pinkham Notch Camp suspecting that some of Dodge's hut-crew members had been involved in stealing highway signs, Dodge covered for them long enough to get the authorities off their backs. Then he charged into the bunkroom where the guilty parties were pretending to be asleep and bellowed, "Get those signs right back to where you took them... and don't come back on your days off again." And, of course, the young men did exactly as they were told.

Mountain Firsts

The circuslike atmosphere of the crowded summit and the congeniality of the valley hotels contributed to some daredevil exploits on the mountain. Records for accomplishments on Washington were intentionally set as early as 1850, when guests of the Glen House vied for who could post the fastest time walking up the carriage road. The first auto ascent was by Freelan O. Stanley and his wife, Flora Tileston Stanley, in 1899, in a steam-powered predecessor of the Stanley Steamer called a Locomobile and invented by Freelan and his twin brother.

About 1900, Edgar Welch of Maine, after having "loosened up" in the Tip-Top House tavern, ran down the carriage road in about forty-five minutes. Thereafter, the road became the ultimate challenge to a variety of eccentrics and athletes. Bicycles were pushed up the mountain for records; bicycles were raced down for records. People walked and ran; skied and snowshoed; drove dogsleds cars, and motorcyles; and flew airplanes, all for the recognition of being first or fastest to do such a thing. Ever more difficult feats are attempted each year, now focusing on winter records, which are the toughest of all. For instance, the first all-women party to make a wintertime Presidential traverse—a trek across the summits from Madison, over Washington, to Eisenhower—succeeded in 1980. A winter traverse of these mountains rates as a significant feat for any alpine climber.

The first known use of skis on Mount Washington took place in February of 1905 when Norman Libby climbed the mountain from the base station and slid down, but here as elsewhere real skiing began in the 1930s, when the energetic and daring began skiing at Tuckerman Ravine. The glacial bowl collects deep snow, which persists here late into the spring. There has never been a lift or tow on Washington, and skiers then, as now, had to shoulder their boards and climb up the steep face of the snow bowl for every run they made.

The American Inferno, among the most famous of downhill skiing races, was held in the ravine from 1933 until 1939. The first year the race was held, the only finisher posted a time of seventeen minutes. In 1939, an Austrian named Toni Matt destroyed all previous records and left spectators awestruck when he "schussed" (going almost straight down with no turns to control his speed) the head-

Spring skiing in Tuckerman Ravine has always been a sport for the determined few who hike in the ravine to make runs down the steep face of the glacial cirque. Appalachian Mountain Club/David F. Hoyt.

wall, entered the woods, and made it to the foot of the mountain in six minutes and twenty-nine seconds. After Matt's stunning victory, and the outbreak of World War II the next year, the race was never held again.

The Observatory and the Summit Today

Continuous monitoring of the weather at the summit was renewed in 1932 with the establishment of the Mount Washington Weather Observatory. The idea to reoccupy the summit was first proposed in 1926 by Robert Monahan of Dartmouth College and Joe Dodge. The two continued to nurture their dream as they sought funding for the weather station. Dodge, a radio man since his World War I days in the navy, and Monahan, a Yale-trained forester and accomplished skier, enlisted support from international scientific circles as well as such established institutions as MIT and the U. S. Weather Bureau. The stage office at the summit was offered to them, and slowly other sources of support were found. Two other well-suited men were selected to be part of the project, both experienced mountain climbers— Alexander McKenzie, from Dartmouth, and Salvatore Pagliuca, a former General Electric employee trained in mechanical and electrical engineering.

The station prospered and grew, warranting incorporation by the state of New Hampshire as the Mount Washington Observatory in 1936. The next year, "the strongest frame building in the United States" was fabricated of railroad timbers and bolted right to the rocks of the summit, to become the observatory's new home. In 1980, the observatory moved to larger quarters in the state's new Sherman Adams summit building, where there is a museum open to the public.

But it was in the old weather station, now demolished, that their most memorable feat was accomplished. On April 12, 1934, amid a fierce storm, the observatory crew measured the wind speed at 231 MPH, the highest surface wind speed ever recorded on earth, and a record that stands to this day. Had the instrument not broken, perhaps the record would have been even higher.

What began as meager corporate support for the observatory has grown into cooperative ventures, with dozens of companies

Mt. Washington's summit today. The cog railway and auto road are in the foreground and the Sherman Adams summit building is at right. Photo courtesy state of New Hampshire, Office of Travel and Tourism Development.

testing their products in the severe conditions at the summit. Polaroid, General Electric, Pittsburgh Plate Glass, and Douglas Aircraft were just a few of the companies active during the winters on Washington before 1950. During World War II, experiments with icing on aircraft were conducted, along with related products such as paints, tires, and all kinds of clothing and footwear.

Today, manufacturers of climbing and camping gear not only test products here, but often shoot pictures for promotional or advertising campaigns as well. The advantage of a complete facility amidst arcticlike conditions is rare, and advertising directors know that they can give their products a severe workout while at the same time have a warm shelter, telephone contact, and transportation back to civilization, all close at hand.

As with other mountaintops that can be reached by road, broadcasting antennas have also found a home on Mount Washington. A radio network built a transmitting station for FM radio in 1941. To supply the staff with water a 1,080-foot well was drilled, but the water froze on its way up. To a depth of 200 feet the rock beneath the summit is permanently below the freezing point—heat cables are necessary to bring water to the surface. Every structure raised on this range must be built against difficult odds to withstand tremendous punishment.

The FM station ran continuously during World War II to warn other New England stations to go off the air in the event of an air raid. Though this pioneer station was a technical achievement, it did not succeed commercially and shut down in 1948. Northern New England's first television station, WMTW, went on the air in 1954 broadcasting from an antenna on Mount Washington. Today, radio and television personnel live and broadcast from their own studios at the summit.

The state of New Hampshire acquired title to the summit in a long process that has led to the creation of a state park there. In 1964, they began to plan for an orderly transition from scattered multiple-use buildings to a single multipurpose facility. They removed the third Summit House (built in 1915) and dedicated the new Sherman Adams Summit Building on September 5, 1980.

Adams, a New Hampshire native, had been an aide to President Eisenhower, but had earned a place in mountain history by virtue of his many accomplishments beginning as a Dartmouth undergraduate. He served as congressman and governor, and worked tirelessly to promote interest in and appreciation for the mountains he loved. The building named in his honor, sited just below the true summit, is a two-story crescent of concrete with observation decks facing out over the Great Gulf Wilderness Area. Within its 240-foot length, the Mount Washington Observatory occupies the west end of the building. A restaurant, gift shop, and even a post office are open from mid-May to mid-October, and weather permitting, the auto road and cog railway bring visitors right to the door.

The harshness of the weather is perhaps the single most important characteristic of Mount Washington besides its height. Including the deaths of Frederick Strickland and Lizzie Bourne, one hundred and fifteen fatalities have been recorded on this peak, many of them accidents that could have been prevented had hikers taken seriously the warnings that are posted at the start of every trail. Access to Washington cannot be closely monitored, given the roads surrounding it and the many trails leading up it. It is part of human nature to want to test the limits, and on Washington, those limits can be changeable and utterly unforgiving. To meet them and succeed is great reward indeed.

Suggestions for Visitors

For information about hiking in the White Mountains, refer to the latest edition of the AMC *White Mountain Guide*. The Pinkham Notch Visitor Center, located on the White Mountain National Forest and run by the Appalachian Mountain Club, has a good bookstore and offers an array of programs and services for outdoors-oriented visitors to Mount Washington. Information on hiking is always available there. The telephone number for hut reservations is 603-466-2727.

About a third of the people who climb Mount Washington do so on foot, out of a total of approximately 250,000 summit visitors per summer. The claim of the oldest continuously maintained footpath is attached to the Crawford Path, which makes a long approach to the summit over Eisenhower, Franklin, and Monroe. There is little opportunity to escape from sudden bad weather along this ridgeline route, but it offers a historic and rewarding climb. A second suggested historic route is through Tuckerman Ravine on the Tuckerman Ravine Trail, one of the most popular on the mountain. This route, which departs from the AMC's Pinkham Notch Visitor Center, is the one taken by thousands of spring skiers on their pilgrimages to the famed bowl.

The cog railway is still very much in business on the west side of the mountain (800-922-8825, ext. 6, for advance reservations). The Mount Washington Hotel is now under the same ownership as the cog railway. Its number is 800-258-0330.

Pinkham Notch Visitor Center, nestled at the eastern base of Mt. Washington, has been the AMC's northern headquarters since 1920. Appalachian Mountain Club/Jerry Shereda.

The Mount Washington Auto Road begins in Pinkham Notch, opposite the site of the Old Glen House. Guided tours are available in auto road vans. For more information, call 603-466-3988. Both the cog railway and the auto road are open only from May to October, weather permitting.

The Mount Washington Observatory is a private, nonprofit organization which, in addition to weather monitoring, equipment testing, and other projects, is also involved in public educational efforts. It maintains a museum display in the summit building and a more accessible facility on Main Street in North Conway. The observatory benefits from the support of interested people through its membership program. For more information on volunteer opportunities or winter educational trips to the summit, write the observatory at P.O. Box 2310, North Conway, NH 03860; 603-356-8345.

Cadillac ⋀⋀⋀

The story of the mountains of Mount Desert Island is also a story of the ocean. On an island barely separate from the Maine coast, a range of mountains rises almost directly out of the sea, the only location on the East Coast of the United States where the shoreline has a mountainous character. Early explorers marked their position by these hills; during wartime, ships escaped enemy detection in the protection of the steep-walled inlets. Farming and logging in the nineteenth century gave way to tourism that outlasted the interest in many other New England mountains. Some of America's wealthiest families invested in summer "cottages" here and eventually spearheaded a movement to set aside in public ownership about one-third of Mount Desert Island. Today, about four million people annually visit the 35,000 acres known as Acadia National Park.

Mount Desert was named by the French explorer Samuel de Champlain, who called it Isle des Monts Deserts, a reference to the lack of vegetation on the mountains' summits. The French pronunciation stressing the second syllable has persisted even in the Anglicized form, so that the name sounds more like the after-dinner treat than the barren place originally intended. According to locals, both ways of saying the word are acceptable. To add to the confusion, there is no hill or peak named Mount Desert—that is the name of the island.

Instead, each hill carries its own name: Pemetic, Penobscot, Sargent, the Bubbles, Parkman, and the greatest of them all, Cadillac.

At 1,530 feet, Cadillac marks the highest point on the eastern coastline of the United States (and is, in fact, the highest point on the Atlantic coast as far south as Brazil). The rays of the rising sun first touch the United States on Cadillac Mountain in some seasons;

The highest of Mount Desert Island's seventeen rocky hills is Cadillac Mountain, named for the famous early eighteenth-century French proprietor of the island, Sieur Antoine de la Mothe Cadillac. Here, it rises gently above Eagle Lake. Kurt Stier.

other points in Down East Maine share that distinction as the sun moves through its annual cycle. For years Cadillac was called Green Mountain and, before that, Bauld, but when the national park was created, the first superintendent renamed the highest point for Sieur Antoine de la Mothe Cadillac, who had received the lands of Mount Desert from King Louis XIV of France in 1688.

Geography and Geology

Mount Desert Island is located in the middle of Maine's coastline just above Penobscot Bay and the mouth of the Penobscot River. The island is a great knob of granite, cut from north to south by parallel glacial valleys, many of which hold freshwater lakes. On the south side, the largest valley opens onto the Atlantic. Called Somes Sound, this valley is considered to be the only true fjord on the East Coast of the United States. Elsewhere on the coast, the jagged contours of the land form a fringe of small coves and harbors typical of most of the Maine coastline.

The geologic history of Mount Desert Island began about 400 million years ago. Magma, welling up through fissures in the sediment, forced aside the preexisting, or "country," rock and created an eleven-mile-long subterranean mass. At the boundaries of this intrusion, where the cooled molten rock, now granite, met the country rock, is the "shatter zone," forming a unique mixture. Volcanic rocks add even more variety to the mix. The whole mass rose, became exposed, and has been shaped ever since by the slow forces of erosion into what we see of the island today. Mount Desert granite, the rock created by slowly cooling magma, ranges in color from greenish gray, caused by the presence of feldspar, to a rosy pink.

Glacial flow and ebb affected Mount Desert in several ways. The grinding movement of the ice carved the typical U-shaped valleys between the island's peaks, scratched ledges, transported boulders, and hollowed ponds. At the ocean's edge, the effect of the glaciers was magnified. As the heavy ice reached the continent's edge, it depressed the land, by some estimates as much as one foot lower for every three feet of ice—and the ice was likely a half-mile thick in some places. Also, because so much of the earth's water was trapped in continental glaciers, the oceans were considerably lower than they are now. The

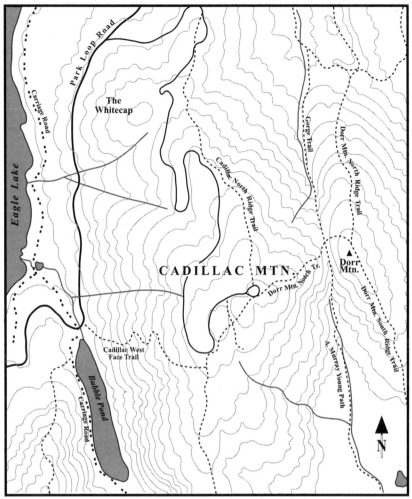

Cadillac Mountain

sea may have been about 330 feet lower than its present level, with great swaths of the continental margin exposed as dry land.

Sea level, therefore, at Mount Desert has been at many different points in the 13,000 years since the edge of the glacier retreated. When ice covered Somes Sound, the sea was miles away. As the Ice Age ended, the sea flooded back about 200 feet higher than its present level, covering the lower parts of the island. The crust of the earth gradually rebounded from being depressed by the ice, and little by little over the millenia, the island rose above the waves. Along the margins, the lobsters surrendered some of the sea to the land creatures. For the last 2,000 years, however, the sea level has been rising slowly again, and the lobsters have started to return to their old territory.

Early History

Mount Desert may have been an occasional year-round dwelling place for the Penobscot Abenaki, who called it Pemetic. Evidence of the Abenaki and their prehistoric ancestors dates back at least six thousand years. Shell heaps along the shore are the best indicators of their lifestyle. There clam shells, and bones from deer, fish, birds, and seals indicate the native peoples' diet during their months of occupation. Disc-shaped shell beads have also been found.

The mountains of the island have so far yielded no archeological discoveries, but native peoples likely combed these inland regions for game and furs, which were traded with Europeans at coastal sites. Unlike much of New England, Mount Desert has few Indian place names remaining, testimony to the island's thorough takeover by both French and English at an early date.

The French laid claim to this part of the New World at the end of the 1500s. King Henri IV placed Pierre du Guast, Sieur de Monts, in charge of the French claim, which extended between the present cities of Montreal and Philadelphia. Because this expanse overlapped with English claims, for the next century and a half Mount Desert was disputed territory. Much blood was shed over who would gain the right to control these northern lands.

Du Guast employed as his pilot an intelligent and adventurous sailor named Samuel de Champlain, whose earlier voyages had won him the post of royal geographer. In the summer of 1604, de Monts started a colony at Saint Croix in Passamaquoddy Bay, and dispatched Champlain to explore west and south along the coast. Champlain wrote of his investigations:

> We passed near to an island some four or five leagues long, in the neighborhood of which we just escaped being lost on a rock that was just awash and which made a hole in the bottom of our boat. From this island to the mainland on the north the dis-

tance is not more than a hundred paces. The island is high and notched in places so that from the sea it gives the appearance of a range of seven or eight mountains. The summits are all bare and rocky. The slopes are covered with pines, firs, and birches. I named it Isle des Monts Deserts.

Du Guast's proprietorship passed into the hands of Antoinette de Pons, marquise de Guercheville, who, in typically French fashion, was eager to establish a Jesuit mission to the natives of America. She sent Father Pierre Biard, a professor of theology at Lyons, into the wilderness from there in 1613. Biard and his party intended to sail up the Penobscot River and establish themselves at Kadesquit, today Bangor. But they were caught in fog off the eastern coast of Mount Desert and were persuaded by the sachem Asticou to settle there instead. Naming the place Saint-Sauveur, they began construction of a fort, but British warships with orders to eliminate French settlements intervened. An armed attack forced the French who had not been killed to surrender. The newborn colony was abandoned.

When John Winthrop came to New England in 1630 to assume the governorship of the Massachusetts Bay Colony, Mount Desert Island was the first land sighted by sailors on the *Arbella*. The island appears again in Massachusetts history during King Philip's War (1675–76), when a man named Thomas Cobbet was taken there as a captive. After nine weeks on the island, Cobbet's release was negotiated through the efforts of a diplomatic Indian named Mugg. The Penobscot sachem Madockawando is said to have received an excellent coat in exchange for the prisoner.

The tug of war for control continued throughout the 1680s, as the French again laid claim to the island. James II of England had put all of his New England possessions, including the disputed Down East territory, under the governance of Sir Edmund Andros. Meanwhile, Louis XIV of France gave Mount Desert Island to the enterprising Sieur Antoine de la Mothe Cadillac, who, according to a census taken by Andros in 1688, was actually living on the island at that time. Cadillac went on to greater fame as the leader of the expedition that founded present-day Detroit, and later served as a governor of French Louisiana.

The mountains on the island offered visual protection for sailing ships during the French and Indian Wars. Prevailing winds would carry the opponents' vessels past the bay on the leeward side of the island, a harbor that offered safety, shelter, and a rendezvous point for French ships. The British navy gathered in the harbor in the mouth of Somes Sound, south and west of the mountain. Since that period, the bay to the east of the island has always borne the name Frenchman Bay.

When the English claimed final victory over France, Maine lands were placed under the jurisdiction of the colony of Massachusetts. In 1762, as part of a convoluted political maneuver, the General Court gave half of Mount Desert Island to its unpopular British overlord, Governor Bernard. He encouraged settlement, and Abraham and Hannah Somes and their four daughters moved from Gloucester, Massachusetts, to become the first permanent colonial settlers.

But Bernard was not destined to control the island's fate for very long. During the American Revolution, Bernard temporarily lost title to his American property. Then, another land claim from the granddaughter of M. Cadillac, Maria Theresa de Grégoire, ended up splitting ownership of the island in two. Bernard's family retained the western half of the island and Mme Gregoire took title to the eastern half, including the mountain that now bears her grandfather's name. American settlers, in a fitting twist of fate, had to acquire their land from the heirs of either a British or a French colonial governor.

Other settlers followed Somes, built their homes near the shore, pastured their livestock on the lowlands of the island, and fished the sea. Timber harvested from the mountainous areas went into ships or was traded as lumber along popular coastal shipping routes. Smooth stones from the shoreline traveled as ballast on ships to Boston, where they paved the streets of the fashionable Louisburg Square on Beacon Hill. Mount Desert had its own tradition of a beacon hill, as one historian writes that signal fires to summon doctors from the mainland were sometimes lit on the highest peaks. But the island was a quiet place, and the population saw only slow growth each year.

Tourism and the Arts

Mount Desert Island was rediscovered in 1844 by a new wave of inhabitants who would come only for the summer months. As he had in the White Mountains, the well-established American painter Thomas Cole came here in search of inspiring landscapes, and sounded the island's praises to his colleagues. "These were the vanguard," wrote Samuel Eliot Morison, "who made Mount Desert known to the great world by their talk as well as their paintings."

Artists rambled all over the island, filling their sketch books with the uniquely beautiful combination of mountain and ocean scenery. They congregated in private homes in Bar Harbor, Somesville, Southwest Harbor, and Northeast Harbor. For many of these artists, accustomed to inland mountains and rivers, Mount Desert presented a completely new opportunity to include the ocean

The advent of tourism on the island in the 1850s marked the beginning of interest in Acadia's mountains here. This view of Jordan Pond House, painted after midcentury by an unknown artist, captures the sense of leisure and great natural beauty that were the island's hallmarks. Photo courtesy William Benton Museum of Art, Storrs, CT.

in their compositions. They seemed to concentrate their efforts on the coast; larger and wilder mountains like the Catskills and the White Mountains, which they knew well, far surpassed these hills for drama. Yet being accustomed to climbing these other mountains, it is not surprising that at Mount Desert, the artists would often go up into the hills to obtain a better view of the ocean.

Frederick Church, Cole's talented pupil, produced a series of pictures of Frenchman Bay during several seasons. Fresh from his investigations of Humboldt and geographic theory, Church departed from Cole's formula of investing nature with human emotion and saw it simply as an expression of the cosmos. His realism and scrupulous attention to scientific detail produced some remarkable paintings of the surrounding mountains and rocky coast.

Church wrote after his first visit: "We have not come thus far to be disappointed. . . . There is an immense range of mountains running through the island, one some two thousand feet high, of admirably varied outline—in some places covered with forest, and broken with rocks and precipices overhanging gems of lakes, and in others showing nothing but bare rock from summit almost to base."

Besides Cole and Church, other prominent names of the era were here, too: Bierstadt, Alvan Fisher, Sanford Gifford, William Hart, and the marine artists Thomas Birch and Fitz Hugh Lane, who created a beautiful pictorial record of this island. Though their fame was all but forgotten by the turn of the century, they left a legacy of fanciful names for such natural landmarks as Porcupine Islands and the Beehive.

Following the first wave of artists came the scientists, a natural progression for mountainous regions. At midcentury, the United States Coast Survey set up its triangulation tower at the logical Down East point—the summit of Cadillac, then called Green Mountain. From 1853 to 1860, surveyors used Cadillac's signal station, providing data from which navigation charts were drawn well into the twentieth century.

In order to get their instruments to the top of the mountain, the Coast Survey's crew cleared a road up from Bar Harbor, then known as the town of Eden. Deputy Collector of Customs Daniel Somes paid a local carpenter fifty dollars to build "in a sheltered place near the top," a "house 10 x 12 square & 9 feet high of boards battened with 3 x 1 inch battens on the roof and sides, floored with table & 2 bunks inside, to have one window with 8 lights and a sliding shutter or dead-light to secure it." Thus specified, the mountain received its first structural imprint from the human inhabitants in its vicinity. Later, as a hotel, this humble building would be expanded or remodeled four times, ultimately being known as the Mountain Tavern.

But it was the artists of midcentury, not the surveyors, who proved to be effective, if unintended, publicists for the area. As their paintings spread the reknown of the ocean and mountain scenery, more and more Mount Desert visitors began to appear from New York, Philadelphia, and Boston. At first they boarded in local homes. Those homeowners gradually expanded their accommodations and began to advertise as hotels. Mount Desert was still hard to reach, however. In 1880, it took twelve hours to go from Boston to Bar Harbor, and at least two days traveling from Philadelphia. A Mount Desert vacation was limited to those who could afford the long trip, and once there, to stay long enough to make it worth the trouble.

Many of these regular Mount Desert summer people, after a few seasons boarding in hotels, bought land and became "cottagers." Mount Desert's unique fusion of the charms of mountain and seaside attracted some powerful and well-connected seasonal residents during its peak years, 1890–1920. These included Mrs. John Jacob Astor; Harvard College President Charles W. Eliot; John D. Rockefeller, Jr.; and George B. Dorr, bachelor heir to a Boston textile fortune, avid outdoorsman, and amateur naturalist.

Summer life on the island was relaxed and informal, filled with parties and social activities, yachting and boating, and frequent canoeing excursions around Frenchman Bay. Particularly popular with the young people was a pastime known as "rocking," an ostensible search for unusual geological specimens that took groups or couples up into the hills in search of interesting treasures without the traditional accompaniment of an adult chaperone.

The summer people's attraction to the mountains, distinctive because the broad panorama of the Atlantic Ocean was close at hand, opened the hills up to more recreational activity. Paths crisscrossed the island and its many hills and fields, and several guidebooks provided an introduction to walking about the island. In the last decade of the century, "village improvement societies" in several towns maintained the trails, marked them with paint blazes, and prepared maps.

After 1912, some truly daring trail construction took place. On Newport (later called Champlain) Mountain, iron ladders were drilled and secured to the rock along a route called the Precipice Trail, permitting ascent of the 1,000-foot-high, otherwise inaccessible cliffs.

The Green Mountain Railroad

Typical of the period, entrepreneurs eager to accommodate public demand and anxious to turn a profit came up with a way to reach the summit of the highest mountain by mechanical means. Frank Clergue, a Bangor businessman, seized the opportunity that lay on the slope of Mount Desert's Green Mountain (later Cadillac). Arranging a lease, in 1881 Clergue quietly began to obtain the necessary permis-

Between 1882 to 1893, a cog railroad patterned after that on Mount Washington carried visitors to the summit of Cadillac. Photo courtesy Bar Harbor Historical Society/Kurt Stier.

In its heyday, the Mountain House on Cadillac accommodated 150 people in its dining room, with sleeping quarters for 50. Photo courtesy Bar Harbor Historical Society/Kurt Stier.

sions to construct a railway there. In the spring of 1883, rails were bolted to bedrock, ox teams hauled ties, and trestles were erected over the grades requiring smoother crossings. Workmen stayed at the summit hotel. Later this building was renovated to include a new restaurant with a capacity of 150 people and sleeping quarters that accommodated 50 overnight guests.

The cog railway on Mount Washington seems to have been Clergue's prototype. Both railroads had the same gauge (Mount Washington's having been changed by an act of the legislature in 1883), and both had the same design of a central cog in the track that held the locomotive's drive wheel. Even before Clergue's specially ordered locomotive arrived from Bangor, workmen were making the descent by Washington-type slideboards. Record time for the one-and-one-eighth-mile track was seventy-five seconds.

A gala celebration marked the opening of the Green Mountain Railroad on June 23, 1883. Invited guests traversed a well-planned route that customers would take—later a steamship took them to Bar

Harbor, then a horse-drawn wagon to Eagle Lake, across Eagle Lake by steamer, then up the railway to the summit. But all was not well with Clergue's enterprise. The carriage road was cutting into his business too much, he thought, and twice he attempted to squelch competition from that quarter. Once he blocked the route by putting up locked gates, and another time he dynamited part of the road. None of this endeared him to the local citizenry, and when Clergue announced plans to construct an electric railway, or trolley line, to replace the horse-drawn wagon from Bar Harbor to Eagle Lake, summer residents rallied to oppose him.

After 1890, Clergue abandoned his bankrupt cog railway and moved on to other enterprises where he felt more welcome. The hotel, rebuilt in 1884 after a fire, was finally torn down in 1897. The railroad tracks were torn up and the remaining ties and spikes were salvaged for other uses. Only the locomotive survived, finding new service at Mount Washington, where a devastating fire in 1895 destroyed four of the cog railway's seven locomotives.

Preservation

Perhaps it was the hotel that first caused residents of neighboring islands and peninsulas to remark that some people didn't know any better than to sit on their scenery. The newly invented portable sawmill began to threaten the remaining forests of the more inaccessible mountains in the interior. Certainly the railroad galvanized opinion on what sorts of recreation seemed appropriate. The very characteristics that had attracted Mount Desert's devoted summer residents suddenly seemed in jeopardy. Financially resourceful, they joined together in a unique reaction.

Led by the potent team of Charles Eliot and George Dorr, a movement began to preserve the island from further development, promoting a simple way of life and an appreciation for the island's natural beauty free from man-made distractions. This group of exemplary conservationists agreed on one principle, expressed by Charles Eliot in his 1904 statement called *The Right Development of Mount Desert:* "The whole island ought to be treated by every resident and by the body of voters as if it were a public park; that is, the beauty and convenience of the place as a health and pleasure resort ought to be kept constantly in mind to guide the policy of the towns and the habit and customs of the population....What needs to be forever excluded from the island is the squalor of the city, with all its inevitable bustle, dirt, and ugliness."

Eliot had resolved to see what could be done to preserve Cadillac Mountain and other scenic portions of the island. His son, Charles Eliot, Jr., a prominent landscape architect, had established the Trustees of Reservations in 1891 as a pioneer private land-conservation organization in Massachusetts. On his son's advice, Eliot brought together a group of conservation-minded islanders, including George B. Dorr, to create the Hancock County Trustees of Public Reservations, chartered in 1903 by the Maine legislature. In Mount Desert, Dorr found a cause worthy of his life and his considerable fortune, and these he devoted fully from 1901 until his death in 1944.

George B. Dorr spearheaded an unprecedented effort to preserve the land on Mount Desert from further development, acquiring much of the acreage that later became Acadia National Park. Photo courtesy Bar Harbor Historical Society/Kurt Stier.

Dorr and others purchased key tracts of land, including Cadillac Mountain, and gave them to the new land trust.

Local citizens nearly thwarted Dorr's ambitions. Alarmed by the fact that lands held by the trust were not taxable, they initiated a move to rescind the charter of the Hancock County Trustees of Public Reservations. Dorr fought off this attack, but it taught him that the land trust was a fragile entity, and he resolved to campaign for federal protection of the land he loved. In 1914, Dorr went to Washington and succeeded in making his case.

President Woodrow Wilson established Sieur de Monts National Monument by presidential proclamation in 1916. Justification for the designation included the island's early association with Samuel de Champlain and recent scientific interest in its topography, geology, fauna and flora. But National Monument status proved inadequate for Dorr, who had been following the progress of the fledgling National Park Service and realized that it could offer even greater protection for his park.

The persuasive Dorr decided to approach Congress once more with his idea, and again he succeeded. In 1919, the National Park Service formally christened its first park east of the Mississippi. It was to be called Lafayette National Park in an effort to strengthen public support for it, just as World War I was ending, by linking it symbolically with a great French war hero. A decade later it was renamed Acadia, from l'Acadie, the French designation for the Down East coast of Maine and the Canadian maritimes. It was the first and only national park donated wholly by private interests to the federal government.

Meanwhile a strong new hand had come into the game. John D. Rockefeller, Jr., purchased a house southwest of Cadillac Mountain at Seal Harbor in 1910, and in 1914 George B. Dorr recruited Rockefeller's support to help preserve the natural beauty of Mount Desert. Rockefeller befriended Dorr and came to regard Eliot, much his elder, as a mentor.

Rockefeller's particular interest, beyond his own 104-room mansion and acres of well-tended grounds, lay in the natural scenery of the island's woods. Inspired by the principles of Frederick Law

The network of carriage roads created by John D. Rockefeller, Jr., on Mount Desert between 1913 and 1940 expressed his belief that natural beauty could be both preserved and made accessible to the public. Kurt Stier.

Olmsted, he laid out and constructed a system of extraordinary carriage roads throughout the park, everywhere framing views of the ocean or mountains by careful native plantings. The roads were an expression of Rockefeller's belief that the beauty of the park should be available to all, not just to those able to hike through it, and should not be marred by man-made intrusions. From the first, automobiles were excluded and only horse-drawn vehicles were allowed.

Through many years of painstaking design, meticulous construction, and extravagant expense, Rockefeller's road system became a reality. Some of the roads he built on land he owned, much of which was later donated to the park. But Rockefeller also financed and supervised construction of carriage roads within the park and on land held by the Hancock County Trustees of Public Reservations. Eventually the network included fifty-seven miles of carriage roads, sixteen beautiful stone bridges, and two gate houses built between 1913 and 1940. He was also responsible for "motor" roads like the Park Loop Road and for improving the road to the summit of Cadillac Mountain. Rockefeller's donations to the park make up almost one-third of its land—11,000 acres.

The Great Fire

Rockefeller, Dorr, and Eliot's vision for Mount Desert—of preserving nature and encouraging quiet recreation within its pristine embrace—suffered a critical blow in 1947. Following months of dry weather, a raging October fire swept across most of the eastern half of the island, including Cadillac Mountain. For the first three days, the blaze traveled slowly, consuming only 169 acres. But then, high winds descended and fanned the flames into an out-of-control inferno.

The town of Bar Harbor lay directly in the path of destruction, and the Coast Guard had begun to evacuate the population when the wind suddenly shifted and spared the town. But the devastation of the two-week-long fire was staggering—18,000 acres of the island burned, including Cadillac Mountain and 10,000 acres in the park. Nearly 250 homes, summer cottages, and hotels were lost, as well as the Jackson Laboratory, a world-famous research station that bred mice for scientific experiments.

In 1947 a terrible forest fire swept Cadillac Mountain and most of the rest of the eastern end of the island. Seventeen thousand acres were burned with the loss estimated at $23 million. Photo courtesy Bar Harbor Historical Society/ Kurt Stier.

Many thought the island would never recover. But fire can be a restorative to nature, clearing out accumulated underbrush and stimulating the growth of a broad variety of species. Today the forests have reestablished themselves and the burned-over parts of the island support healthy ecosystems. The old woods can be seen in only a few places: along the southern part of the Park Loop Road and in the mountains on the west side of the island.

The Island Today

Declining budgets at the National Park Service (NPS) beginning in the 1970s and an unrelenting tide of more and more visitors to the island forced Acadia's trails onto *Backpacker* magazine's top-ten list of the country's critically endangered trail systems. An inventory of the

250-mile system, conducted by the Appalachian Mountain Club for the Park Service in 1988, resulted in the discouraging report that only 100 miles of those trails were actually usable.

Recognizing their shared goals and complementary resources, however, the Appalachian Mountain Club and the National Park Service teamed up in 1992 to become partners at Acadia. AMC members perform much-needed trail work and help with nature programming during the peak season in the park. Echo Lake Camp, a gift to the AMC from George Dorr in the 1920s, serves as an overnight base for trail workers and as the center for joint AMC-NPS environmental-education offerings. Another group, the Friends of Acadia, and unaffiliated volunteers, make important contributions toward the ongoing work of clearing brush, marking trails, and controlling erosion.

The National Park Service has undertaken another initiative to renew and respect the Native American connection to the land of Mount Desert. Its efforts include cooperation with several groups of Native Americans, including the Penobscot and Passamaquoddy, who have begun holding private spiritual and ceremonial activities on Cadillac Mountain. For the past several years, one of the more publicized Native American activities is a vision quest held each year on Earth Day in April on the summit of Cadillac.

Suggestions for Visitors

Not all of the island of Mount Desert is publicly owned, and the protected lands, some 35,000 acres that make up the park, are intermixed with privately owned lands. The Schoodic Point peninsula and nearby Isle au Haut are also part of the park. The former can be reached both by car and by water; the latter only by a forty-minute boat ride.

Acadia is a walker's paradise. The natural beauty of the island, the almost constant cooling breezes, and miles of interconnected trails of varying degrees of difficulty virtually guarantee a pleasant experience here. The visitor center, staffed by the NPS, even has a Difficulty Ratings Chart for the 120 miles of trails that are currently marked and maintained. The visitor center has weekly talks on subalpine botany on Cadillac and the other peaks, as well as programs on

View of the Porcupines, small islands in Frenchman Bay, from Cadillac summit. Kurt Stier.

history, glaciation, natural history and even stargazing. The park publishes a newsletter during the summer and fall listing all island events. Observations of the night sky from Cadillac, as well as the sunsets, have always been very popular.

Because of the auto road on Cadillac, that mountain receives more use than any other on the island. At the summit, besides a parking lot, are restroom facilities and a small gift shop contained within a single-story wood-frame structure.

A moderate 4.4-mile hike of Cadillac Mountain follows the North Ridge Trail, from North Ridge Cadillac Parking Area. A mix of steep grades and level stretches, it ascends the mountain just east of the automobile road, with clear views from the ridge much of the way. The reward of the view at the summit is unsurpassed.

The Precipice Trail on Champlain still utilizes ladders and handrails to scale a nearly vertical rock face. For bird watchers an added incentive in exploring this route is the possibility of sighting a peregrine falcon, a species extirpated from the island in the 1950s and reintroduced successfully in the 1980s. A pair of birds has nested for the past two years on Champlain Mountain, one of two known historic locations for the birds on the island. During their nesting season, the Precipice Trail is closed to protect their habitat.

An island tradition is tea and popovers at the Jordan Pond House, located near the distinctive double-humped mountain known as the Bubbles. Jordan Pond can be approached by footpath or, for the less adventurous, by car from the Park Loop Road.

The Abbe Museum, at Sieur de Monts Spring, houses collections and exhibits relating to the native peoples of the island and is open seasonally. Near the museum is the Nature Center and the Wild Gardens of Acadia, a garden of native plants. Attending NPS ranger-led programs and visiting the Natural History Museum at the College of the Atlantic are good ways to learn more about the wildlife, geology, and botany of the island.

For overnight accommodations, there are both park-run and private campgrounds. Trailside camping is strictly prohibited. Acadia is a popular place, so expect crowds during the summer season. Some campgrounds take reservations; others are run on a first-come, first-served basis. Detailed information is available from Acadia National Park, P. O. Box 177, Bar Harbor, ME 04609; 207-288-3338.

Katahdin

Katahdin stands above the surrounding plain unique in grandeur and glory. The works of man are short lived. Monuments decay, buildings crumble and wealth vanishes, but Katahdin in its massive grandeur will forever remain the mountain of the people of Maine. Throughout the ages it will stand as an inspiration to the men and women of this State.

—Percival Baxter, 1931

Katahdin is New England's wilderness mountain. Its remote location, its great size, and the lack of man-made intrusions around it attract lovers of mountains as to a sacred place. They have been told this mountain will inspire awe, and it does. Its mighty presence lifts the spirit and fills the eyes with delight. Katahdin is spectacular, both to look up at and to look down from.

The record of its history demands respect, too. The last of New England's major peaks to be explored and mapped, it remained almost exclusively the domain of loggers, woodsmen, and serious sportsmen well into the twentieth century. No structures have ever been built on its summit. Low-growing alpine grasses and plants cling precariously to the tumbled rocks along with krummholz, the distinctive stunted tree growth typical of New England's highest areas.

Baxter Peak, the highest point on Katahdin, stands to the west of Pamola and Chimney Peak. Kathy Tarantola.

The idea of preserving Katahdin as a wilderness refuge took hold of a native son who would stop at nothing less than complete protection for the mountain and the region around it. Percival Baxter made Katahdin his life's work, and expended much of his personal fortune to acquire more than 200,000 acres that would later be named in his honor. Baxter State Park, unrivaled in the East, stands as just protection for a majestic mountain.

Geography and Geology

Katahdin is synonymous with the wild mountain lands of northern Maine. Remote from the coast, in a densely forested region of few towns and roads, it towers above the relatively low land surrounding it. The mountain is actually a series of peaks arranged in a fishhook shape: Hamlin and Howe peaks to the north and Pamola and Baxter peaks (joined by a dramatic ridge called the Knife Edge) on the south. Baxter Peak, the highest of the summits and second in height among New England mountains only to Mount Washington, reaches 5,257 feet. An alpine plateau called the Saddle joins the northern and southern sections, and the East and West branches of the Penobscot River drain the slopes.

The Katahdin massif forms the northern extremity of the Appalachian chain. A convoy of lesser mountains have Katahdin as its flagship. South Turner Mountain (3,122 feet), Doubletop Mountain (3,488 feet), North Brother (4,143 feet), and the Traveler (3,541 feet) are among the escorting peaks that, taken together, make up the nearby range.

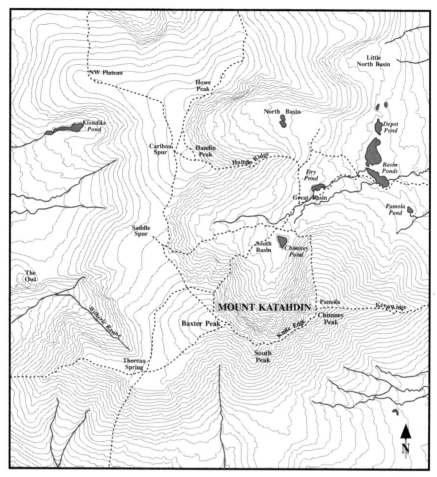

Katahdin

The Katahdin Range originated from a great inland sea, where layers of debris built up in deposits along the bottom. About 350 million to 400 million years ago, these sediments were disturbed by erupting volcanoes that spewed lava and ash. To these two events, each responsible for rock formations on the Katahdin Range today, was added a third: Magma (or molten rock) swelled up through underground faults where it cooled slowly into coarse-grained granite.

Then, mountain-building forces of pressure, folding, and faulting raised up what was once the sea floor into the ripples and ridges of the Appalachian chain. Erosion, working infinitely slowly on the different rock compositions, wore down the mountains at different rates. Katahdin granites, wearing away less quickly than the softer sedimentary and igneous (volcanic) rocks, form most of the mountain's bedrock today. Often, because of the presence of feldspar, this rock takes on a reddish color.

The movement of glaciers during the Pleistocene era (beginning about a million years ago) created the outline of the mountain as it stands today. Evidence of glacial activity is unusually pronounced on Katahdin. The sharp jagged profile of the summit ridge was not worn by ice and erosion in the same way that the mountains in the other New England states have been. Here, instead, the top of the mountain protruded above the ice sheet, escaping the ice's grinding action and leaving it jagged rather than rounded.

Perhaps Katahdin's most distinctive feature is the steep-walled gulfs on the mountain's flanks. These are glacial cirques—deep three-sided ravines formed by the action of tremendous accumulations of snow during the Ice Age, when summers were too short and too cold to melt the previous winter's snow. Year after year, snow piled upon itself, compressing the lower layer into a viscous form of ice that seized rocks weighing tons, plucked them from the mountainside, and bore them into the valley.

When the ice disappeared, some 12,000 years ago, Katahdin bore gouges in its flanks resembling giant bites from an apple. Named the Great Basin, the Northwest Basin, and the North and South basins, each of these is drained by small streams that collect in individual ponds at its foot.

Early History and Exploration

The name Katahdin is of Indian origin, and the sense of an Indian presence is still strong here. The Penobscot Abenaki named most of the land features here, and their descendants still live in the valley of the Penobscot River. These many-syllabled names often test visitors' pronunciation to the limit. Abol Stream, which drains the south side of the mountain, is short for Aboljacknagesic, meaning "open land stream." To Charles Turner, the first white man known to have stood atop Katahdin, the mountain's name sounded like No-tar-dn or Cata-din, which means "the primary or greatest mountain." A variant contemporary spelling is Ktaadn.

The Penobscot were masters of their woods and their river but believed that the mountaintops belonged to the gods. Therefore, while the Indians hunted Katahdin's broad shoulders, they avoided any invasion of the sanctified naked peaks. Katahdin might be compared to the Greeks' Mount Olympus. According to their beliefs, passed down through legends and accounts of white travelers in the region, the mountain summit was the home of a many-faceted god called Pamola, whose name, according to contemporary Indian sources, meant "comes flying." Pamola was vengeful, and to violate his domain meant certain punishment.

Images of Pamola, the native deity of Katahdin, have captured the interest of visitors to the mountain ever since the Abenaki told the early explorers about him. According to John Gyles, a Maine settler captured by Indians about 1690, the mountain god resembled "a great speckled bird, like an eagle, though somewhat larger." Pamola's size increased in later stories. John Neptune, an Indian guide, said Pamola had "a head and face as large as four horses, and shaped like that of a man. His body, form and feet were those of an eagle, and his strength was such that he could take up a moose with one of his arrow-like claws." In a different incarnation, the god is a storm bird whose wings pummeled intruders with wind, clouds, lightning, and torrents of rain and snow.

One Indian legend portrays the milder aspects of the god. When an Indian woman wished that the mountain were a man so she could marry him, the spirit of Pamola appeared in human form and took her to live inside Katahdin. The woman bore two children, a boy and a girl. When she asked her husband for permission to visit her family on the river to show them her children, Pamola granted the wish, giving each child a magic power. The boy could strike dead anything at which he pointed, and the girl, if she passed her fingers over her lips before she spoke, was able to make anything she said come true.

As the small family approached their former village, they were dismayed to see heartbreaking evidence of famine. Thanks to the powers Pamola had given the daughter, food supplies were restored to the people. But, alas, the young boy for some reason raised his finger and pointed at a man. No harm had been intended, but the god's promise was fulfilled and the result was fatal. In shame, the woman and her children were sent away from the Penobscot to live forever within the mountain.

Representations of Pamola, perhaps because his form was so changeable, are lacking in Indian iconography. Only two attempts to capture the appearance of this god are known, the first drawn by a historian in 1866. The second and better-known rendition shows a friendly, fanciful creature: part man, part moose, and part eagle, chatting with a well-known Katahdin guide, Roy Dudley. The artist of

Local artist and devoted Katahdin climber Jake Day drew this humorous pictorial representation of the Indian spirit Pamola chatting with ranger Roy Dudley at the Chimney Pond Campground in the 1930s. Photo courtesy Baxter State Park.

this cartoon was Maurice "Jake" Day, who drew the sketch in 1933 while listening to Roy Dudley spin stories about Pamola at Katahdin's Chimney Pond.

Early History

Katahdin was the last great peak in New England to be explored by white settlers. Because Penobscot leaders maintained neutrality during the French and Indian Wars and were skillful diplomats, colonial authorities allowed these tribes to stay on their land at a time when whites were eliminating the native presence elsewhere in New England.

Being so remote from the coast and so far from the centers of population, the river valleys of northern Maine offered no incentive to settlers. Therefore, paid surveyors, rather than curious adventurers, military tacticians, or would-be farmers, were the first whites to explore the Katahdin region. Working for state or national governments to chart land claims or settle boundary disputes, these men helped to open up the vast wilderness of inland Maine.

The Massachusetts governor, who had jurisdiction over Maine until separate statehood was granted in 1820, speculated that a road passing through the valley of the Penobscot could link the city of Quebec, then an English possession, with the Atlantic seaboard, bringing great prosperity to his territory. As the first step in realizing that dream, he hired Joseph Chadwick in 1763 to map the Penobscot River. Chadwick noted that Katahdin was the highest of the area's mountains, according to the Indians, but he did not climb it. All his surveying work came to naught. After the Revolution, when Canada became a French possession, the idea of an international roadway was abandoned.

It was not until 1804, when the Lewis and Clark expedition was well on its way up the Missouri River, that Katahdin was first climbed by whites. Charles Turner and his group of eleven surveyors ascended the Penobscot River's West Branch in canoes, then drew closer to the mountain by paddling up a tributary now called Katahdin Stream. At 8:00 A.M. on the morning of August 13, they left their boats and began a laborious trek along Katahdin's western spur, probably following the approximate route of the present-day Hunt Trail. They made their way through the rising forest, then, leaving the trees behind, ventured onto the treeless and windy ridge. At 5:00 P.M., Turner's group triumphantly reached the summit, where they left a bottle of rum and a sheet of lead inscribed with their initials.

The next group to climb the mountain successfully was led by Colin Campbell. His team of British surveyors were trying to gain an edge for Canada in a boundary dispute with Maine. From their camp at the mouth of Katahdin Stream, Campbell twice tried unsuccessfully to find a route up the mountain. Then, on October 13, 1819, Campbell followed Abol Stream and discovered a three-year-old landslide. He followed the steep, wide path to the "table land" west of the summit then on to the peak itself. His newly gained expertise put him in demand as a guide, and Campbell returned the following year to lead a group of British and American surveyors up the same route to the summit. The path of the 1816 landslide on Katahdin's south face, named Abol Slide, created a naturally cleared ascent route that is still in use today.

The results of these early surveys led to a somewhat different pattern of establishing townships compared to elsewhere in New England. The government of Maine decided to divide its largely uninhabited interior into a grid of numbered townships, each six miles square. In order to start the grid, a base line had to be drawn above the existing named towns. Joseph Norris and his son were hired in 1825 to survey this base line. Their starting point was at the head of the Saint Croix River on the eastern border of Maine. From a "monument" there, a yellow birch tree banded with three iron hoops, they were to survey and mark a straight line west to Quebec.

Norris and his son set out late in 1825 to survey the Monument Line in accordance with their contract with the state. Their compass led them through Maine's roughest country. They had to go straight over the top of East Turner Mountain, not far from the summit of South Turner, and then across Katahdin's northern spur. As autumn changed to winter, the surveyors, still many miles from Quebec, found themselves at the headwall of the Northwest Basin, facing a precipitous drop. Norris decided that it was time to bail out. He piled rocks into a cairn to mark the point at which his line had reached the precipice, and ordered a withdrawal. They retreated to the south, climbing to Hamlin Peak, crossing the saddle, and making the fourth recorded ascent of the summit called Monument Peak (renamed Baxter Peak in 1931). The next day the group descended Abol Slide and returned to civilization by way of the Penobscot.

Edwin Rose came back in 1833 to complete the Katahdin segment of the Monument Line between the Northwest Basin and Doubletop Mountain, six miles to the west. In the intervening years, the rest of the line had been surveyed to Quebec, and when the middle section was finished, calculations proved to have been slightly off. The westbound line from Katahdin failed to meet the Quebec line precisely, so the Monument Line makes a half-mile jog just west of Doubletop. Nevertheless, towns were assigned numbers and letters to designate their position from the line, TR for township (running vertically), and R for range (running horizontally). The Rose expedition accomplished more: It also made the first detailed map of Katahdin.

In the decade of the 1830s, surveying and mapping yielded to timber harvesting and scientific exploration. Logging roads created to harvest the virgin white pine made access to Katahdin easier for a group of three professors who arrived on horseback at a logging camp in August of 1836. Two of the scientists were from Colby College, George Washington Keely and Phineas Barnes, and the third, Jacob Whitman Bailey, came from the military academy at West Point. They hired two men to guide them and to carry supplies that included tea, hard bread, pork, and salt. The mountain elements tested them with unpleasant conditions. After a difficult bushwhack on their first day of hiking, they slept in drizzle at the foot of Abol Slide. Rain continued as the five began their climb the next morning. Bailey and Keely turned back, but Barnes and the guides made the summit.

More scientific scrutiny of this giant of a mountain followed the Colby College expedition. In 1836, the state commissioned its first official geological survey. Geologist Charles T. Jackson, brother-in-law of Ralph Waldo Emerson, already had conducted a similar survey for New Hampshire, and in 1837 he set out to explore the region around Katahdin. There were still no real roads to the area. At Old Town, Jackson hired a Penobscot guide, Louis Neptune, and a group to handle their canoe. The party arrived at the base of Abol Slide in late September and ascended the next day into a storm. Neptune's warnings about Pamola's powers did not dissuade them, and part of the group reached the summit. They would have been lost in the clouds had the guide not taken care to mark their path with cairns, enabling them to regain the top of the slide. One important accomplishment came out of Jackson's survey—a surprisingly accurate estimate of the altitude of the summit at 5,300 feet, only slightly exceeding the current measurement of 5,267 feet.

The remote and rugged terrain around Katahdin almost required that parties wishing to explore the mountain hire an experienced guide. Woodsman guides themselves made many new discoveries and accomplishments on Katahdin.

The Rev. Marcus Keep, a powerful, boastful, eccentric character, stands out among the earliest of Katahdin's expert guides. A Middlebury graduate who preferred missionary service in the wilds of Maine to a more traditional pulpit, he failed in his first attempt to climb Katahdin in 1846. But the next year, he and a group of fellow ministers climbed Katahdin's east shoulder, a ridge that now bears his name. From there, they traveled to Pamola Peak, which marks the upper end of this spur, and then on to the summit via the Knife Edge, a mile of narrow, jagged ridge. Keep's party became the first to cross the Knife Edge in conquering Katahdin. He would accumulate another first as well, returning just a few weeks later to become the first person known to have reached Chimney Pond.

Keep created the first real trail on Katahdin, the Keep Path, in 1848, and guided groups up the mountain every year until 1861. In that year, he worked with a geological-survey team headed by Charles Hitchcock (who also worked in the White Mountains). Keep made his last trip up Katahdin in 1881, guiding Charles E. Hamlin, a Harvard geologist who had made at least five previous visits to Katahdin. Hamlin, for whom one of Katahdin's summits is named, made an exhaustive study of Katahdin that generated many published articles and a large-scale relief model of the mountain. Hamlin was also responsible for forging an early link between Katahdin and the Appalachian Mountain Club, joining the fledgling Boston-based organization in 1877, the second year of its existence.

Authors Laura and Guy Waterman have captured the distinctive character of the Katahdin experience in these years in a passage in *Forest and Crag*, pointing out the contrast with the gentility of the White Mountain tourist experience.

> These tales of bushwhacking through blowdown, burnt-over brush and bogs, with pork and bread slung over the shoulder in blankets, cold and damp bivouacs on the open slides, clambering over the Knife Edge, lengthy approach marches, and smoky lumber camps—all speak of a world different from the fashionable tour of other Northeastern mountain regions. Katahdin remained, right up to the Civil War, a test for the adventurous—a long, long way from the elegance of the Glen House ballrooms, the Catskill Mountain House's columned piazza, or Mr. Bingham's "Astor House of those altitudes" on Mansfield.

The Logging Camps

Much of the lore associated with the Katahdin region is drawn from its logging camps. The Penobscot River was the origin of America's logging culture, and in the lumber industry's early, innocent days, small independent companies sent the plentiful white-pine logs downriver to sawmills in the towns of Orono and Bangor.

French bateaux, or bark canoes, made by and purchased from the Abenaki, were used by the loggers to go up the rivers. Scouts "cruised" the woods to find good stands of pine. When lost in the trackless forest, they climbed to the tops of trees to look for landmarks. Camps were built at promising locations, and the enormous trees, up to two hundred feet tall and ten feet in diameter, were felled, limbed, sawed into manageable lengths, and branded with a mark that identified the mill's ownership of the log. These were the occupations of the summer and fall—plus the cutting of wild meadows to be dried into hay to feed the oxen required in the next stage of the operation.

As soon as the river froze, teams of oxen were marched up the icy highway to the camps, and there spent the winter dragging logs to places where spring waters could reach them. Henry David Thoreau,

Bateaux such as this carried the first explorers up the rivers and streams close to the mountain, from where they planned their bushwhacking ascents. Henry David Thoreau traveled to Katahdin in 1846 in a similar boat. Photo courtesy Northeast Archives of Folklore and Oral History, Orono, ME.

the Concord naturalist, described this work in 1846 after ascending the West Branch of the Penobscot on his journey to Katahdin.

> All winter long the logger goes on piling up the trees which he has trimmed and hauled in some dry ravine at the head of a stream, and then in the spring he stands on the bank and whistles for Rain and Thaw, ready to wring the perspiration out of his shirt to swell the tide, till suddenly, with a whoop and halloo from him, shutting his eyes, as if to bid farewell to the existing state of things, a fair proportion of his winter's work goes scrambling down the country, followed by his faithful dogs, Thaw and Rain and Freshet and Wind, the whole pack in full cry, toward the Orono Mills.

Brave and skillful men were required to shepherd the load of logs downriver and across lakes to the mills. Obstacles to the smooth passage of the logs often presented a life-or-death situation for the logger, but only a safe delivery of logs meant payment for the year's work. If the logs caught on rocks and caused jams, loggers with spikes on their boots chopped loose the key log, releasing the others. They trusted their wits and agility to be able to jump free before the newly released logs rushed downstream with them.

Where the river current flowed smoothly, an endless train of mill-bound logs was kept in order by drivers and their pikes. Invented in 1858, a special implement called a peavey was used by these men to help loosen any jammed logs in the massive flow. Balanced on the unstable surface of floating logs, sometimes it chanced that the driver's spiked boots failed him, and he slipped through a space that opened momentarily between two logs. Alas for him, the little window of light often moved downstream beyond his reach, and the darkness of the great log flow covered him. Loggers did not expect to die in bed.

Henry David Thoreau, with his cousin George Thatcher of Bangor and several Indian guides, had loggers pole them up the West Branch in 1846. Tying their bateau to a tree in Abol Stream, the group set off overland for Katahdin with Thoreau at their head. Ignoring the advice he no doubt received, Thoreau insisted on planning the route of ascent himself. Using his method from home, he set a direct compass line toward the summit and proceeded to follow it. Somewhere to the right of Abol Slide, they spent hours in the woods and still had not gained the summit. Fearing they were lost, a logger in the group named McCauslin climbed a tree to check their bearings. He stretched out his arm and pointed toward the summit; their line of march was correct. But they still had hours to go, pressing on through the tangled, steep, rocky woods in what Thoreau called the "worst kind of traveling."

As Thoreau's companions pitched camp that night on the mountainside, Thoreau scouted ahead, walking atop the stunted spruce trees in the failing light, until a cloud turned him back. Their camp was not a comfortable one:

> the trees here seemed so evergreen and sappy, that we almost
> doubted if they would acknowledge the influence of fire; but fire
> prevailed at last, and blazed here, too, like a good citizen of the
> world....Some of the more aerial and finer-spirited winds rushed

and roared through the ravine all night, from time to time arousing our fire, and dispersing the embers about. It was as if we lay in the very nest of a young whirlwind.

The next morning a determined Thoreau outdistanced his companions and climbed on alone, above the treeline, on boulders shattered from Katahdin's solid bulk.

They were the raw materials of the planet dropped from an unseen quarry, which the vast chemistry of nature would anon work up, or work down, into the smiling and verdant plains and valleys of earth....The tops of mountains are among the unfinished parts of the globe, whither it is a slight insult to the gods to climb and pry into their secrets, and try their effect on our humanity.

Alone in the mist, short of the peak by an unknown distance, Thoreau ended his climb. He was worried about becoming completely separated from his companions—and perhaps he chose to spare Pamola even the "slight insult" of reaching the summit. For whatever reasons, he retreated from the clouded height, found his friends, and together they escaped to the river.

Thoreau's Katahdin experience, which he chronicled in "Ktaadn," part of his book *The Maine Woods*, published in 1864, changed his life. Where once he had imagined the mountain as an idyllic retreat from the constraints of urban society, he had come to a different understanding of the power of the elements. Summing up his travels to Katahdin, Thoreau wrote: "It is even more grim and wild there than you had anticipated."

Art and Artists

Despite Thoreau's mixed review, by the second half of the century Katahdin's appeal to recreational hikers was broadening. Although Alden Partridge never climbed Katahdin, America's celebrated landscape artists made their way there and were among the first to participate in the backwoods movement at Katahdin. Their search for wilderness subjects had begun with the Catskills, took in the Adirondacks and White Mountains, ranged westward with the discovery of Yosemite, and ultimately included Central and South America and even the Arctic. In the mountains of Maine, they found a pure wilderness voice. At Katahdin, Creation was laid out for them to appreciate and paint. The mountain became a symbol for the strength and nobility of the American continent, bearing the message of America as a God-given paradise.

Experiencing Katahdin at midcentury was a hard-won reward. Getting there required several days' journey over rough logging roads. Loads were hauled on wooden sleds. Camp comprised two lean-tos, one for the guests and one for the guides, arranged on opposite sides of a cooking-and-dining cabin, with a log fire between that consumed three-quarters of a cord of wood per day. Bedding consisted of rubber mats and a few blankets laid on a bed of evergreen boughs. Food was meager, to be supplemented by a catch of fresh trout or just-picked berries as often as possible.

As described in a *Scribner's Monthly* article published in 1878, the basics included pork, hard bread, tea, sugar, a few lemons (antiscorbutic), beans, wheat flour, baking powder, rice, potatoes, raisins, Indian meal, and "occasional luxuries"—canned meats, vegetables, and butter. "With regard to spirits, rum is probably the best adapted, and while a little is necessary in case of exhaustion or chill, and often has a hygienic importance, it is a very serious mistake, as the hardy lumbermen well know, to use it as a stimulant before exertion, or freely at any time."

The painter Frederick Edwin Church made several trips to Katahdin, finding in the mountain the culmination of his search for the quintessential image of America. Church and his friend Theodore Winthrop journeyed to Katahdin in 1856 on a voyage of personal discovery, seeking contact with the "wildest wilds" of a "fresh world" so that they "might be re-created to a more sensitive vitality." Making dozens of sketches of the mountain from different vantage points, Church celebrated the wild power of nature and the textured beauty of its forms. Church's art echoed the Transcendental philosophers of the same era in expressing a knowledge of God uniquely available to Americans through the direct experience of nature.

Frederick Church made dozens of sketches and several major paintings of Katahdin. This small oil painting accentuated the craggy glaciated slopes and symbolic grandeur of this wilderness icon. Photo courtesy Addison Gallery of American Art, Andover, MA.

Recreation

Logging activity here, as in the White Mountains, made it possible for more visitors to get to Katahdin and largely determined the approaches that were used. In the early 1880s, timber cutting shifted from small-scale operations to a true industry, supplying the paper-pulp industry with spruce and fir in addition to the pine cut for lumber. Activity on Katahdin shifted from the south side of the mountain to its northern slopes. A new center for logging activity developed there around Wassataquoik Stream, which drains the lands immediately to the north of the mountain.

Foster Tracey and his son-in-law, Hugh Love, began building dams and camps here, making far-reaching changes to the relatively untouched landscape north of Katahdin. The first Tracey and Love camp, located at the junction of Pogy Brook and Wassataquoik Stream, became known as Old City. A second camp near Russell Pond was called New City. From there loggers created a radiating network of trails and roads that is still in use as part of Baxter State Park.

The loggers' sideline of accommodating tourists meant more recreational use of the mountain. In 1884 Foster Tracey cut a bridle path to the summit of Katahdin from his camp six miles north of the mountain, where the gradient was more gentle than elsewhere on the mountain. Even though he envisioned a "resort" here, Tracey's clientele was not the type for large hotels or well-graded paths. Rustic camps have remained, then, as now, the only order of the day, and by New Hampshire or Vermont standards, the hiking trails are primitive. The Appalachian Mountain Club initiated a long-term relationship with the mountain in 1887, shortly after its founding. Participants at an annual group outing called August Camp worked to cut and maintain trails there, and had their own shelter at Kidney Pond on Katahdin.

Both logging camps and tourists led inevitably to fires. One of the biggest occurred June 2–9, 1903. A blaze swept the area north of Katahdin, including the neighborhoods of Wassataquoik Stream and Russell Pond, destroying many of the camps and trails in that area. After a second major forest fire in 1908, timber interests formed the Maine Forestry District and created a network of fire lookout towers that remained in service until 1972. At one point a tower was erected on Abol Slide, but Katahdin was too frequently in fog and clouds to be a practical location for a lookout.

Although the last of the logging rights around Katahdin have now expired, forest fires still pose a constant threat. In 1977, for instance, a severe fire southwest of the mountain burned 3,588 acres, the scars of which will be visible for a long time to come. Lasting for fourteen days, the blaze raged out of control between the foot of the mountain and the West Branch of the Penobscot, reaching as close as Foss and Knowlton ponds.

Protection

When the national-park system was created in 1893, some groups in Maine saw it as a way to assure Katahdin's ultimate preservation, at that time still largely at the mercy of the logging companies. The idea was first proposed by the Maine Hotel Proprietor's Association in 1895 and drew support from other tourist-oriented interests. Then in

1904 the Maine State Federation of Women's Clubs took up the cause, and their broad-based support convinced others that this spectacular centerpiece of the north woods was worthy of federal protection and promotion. They asked Congress to create a national park at Katahdin, but the legislators refused to act, recognizing that to do so would alienate the considerable political interests in the state opposed to a federal takeover of these lands.

Percival P. Baxter, a wealthy bachelor from Portland, single-handedly led the effort to preserve Katahdin, but as a state park rather than a national park. In 1918, while he was a state legislator, Baxter made his first attempt to have the state of Maine acquire the Katahdin area. When he first climbed the mountain two years later, he vowed resolutely, "This shall belong to Maine if I live." It took him nearly a lifetime and much of his personal fortune, but Baxter made good on his promise.

Percival P. Baxter single-handedly preserved the Katahdin wilderness "for the people of Maine" with his purchase of more than 200,000 acres. Photo courtesy Baxter State Park.

As a two-term governor from 1921 to 1925, Baxter tried again to persuade the legislature to purchase the mountain. They refused. Then in 1930, as a private citizen using his own money, Baxter bought almost 6,000 acres of the mountain and donated the entire parcel to the state of Maine. In return, an appreciative legislature honored Baxter by naming the newly created state park after him and changing the name of the range's highest peak from Monument Mountain to Baxter Peak.

Baxter enlarged the park with another gift in 1937, and made continual additions throughout the 1940s and 1950s. He donated the twenty-eighth and final parcel in 1962, when he was eighty-seven years old, bringing the total acreage to 201,018 and making it the country's fourth largest state park. It is the only state park in the country to be acquired completely through individual purchase.

Baxter was a patient and skillful negotiator, making many of his purchases directly from lumber companies and sometimes buying land he did not want to trade for land he did. While the Great Northern Paper Company still controls most of the vast acreage of Maine's north woods, because of Baxter's efforts a huge chunk, where logging is prohibited, is set aside for public recreation and wildlife preservation.

As testimony to the foresight of this simple man, a bronze plaque was mounted on the summit of Katahdin. Its inscription is quoted at the beginning of this chapter. Baxter has elaborated on his devotion to the cause of preserving this mountain:

> Katahdin always should and must remain the wild stormswept, untouched-by-man region it now is; that is its great charm. Only small cabins for mountain climbers and those who love the wilderness should be allowed there, only trails for those who travel on foot or horseback, a place where nature rules and where the creatures of the forest hold undisputed dominion.
>
> As modern civilization with its trailers and gasoline fumes, its unsightly billboards, its radio and jazz, encroaches on the Maine wilderness the time yet may come when only the Katahdin region remains undefiled by man. To acquire this Katahdin region for the people of Maine has been undertaken by me as

my life's work, and I hope as the years roll on that this State Park will be enjoyed by an ever-increasing number of Maine people and by those who come to us from beyond our borders.

The Appalachian Trail

Before it was fully protected as a state park, Katahdin became the obvious choice for the northern terminus of the Maine-to-Georgia Appalachian Trail (AT), which in 1927 linked existing trails on well-known peaks into a long-distance traverse of the entire Appalachian ridge.

The northern end of the 2,100-mile Appalachian Trail is on Katahdin, marked by a modest signpost and the crossing of an average 150 successful end-to-enders a year. Appalachian Mountain Club/David Hoyt.

Benton MacKaye is credited with conceiving the idea of the Appalachian Trail. With a degree in forestry from Harvard in 1905, MacKaye cut his teeth climbing Monadnock and the Green Mountains a decade before the Long Trail was begun. In June of 1921 he began to formulate an idea for the AT, envisioning not just a connected network of trails but a series of community camps along the mountaintop footpath as well, where healthful activity and self-improvement would be the key goals.

MacKaye took the initial step toward his dream's realization at the first Appalachian Trail Conference (ATC) in March 1925, in Washington, D. C. Here he presented his ideas and planted seeds for the formation of Appalachian Trail clubs along the entire Maine-to-Georgia corridor. A young man named Myron Avery, a native of Maine, a career navy officer in Washington, and a member of the Potomac Appalachian Trail Club, stepped forward to shepherd the plan from concept to reality. Through Avery's dedication to the skyline trail, the route was laid out, marked, and completed.

Much of the actual trail work in Maine was done by a young man named Helon N. Taylor. A blitz of trail cutting during the summer of 1933 completed the Appalachian Trail segment from the summit of Katahdin along the Hunt Trail, and from there halfway to Saddleback, an impressive 118 miles. Taylor went on to become supervisor of Baxter State Park from 1950 to 1967.

Avery also played an important role in the history of Katahdin and Baxter State Park. Born and brought up in Lubec, Maine, he spent countless hours exploring the Katahdin region and coming to know it thoroughly. Ultimately, he became a leading authority on the mountain, writing and editing the original AMC trail guide to Katahdin and numerous other articles on the mountain's history.

In the 1930s, as chairman of the ATC (a position he held for twenty-two years), Avery resurrected the idea of national ownership of Katahdin, believing that the state of Maine ought to relinquish control of Katahdin to the National Park Service. Avery had good reason to want the change, but he faced some serious opposition. With state resources at a low ebb because of the Great Depression and federally funded CCC crews doing the only regular maintenance in the park, and with agressively funded land-acquisition programs by the National Park Service, it seemed in the best interests of the park to become part of the federal system. Avery's chief argument was that the state provided inadequate supervision of campers and maintenance of facilities.

Percy Baxter, however, was vehemently opposed to Avery's plan, which one supporter admitted included "great log cabin hotels similar to those ... in Yellowstone and Yosemite." Robert Sterling Yard, head of the newly formed Wilderness Society, joined with Baxter in lobbying to keep Katahdin under state control, and used his influence to appeal directly to President Franklin Roosevelt.

A controversial bill to create a national park at Katahdin finally died in Congress in 1938, a victim of Maine's stubborn reluctance to yield control, its distrust of federal politics, and Baxter's continuing claim that, should the federal government take over, his trust would be invalidated and all lands once given to the state of Maine would revert to his personal ownership. Indirectly, the controversy benefited the park. State officials hired a full-time ranger for the park, improved existing roads and facilities, and within a few years appointed an official administrative body for the park.

Mountain Lore

Katahdin's regulars have a unique camaraderie; the mountain's challenges and quiet camps forge strong friendships. A group of local businessmen and recreational hikers who, throughout the middle of the twentieth century, kept alive the spirit of the old days became known as Jake's Rangers, after their leader, Jake Day. Spinning yarns, swapping fish stories, and ranging over the streams, ponds, and peaks of the park on a regular basis, these men were unofficial assistants for the park's regular staff in patrolling the area and helping to maintain trails.

Jake Maurice Day (1892–1983), the leader of the group, was a Maine native who worked for Walt Disney Studios in California as an animation artist. For the production of *Bambi*, Felix Salten's moralistic tale about a young deer originally set in Germany, Day convinced Disney to use the northern woods of Maine as a setting. He volunteered to make photographs of the wildlife and the forests for reference by the artists.

The trip home reawakened Day's kinship with Katahdin and Baxter State Park. Day returned to Disney only long enough to complete his assignment, recognizing that his heart belonged back in Maine. Jake Day went on to become a well-known painter of the Katahdin area, depicting forest and mountain scenery as well as the loggers and their camps. A devoted hiker, he climbed the mountain for the last time at the age of eighty in 1972.

Modern Park Management

The close of World War II marked the start of the modern era on Katahdin. During the long tenure of park supervisor Helon Taylor, 1950 to 1969, the trail network on Katahdin doubled from about 50 miles to nearly 100 miles. Volunteers and financing from the AMC helped to do much of the work of cutting new trails and rerouting eroded parts of others. In honor of Taylor's important leadership contribution, a new route to the summit of Pamola was named in his honor in 1964.

Katahdin's location, as well as its formidable height and steepness, dissuades many of the hikers attracted to the more accessible peaks in New England. Even so, overnight campers in the park number about 83,000 per year, and the total yearly visitor count is about 115,000.

Besides the rigors of hiking here, Katahdin's ridge sees extremes of weather not unlike Mount Washington. Summer storms can be especially violent, and the temperature can drop suddenly at any time. In comparison to Washington, Katahdin's total of sixteen recorded fatalities may seem surprisingly low. But the number of climbers here has always been smaller than in the Presidentials, and winter ascents are prohibited.

The first fatal accident since the creation of the park in 1931 took place in 1963. Two women, one more experienced than the other, had begun their hike of Baxter Peak along the Cathedral Trail on Monday morning, October 28. After reaching the summit, they decided to walk across the Knife Edge and maybe take the Dudley Trail back down from there. The less experienced climber of the two, Margaret Ivusic, insisted on taking a shortcut to pick up the new trail, while the other, Helen Mower, who had been climbing since childhood, chose to stay on the trail.

The women were in voice contact with each other, so when Ivusic became trapped on the steep face near the Chimney (today a technical climbing route), she was able to reassure her friend that she was not hurt. Mower went down to the Chimney Pond camp and alerted ranger Ralph Heath, who went up onto the mountain well after dark in his first rescue attempt. His eighty feet of rope proved insufficient, but the climber was still uninjured, so a second rescue attempt was not mounted until after breakfast on Tuesday.

That morning the weather turned suddenly cold and snowy, side effects of Hurricane Ginny which descended with brutal winds and more than a foot of snow. The ranger did not return to camp. Search parties were delayed because of the severe weather. Volunteers from Maine and Vermont ultimately recovered one body, but after a week gave up the search for Ranger Heath, whose body was never found.

The much-publicized double fatality highlighted the risk all rescuers assume when they go after others whose lack of judgment or poor preparation leads them into trouble. The tragedy might have been avoided had the climber not chosen to leave the trail to find a shortcut and had the possibility of severe storms, in this case bringing snow out of season, been anticipated. An immediate result was the adoption of stricter regulations governing use of the park outside the summer season, as well as a more carefully prepared search-and-rescue plan.

Percival Baxter played a key role in policy decisions at the park up until his death in 1969, and he provided generous, sometimes anonymous financial support for its activities. He had set up a three-part administrative board consisting of the forest commissioner, the commissioner of Inland Fisheries and Game, and the attorney general. Park supervisors managed the campground operation and maintenance. With small staffs and modest budgets, however, little attention was paid to long-range planning or future opportunities.

The establishment of a citizen's advisory committee in the 1970s marked a turning point in park management. Such divisive issues as the rights of snowmobilers, trash disposal, and the use of pesticides had to be resolved in light of Baxter's wishes for the park. A long-range master plan followed, along with the appointment of the park's first full-time director. Negotiations with timber companies concluded all logging around Katahdin, removing this activity to the northwestern section of the park. Low stone walls were constructed above treeline to direct hikers away from the fragile alpine areas on the summit ridge. Another concession was made to handle access to overnight camping in the park; each campground is ranger-patrolled and accessible only by prior reservation. If hiking conditions are dangerous, rangers can even prohibit attempts to climb Katahdin.

Wildlife

Preserving and protecting wildlife habitat is equally important to providing recreational opportunities for people within the park. In fact, the chance to see wildlife is one of the main reasons people come to Baxter. Moose are ubiquitous, particularly around the shores of the ponds and along the stream banks. Black bear, though timid, are common, though visitors are cautioned to avoid them. White-tailed deer are here, too, and in the 1960s caribou from Canada were

Wildlife is plentiful in Baxter State Park and around Katahdin. The best moose watching is at Sandy Stream Pond, near Roaring Brook Campground. Photo courtesy Baxter State Park.

reintroduced into the park. Several survived the first few years, but the experiment ultimately failed. In 1988, a two-year program to reintroduce caribou was tried again, without success. Wildlife experts ascribed the failure of the caribou to survive to two major factors, predation from wild bears and a brain-damaging meningeal worm carried by moose for which the caribou lacked any resistance.

Beavers continue to modify the natural environment with their stream damming and flooding activities. Fox, porcupine, rabbits, and such less frequently seen species as coyotes, fisher, mink, and weasels inhabit the lower elevations, too. As on Washington, there is little wildlife in the alpine zone on the rocky crest of the mountain.

Protection of the wildlife is guaranteed. As a condition of Baxter's gift to the state, "said premises shall forever be used for State forest, public park and recreational purposes, shall forever be left in the natural wild state, shall forever be kept as a sanctuary for wild beasts and birds." In the case of fishing, however, recreational interests prevail over wildlife preservation, and brook trout are one of the main attractions drawing fishermen to the park.

No more eloquent appreciation of Katahdin has been written than that of Chief Justice William O. Douglas in his chronicle of the Appalachian Trail, My Wilderness, East to Katahdin.

> Katahdin has been like a haunting melody since the days in the late twenties when I first saw it against a buttermilk sky. For some years, I explored the dark woods and marshy lakes at its feet, and climbed its rough points. Then came a long period of absence. But the pull of Katahdin, like that of an old love, was always strong. The memories of it were especially bright every May, when the ice went out and the squaretails started jumping—every June, when the salmon-fly hatch was on. Fiddlehead ferns—partridgeberries—alpine azalea with tiny cerise flowers—the pitcher plant with fleshy flowers the color of raw meat and its leaves full of water and the debris of insects attracted by its honey glands—bright forests of paper birch—fragrance of pencil cedar—the rushing of white water against a canoe—the hearty welcoming song of the white throated sparrow: all these—and more—were Katahdin.

Douglas's appreciation for the wilderness goes beyond complacency. "If we are to survive," he writes, "we must make Katahdin the symbol of our struggle for independence from the machine that promises to enslave us. We must multiply the Baxter Parks a thousand fold.... We must provide enough wilderness areas so that, no matter how dense our population, man—though apartment born—may attend the great school of the outdoors, and come to know the joy of walking the woods, alone and unafraid.... Baxter Park may only be a tiny island in a sea of cities, cement highways, and factories, but it will be forever a retreat where man can once more come to understanding terms with the earth of which he is only an infinitesimal part."

Suggestions for Visitors

Baxter State Park is closely administered and well organized, and it expects the same of visitors. Rangers at the gatehouses on the four access roads to the park monitor visitors and their intended acitivites. A perimeter road provides vehicular access to all but two of the nine major campgrounds; otherwise travel within the park is by foot. Canoes can be rented at several of the ponds within the park. All camping is by prior reservation, and the choice locations and dates are taken six months in advance. Amenities are few—no stores, hot showers, or gas stations. During winter, use of the park is strictly limited and camping and climbing are by special permit only. For registration information write to: Baxter State Park Headquarters, 64 Balsam Drive, Millinocket, ME, 04462; 207-723-5140.

Hikers need to take the elements seriously here. Lightning strikes are common during the summer, and storms can gather in a matter of a few minutes, bringing rain, wind, hail, or worse. The bare rocks can become slippery and ice coated. Thoreau called Katahdin's summit a "cloud-factory," and even on clear days in the region, the summit itself is likely to be obscured by fog or clouds.

Locales significant to Katahdin's story are dispersed throughout the park. Abol Stream is reached from Abol Campground; the 1816 Abol Slide is still a popular route for ascending the mountain. The sites of the old logging camps are in the vicinity of Russell Pond Campground. The best moose watching is at Sandy Stream Pond, near Roaring Brook Campground.

A sign at popular Chimney Pond reminds visitors to respect the fragile alpine environment.

At Chimney Pond Campground, halfway up the mountain, hikers feast their eyes on the walls of the wonderful cirques from the floor of the South Basin, and thus sleep within Katahdin's embrace. From Chimney Pond, Pamola Peak is reached by way of the Dudley Trail, named for Leroy Dudley, a yarn-spinning mountain guide who held court at Chimney Pond from 1917 until 1942. Another route from Chimney Pond ascends the Cathedral, the nickname of the great mass that divides South Basin from the Great Basin, and is an arduous, direct route to Baxter Peak. The Saddle Trail leads from Chimney Pond up the headwall of the Great Basin, ascending by the Saddle Slide, a mile and a half to the top of the headwall and then a final brutal mile up the treeless summit cone to Baxter Peak. Though steep and challenging (it gains 2,300 feet over its two-and-a-half-mile length), the Saddle Trail is the tamest of the three trails leading up from Chimney Pond. It is the only one recommended for the descent.

Even in this age in which trails are well marked and maintained, reaching Baxter Peak requires fitness and determination. Katahdin's summit is forbidding: hard to reach, uncomfortable to linger on, and unwelcoming in its aspect. Yet of all New England's mountains, because of its height, its long history, and its wild and uncompromised character, perhaps Katahdin takes the strongest hold on the imagination.

Bibliography

Albee, John. *Lake Chocorua*. Washington, DC: McQueen Press, 1910.

AMC *Guide to Mount Desert Island and Acadia National Park*. 5th edition. Boston: Appalachian Mountain Club, 1993.

Baxter Park Authority. *A Guide to Baxter State Park and Mount Katahdin in Maine*. Baxter Park Authority, 1981.

Bigelow, Edwin L., and Nancy H. Otis. *Manchester, Vermont: A Pleasant Land Among the Mountains*. Manchester Center, VT: Rod & Reel Publishing Co., for the Mark Skinner Library, 1961.

Billings, Marland P., Katharine Fowler-Billings, Carleton A. Chapman, Randolph W. Chapman, and Richard P. Goldthwait. *The Geology of the Mount Washington Quadrangle*. Concord, NH: State of New Hampshire Department of Resources and Economic Development, 1979.

Blake, Francis Everett. *Lucy Keyes, the Lost Child of Wachusett Mountain*. Boston: David Clapp and Son, 1893.

———. *History of the Town of Princeton*. Princeton, MA: 1915.

Bonfanti, Leo. *Biographies and Legends of the New England Indians*. Vol. 2–3. Wakefield, MA: Pride Publications, Inc., 1970, 1972.

Brown, J. Willcox. *Forest History of Mount Moosilauke*. Hanover, NH: Dartmouth Outing Club, 1989.

Burke, Edmund. *On the Sublime and Beautiful (1756)*. The Harvard Classics. New York: PF Collier & Son, 1909.

Burns, Deborah E., and Lauren R. Stevens. *Most Excellent Majesty: A History of Mount Greylock*. Pittsfield, Mass.: Berkshire Natural Resources Council, Inc., 1988.

Burt, F. Allen. "A Lost Mountain Railway." *Appalachia* (December 1943).

———. *The Story of Mount Washington*. Hanover, NH: Dartmouth Publications, 1960.

Chamberlain, Allen. *The Annals of the Grand Monadnock*. Concord, NH: Society for the Protection of New Hampshire Forests, 1936.

Christman, Robert A. *The Geology of Mt. Mansfield State Forest*. Vermont Geological Survey, 1956.

A Circle of Friends: Art Colonies of Dublin and Cornish. Durham, NH: University Art Galleries, University of New Hampshire, 1985.

Clement, Daniel Quincy. "Moosilauke." Unpublished manuscript at New Hampshire Historical Society, Concord, NH: probably written between 1876 and 1878. Transcribed by Robert Averill.

Collier, Sargent F. *Mount Desert Island and Acadia National Park*. Camden, ME: Down East Books, 1978.

DeLorme's Map and Guide of Baxter State Park and Katahdin. Freeport, ME: DeLorme Mapping Co., 1989.

Doherty, Paul T. *Smoke From a Thousand Campfires*. Berlin, NH: Smith & Town Printers, 1992.

Douglas, Willliam O. *My Wilderness: East to Katahdin*. Garden City, NY: Doubleday, 1961.

Dwelley, Marilyn. *Trees and Shrubs of New England*. Camden, ME: Down East Books, 1980.

Eckstorm, Fannie Hardy. *The Indian Legends of Mount Katahdin*. Boston: Appalachian Mountain Club, 1924.

Eschholz, Paul A. "The Landlord at Lion's Head: William Dean Howells' Use of the Vermont Scene." *Vermont History* 42 (1974): (44–47).

Evans, Llew. "Mount Mansfield, Capstone of Vermont." *Appalachia* (June 1944).

Fay, Charles E. "Was Chocorua the Original Pigwacket Hill." *Appalachia* (December 1886).

Forbrush, Edward Howe. *Birds of Massachusetts and other New England States*. Massachusetts Department of Agriculture, 1929.

Freund, Thatcher. "Beauty Under Siege." *New England Monthly* (July 1990).

Gilman, Richard A., Carleton A. Chapman, Thomas V. Lowell, Harold W. Borns, Jr. *The Geology of Mount Desert Island*. Maine Geological Survey Department of Conservation, 1988.

Green Mountain Club, *Guide Book of the Long Trail*. 23d edition. Waterbury Center, VT: Green Mountain Club, 1991.

Hagerman, Robert L. *Mansfield: the Story of Vermont's Loftiest Mountain*. Phoenix Publishing, 1975.

Hakola, Dr. John W. *Legacy of a Lifetime: The Story of Baxter State Park*. Baxter State Park Authority, 1981.

Hale, Richard Walden. *The Story of Bar Harbor*. New York: Ives Washburn, Inc., 1949.

Harkey, Sharon, ed. *Mount Ascutney Guide*, 5th edition. Ascutney Trails Association, 1992.

Harkness, Marjory Gane. *The Tamworth Narrative*. Freeport, ME: The Bond Wheelwright Co., 1958.

Harris, Stuart K., Jean H. Langenhaim, and Frederick L. Steele. *AMC Field Guide to Mountain Flowers of New England*. Boston: Appalachian Mountain Club, 1977.

Heise, Anne E. "The Phantom's Mask: Acid Rain and Forest Decline on Camel's Hump." *Appalachia* (Summer 1985).

Hitchcock, John H. "Wachusett Mountain: Landmark from the Past, Challenge for the Future." *Appalachia* (June and December, 1971).

Horwitz, Ellie. "Back from the Brink." *Massachusetts Wildlife* (Summer 1986).

Howarth, William. *Thoreau in the Mountains*. New York: Farrar, Straus, Giroux, 1982.

Ilex, Arbor. "Camps and Tramps About Katahdin." *Scribner's Monthly* (May 1878).

Jorgensen, Neil. *A Guide to New England's Landscape*. Chester, CT: Globe Pequot Press, 1977.

Kendall, David L. *Glaciers and Granite: A Guide to Maine's Landscape and Geology*. Camden, ME: Down East Books, 1987.

Keyes, Donald D., et al. *The White Mountains, Place and Perceptions*. Durham, NH: University Art Galleries, University of New Hampshire, 1980.

Kilbourne, Frederick W. *Chronicles of the White Mountains*. Boston and New York: Houghton Mifflin Co., 1916.

———. "Moosilauke: the Story of a Mountain." *Appalachia* (June 1940).

King, Thomas Starr. *The White Hills: Their Legends, Landscape, and Poetry*. Boston: Crosby, Nichols and Co., 1859.

Kostecke, Diane M., ed. *Franconia Notch, an In-Depth Guide.* Concord, NH: Society for the Protection of New Hampshire Forests, 1975.

Lindner, Brian. *The History of the Camel's Hump Bomber Crash.* Essex Junction, VT: 1978.

Lipke, William C., and Philip N. Grime, eds. *Vermont Landscape Images, 1776–1976.* Burlington, VT: Robert Hull Fleming Museum, 1976.

Little, William. *History of Warren: A Mountain Hamlet.* Manchester, NH: 1870.

Manning, Robert E., ed. *Mountain Passages, An Appalachia Anthology.* Boston: Appalachian Mountain Club, 1982.

Mansfield, Howard. *In the Memory House.* Golden, CO: Fulcrum Publishing, 1993.

Martinelli, Laurie. "The Greylock Glen Project." *Sanctuary,* 32 (January/February 1993).

Mayo, Lawrence Shaw. "The History of the Legend of Chocorua." *New England Quarterly,* 19 (September 1946).

Mazuzan, George T. "Skiing is Not Merely a Schport: The Development of Mount Mansfield as a Winter Recreation Area, 1930–1955." *Vermont History* 40 (1972): 47–63.

McAvoy, George E. *And Then There Was One.* Littleton, NH: Crawford Press, 1988.

McGrath, Robert L., and Barbara J. MacAdam. "A Sweet Foretaste of Heaven": *Artists in the White Mountains 1830–1930.* Hanover, NH: Hood Museum of Art, 1988.

Morison, Samuel Eliot. *The Story of Mount Desert Island.* Boston: Atlantic Monthly Press, 1960.

Morse, Stearns, ed. *Lucy Crawford's History of the White Mountains.* Hanover, NH: Dartmouth Publications, 1966.

National Park Service. *Acadia National Park General Management Plan.* U. S. Department of the Interior, 1992.

Nickerson, Marion L., and John A. Downs. *Chocorua Peak House.* Center Conway, NH: Walker's Pond Press, 1970.

Novak, Barbara. *American Painting of the 19th Century.* New York: Praeger Publishing, 1967.

Nutting, Helen Cushing, ed. *To Monadnock: the Records of a Mountain in New Hampshire through Three Centuries*. New York: Stratford Press, 1925.

Older, Julia, and Steve Sherman. *Grand Monadnock: Exploring the Most Popular Mountain in America*. Hancock, NH: Appledore Books, 1990.

Osgood, James R. *The White Mountains: A Handbook for Travelers*. Boston: Ticknor & Co., 1886.

Palmer, Edwin F. "Camel's Hump." *Vermonter* (April 1910).

Randall, Peter. *Mount Washington*. Hanover, NH: University Press of New England, 1974.

Raymo, Chet, and Maureen E. Raymo. *Written in Stone*. Chester, CT: Globe Pequot Press, 1989.

Rebek, Andrea. "The Selling of Vermont: From Agriculture to Tourism." *Vermont History* 34 (Winter 1976).

Reifsnyder, William. *High Huts of the White Mountains*, 2nd ed. Boston: Appalachian Mountain Club, 1993.

Rich, Nancy. "White Mountain Photography, 1860–1885: The Picturesque Ideal in Eastern American Landscape Photography." unpublished manuscipt at the Society for the Protection of New England Antiquities, Boston: 1988.

Roberts, Ann Rockefeller. *Mr. Rockefeller's Roads*. Camden, ME: Down East Books, 1990.

Rockwell, Landon G. "Concerning the Strange 'Doctor' of Moosilauke." *Appalachia* (June 1941).

Roomet, Louise B. "Vermont as a Resort Area in the Nineteenth Century." *Vermont History* 44 (Winter 1976).

Sharpe, Grant W. *A Guide to Acadia National Park*. New York: Golden Press, 1968.

Speck, Frank G. *Penobscot Man*. New York: Octagon Books, 1976.

Stewart, Chris, and Mike Torrey, eds. *A Century of Hospitality in High Places: The Appalachian Mountain Club Hut System, 1888–1988*. Boston: Appalachian Mountain Club, 1988.

Stowell, Robert F. *A Thoreau Gazetteer*. Princeton, NJ: Princeton University Press, 1970.

Street, George E. *Mount Desert, A History*. Boston: Houghton Mifflin, 1905.

Thomson, Betty Flanders. *The Changing Face of New England*. Boston: Houghton Mifflin, 1977.

Thoreau, Henry David. *Ktaadn*. New York: Tanam Press, 1980.

A Trail Guide to Mount Moosilauke. Hanover, N. H.: Environmental Studies Division, Dartmouth Outing Club, 1978.

Van Diver, Bradford B. *Roadside Geology of Vermont and New Hampshire*. Missoula, MT: Mountain Press Publishing Co., 1987.

Vaughan, Alden T., and Edward W. Clark, eds. *Puritans Among the Indians*. Cambridge, MA: Belknap Press of Harvard University Press, 1981.

Waterman, Guy, and Laura Waterman. *Forest and Crag: A History of Hiking, Trail Blazing, and Adventure in the Northeast Mountains*. Boston: Appalachian Mountain Club, 1989.

Willey, Benjamin F. *Incidents in White Mountain History*. Boston: Nathaniel Noyes, 1856.

Williams, Ted. "The Peregrine Symptom." *Massachusetts Wildlife* (July–August 1972).

Index

[**Note:** Page numbers in italics indicate photo or illustration captions.]

328

336   *Index*

About the Authors

MAGGIE STIER is the former curator of Fruitlands Museums in Harvard, Massachusetts. An authority on New England cultural history, she specializes in interpreting the historical landscape for modern audiences. She has organized exhibitions and presentations on New England artworks and cultural movements such as the art of the White Mountains and the New England Shaker communities. She is a graduate of Vassar College and holds a M.A. from Boston University's American and New England Studies Program. A native New Englander, she is a lifetime hiker with an intimate knowledge of New England's high peaks. She lives with her family in Harvard, Massachusetts.

RON MCADOW is an educator and author of *The Concord, Sudbury, and Assabet Rivers*, *The Charles River*, and *New England Time Line*. A graduate of the University of Chicago, he has worked in environmental education, children's television, and writing projects on local resources. He is currently at work in educational and nature-oriented materials. He lives with his family in Southborough, Massachusetts.

About the AMC

THE APPALACHIAN MOUNTAIN CLUB pursues an active conservation agenda while encouraging responsible recreation. Our philosophy is that successful, long-term conservation depends on firsthand experience of the natural environment. AMC's 64,000 members pursue interests in hiking, canoeing, skiing, walking, rock climbing, bicycling, camping, kayaking, and backpacking, and—at the same time—help safeguard the environment.

Founded in 1876, the club has been at the forefront of the environmental protection movement. As cofounder of several leading New England environmental organizations, and as an active member working in coalition with these and many other groups, the AMC has successfully influenced legislation and public opinion.

Conservation

The most recent efforts in the AMC conservation program include river protection, Northern Forest Lands policy, Sterling Forest (NY) preservation, and support for the Clean Air Act. The AMC depends upon its active members and grassroots supporters to promote this conservation agenda.

Education

The AMC's education department offers members and the general public a wide range of workshops, from introductory camping to intensive Mountain Leadership School taught on the trails of the White Mountains. In addition, volunteers in each chapter lead hundreds of outdoor activities and excursions and offer introductory instruction in backcountry sports.

Research

The AMC's research department focuses on the forces affecting the ecosystem, including ozone levels, acid rain and fog, climate change, rare flora and habitat protection, and air quality and visibility.

349

Trails Program

Another facet of the AMC is the trails program, which maintains more than 1,400 miles of trail (including 350 miles of the Appalachian Trail) and more than 50 shelters in the Northeast. Through a coordinated effort of volunteers, seasonal crews, and program staff, the AMC contributes more than 10,000 hours of public service work each summer in the area from Washington, D.C. to Maine.

In addition to supporting our work by becoming an AMC member, hikers can donate time as volunteers. The club offers four unique weekly volunteer base camps in New Hampshire, Maine, Massachusetts, and New York. We also sponsor ten-day service projects throughout the United States, Adopt-a-Trail programs, trails day events, trail skills workshops, and chapter and camp volunteer projects.

The AMC has a longstanding connection to Acadia National Park. Working in cooperation with the National Park Service and Friends of Acadia, the AMC Trails Program provides many opportunities to preserve the park's resources. These include half-day volunteer projects for guests at AMC's Echo Lake Camp, ten-day service projects, weeklong volunteer crews in the fall, and trails day events. For more information on these public service volunteer opportunities, contact the AMC Trails Program, Pinkham Notch Visitor Center, P.O. Box 298, Gorham NH 03581; 603-466-2721.

Alpine Huts

The club operates eight alpine huts in the White Mountains that provide shelter, bunks and blankets, and hearty meals for hikers. Pinkham Notch Visitor Center, at the foot of Mt. Washington, is base camp to the adventurous and the ideal location for individuals and families new to outdoor recreation. Comfortable bunkrooms, mountain hospitality, and home-cooked, family-style meals make Pinkham Notch Visitor Center a fun and affordable choice for lodging. For reservations, call 603-466-2727.

Publications

The AMC main office in Boston and at Pinkham Notch Visitor Center in New Hampshire, the bookstore and information center stock the entire line of AMC publications, as well as other trail and river guides, maps, reference materials, and the latest articles on conservation issues. Guidebooks and other AMC gifts are available by mail order 1-800-262-4455, or by writing AMC, P.O. Box 298, Gorham NH 03581. Also available from the bookstore or by subscription is *Appalachia*, the country's oldest mountaineering and conservation journal.